Elizabeth Abbott and Claudette Larocque
snapd at CFUW Markham Unionville meeting

# Praise for *Dogs and Underdogs*

"Abbott writes with knowledge and passion about the dogs she has known and loved. Her stories about a cast of canine characters from around the world highlight the challenges they have faced, but more than that, *Dogs and Underdogs* is a call to action that should convince every reader to follow Abbott's lead in trying to help dogs. I cannot recommend this book highly enough."—**Rob Laidlaw, award-winning author of *No Shelter Here* and director of Zoocheck Canada**

"In *Dogs and Underdogs*, Elizabeth Abbott takes us to many places around the world and allows us to see how a rescued dog can save the heart and mind of the dog's rescuer. Some truly touching accounts here may well bring a tear to the reader's eye and a smile to the reader's lips."—**Stanley Coren, bestselling author of *The Intelligence of Dogs* and *How Dogs Think***

"Elizabeth Abbott's *Dogs and Underdogs* is a gem, surely one of the best reads that clearly shows how dogs help and rescue us, and we help and rescue them when we open our hearts to just who they are and what they can do."—**Marc Bekoff, author of *Rewilding Our Hearts***

"*Dogs and Underdogs* can be traced back to the moment a human first looked deep into the eyes of a wolf and saw—a friend. Others probably thought that person was crazy, but they weren't. The kinship they recognized was firmly rooted in a shared social brain chemistry that would deepen into one of the most profound and life-enhancing bonds on this planet. Thirty thousand years on, Elizabeth Abbott brings us a powerful reminder that dogs have always been worth our faith, our generosity, and even our heroics—because to rescue is to be rescued."—**Meg Daley Olmert, author of *Made for Each Other***

"If you are a 'dog person,' you will love this book, which is often funny, and always moving and inspirational. If you don't consider yourself a 'dog person,' you will enjoy it anyway. A fascinating story about an extraordinary life."—**Maureen Jennings, dog lover and bestselling author of the Murdoch Mysteries series**

"Four decades of Elizabeth Abbott's dog relationships and adventures come together in *Dogs and Underdogs*. The book is emotionally captivating and takes the reader on unimaginable real-life journeys. Attention dog lovers—curl up with this book and prepare to be moved."—**Lorraine Houston, director of Speaking of Dogs Rescue Program**

"The dogs in this book come to life as persons who share in the personal, physical, and political worlds of the humans that care about them, and share the same vulnerabilities. We're all in this together, Elizabeth Abbott shows us, through every change of situation in her own life. For me, this is more than a 'my life with dogs' story; it is an epic of commitment and compassion that challenges me to think more carefully about the dogs that pass through my clinic and the shelter where I work."—**Debbie Tacium, DMV, shelter veterinarian at the SPA de l'Estrie in Sherbrooke, Quebec, and animal-issues writer**

To Mary

# DOGS & UNDERDOGS

## FINDING HAPPINESS AT
## BOTH ENDS OF THE LEASH

ELIZABETH ABBOTT

Warmest wishes,

Elizabeth Abbott

**VIKING**

VIKING

an imprint of Penguin Canada Books Inc., a Penguin Random House Company

Published by the Penguin Group

Penguin Canada Books Inc., 90 Eglinton Avenue East, Suite 700,
Toronto, Ontario, Canada M4P 2Y3

Penguin Group (USA) LLC, 375 Hudson Street, New York, New York 10014, U.S.A.
Penguin Books Ltd, 80 Strand, London WC2R 0RL, England
Penguin Ireland, 25 St Stephen's Green, Dublin 2, Ireland
(a division of Penguin Books Ltd)
Penguin Group (Australia), 707 Collins Street, Melbourne, Victoria 3008, Australia
(a division of Pearson Australia Group Pty Ltd)
Penguin Books India Pvt Ltd, 11 Community Centre, Panchsheel Park,
New Delhi – 110 017, India
Penguin Group (NZ), 67 Apollo Drive, Rosedale, Auckland 0632, New Zealand
(a division of Pearson New Zealand Ltd)
Penguin Books (South Africa) (Pty) Ltd, 24 Sturdee Avenue, Rosebank,
Johannesburg 2196, South Africa

Penguin Books Ltd, Registered Offices: 80 Strand, London WC2R 0RL, England

First published 2015

1 2 3 4 5 6 7 8 9 10 (RRD)

Copyright © Elizabeth Abbott, 2015

Manufactured in the U.S.A.

---

LIBRARY AND ARCHIVES CANADA CATALOGUING IN PUBLICATION

Abbott, Elizabeth, author
Dogs and underdogs : finding happiness at both ends of the
leash / Elizabeth Abbott.

ISBN 978-0-670-06825-8 (bound)

1. Abbott, Elizabeth. 2. Dogs—Anecdotes. 3. Human-animal
relationships. I. Title.

SF426.2.A23 2015          636.7          C2015-900172-2

---

eBook ISBN 978-0-14-319448-4

Penguin is committed to publishing works of quality and integrity.
In that spirit, we are proud to offer this book to our readers; however,
the story, the experiences, and the words are the author's alone.

Visit the Penguin Canada website at **www.penguin.ca**

Special and corporate bulk purchase rates available;
please see **www.penguin.ca/corporatesales** or call 1-800-810-3104.

*To my brother, Steve Abbott, for a lifetime of
friendship and shared animal loving*

*To all the dogs (and cats) I've loved, who are the
reason this book could be written. They have filled
my heart and expanded it to include all animals.*

*And to Bonzi, Petey, and Poppy, and Snoopy
and Chanel, who bless my life today.*

*And to the rescue community, those tireless women
and men who save, nurture, transport, and find
homes for needy animals, giving them that second
chance that makes all the difference in the world.*

# CONTENTS

# PROLOGUE

*Until one has loved an animal,*
*a part of one's soul remains unawakened.*
Anatole France

If someone had told me thirty-five years ago that a dog would alter the course of my life forever, I would have shaken my head and laughed. Back then, I couldn't have imagined that a Labrador–German Shepherd Dog mix named Tommy would do anything more than love and protect me. But Tommy did more than that. The powerful, complicated bond between us didn't just mean that I'd come to his aid when he was in trouble; it also awakened in my heart the sense of mission that has since driven me, and that has made me a dog rescuer.

The first dog I ever loved was Mike the Airedale terrier. I was a toddler when I spent two summers with his people—my great-aunt and uncle—in the idyllic Ontario village of St. Marys. Mike would sit with us in an armchair as we took tea and listened to the radio; he'd lope beside me as I played outside. And when I was sad or homesick for my parents in Montreal, he'd lean against me as I hugged him.

As I got older, I began to lobby my parents for a dog. Even after I'd demolished my mother's long list of objections—A dog would need to be walked (I'd walk it!); would shed hair on the living room furniture (I'd keep it in my room); leave muddy paw prints on the floors (I'd mop them up); bark and bother the neighbours (I'd train it not to); and put an end to my summers at camp (So what? I'd give up *anything* for my dog)—Mom adamantly opposed the idea.

My father, who'd grown up with dogs, was no help. "Your mother and I have chosen children over dogs," he'd say. But he did give me a dog of sorts, in the form of a book, *Beautiful Joe,* by Margaret Marshall Saunders. This 1893 novel is based on the true story of an abused terrier crossbreed in Meaford, Ontario, whom Saunders's sister-in-law had adopted. Beautiful Joe's cruel owner, the milkman James Jenkins, smashed in his littermates' brains while their mother, whom he'd beaten and starved, howled in anguish. Afterward she bade lone-survivor Joe a gentle farewell, and then lay down and died.

Jenkins was furious. He kicked the puppy, snarling, "She was worth two of you; why didn't you go instead?" Joe, broken-hearted, lunged and bit Jenkins's ankle. In retaliation, Jenkins hacked off the pup's ears and tail.

This attack changed Joe's life forever. A passing cyclist overheard his anguished shrieks, slugged Jenkins, and then snatched Joe away to safety. His rescuer's young cousin, Laura Morris, cleansed his wounds, and despite his mutilated ugliness, renamed him Beautiful Joe and adopted him.

The story continued in words scorched into my heart. "That animal has been wronged; it looks to you to right it," Laura said, urging someone to alert the police to Joe's abuse. "A child has its voice to tell its wrong—a poor, dumb creature must suffer in silence; bitter, bitter silence."

Even more to the point, Laura's sensible, kindly mother seemed to be appealing to my own when she told a dog-hostile woman whose son longed for a dog: "I should not wish my boys to be without a good, faithful dog. A child can learn many a lesson from a dog."

I read this passage to my mother, certain that she would succumb to the power of its logic, but it only irritated her. "It's a book *about* a dog, Elizabeth. Of course the author sees nothing wrong in having one in the house; she probably has one in hers. But this is *my* house, and my answer remains: No dog."

But I still had Joe, and how I loved him! How I grieved for his battered body and his murdered littermates! How I vowed to be selflessly kind and conscientious in my dealings with dogs, and to give voice to their bitter, bitter silence! And how much more pressing my love for Beautiful Joe made my quest for a real-life dog!

Two years later, suddenly and serendipitously, my family did get a dog—or rather, my father got one. It happened when he fulfilled his dream of becoming a gentleman farmer and bought a two-hundred-acre farm nestled between St. Benoit du Lac monastery and Lake Memphremagog. Astonishingly, Roswell Farm included Sandy, a mature St. Bernard.

But Dad warned me that although Sandy was a trusty watchdog, she was also bad-tempered, nippy, and wanted only minimal contact with the humans who provided her food and shelter. So my siblings and I kept our distance, and whenever one of us forgot and moved too close, Sandy would growl a reminder. But an extraordinary thing happened. Sandy fell in love with Dad, and he loved her right back, lavishing her with treats, companionship, and regular tramps around the property.

Then Sandy surprised us by producing a litter of eight. She was a ferociously protective mother, and only my father could go near her pups. I pleaded to have one. My parents' response was unequivocal: "No."

One day Sandy disappeared. "She did what dogs do," Dad told us kids. "She went off someplace in the woods." I knew what that meant—it was what Beautiful Joe's brother, Old Jim, had done when he felt death approaching. "He wanted to spare [Miss Laura] the greater sorrow of his death. He was always such a thoughtful dog, and so anxious not to give trouble."

Dad must have mourned, silently and privately. Today I regret that I never asked him how he'd felt about Sandy. If dog-yearning and dog-loving are genetic, I know that I inherited those traits from my father. But for years my bred-in-the-bone hunger for dogs remained just that—a hunger. My parents were always generous. They just never gave me the gift I truly wanted.

When I was twenty, a fourth-year undergraduate history student living away from home, I gave myself that gift. Sam was an adult German Shepherd Dog–Irish setter cross-breed, and life with him was as glorious and fulfilling as I'd imagined. But when Sam was middle-aged my partner and I moved to a rural area outside of Montreal, an unfenced doggy paradise—until the afternoon Sam interrupted hunters from the city, who turned their sights on him instead of the deer who got away.

Although I got Sam to the veterinary clinic alive, he passed away minutes later. "The hunter must have held his rifle right up against his chest," the vet told me. "He pulverized your poor dog, Madame. There was nothing I could do to save him."

I grieved for weeks. Sam had been so happy, and I'd loved him so much. But his death confirmed that I didn't want to live without a dog of my own. My next dog was Jean-Paul, a sleek and sturdy standard black dachshund who inspired my lifelong fondness for his breed. His unexpected death at a veterinary clinic treating him for a chronic skin condition broke my heart.

For over a year after JP's death, I lived without a dog. My changed circumstances—a breakup, a new relationship, lodgings that prohibited pets—made it impossible to have one. Plus I was spending an inordinate amount of time in the library working on my doctoral thesis. But I finished it and graduated, and moved into a comfortable, dog-tolerant apartment with the man I would later marry. I soon overcame his objections to sharing his lodgings with a dog and plunged into the task of finding one.

I wanted a dog without any resemblance to JP, whose death haunted me. The English bulldog was such a dog, and my fiancé approved. The SPCA had none, but an ad in the *Montreal Star* included an English bulldog in its list of available puppies, along with a Vermont phone number. When I reached John, the advertiser, he offered me a five-month-old male pup from Kansas. The price was $350, and to confirm the sale, I had to deposit $175 into John's Canadian bank account.

I endured two months of silence, queasy misgivings, and my friends' ominous predictions that I'd never hear from John again. Then, out of the blue, he phoned with a delivery date and a reminder that he expected cash. He arrived hours late, heaving a crated English bulldog into the apartment. After pocketing the second instalment of the purchase price, he demanded an additional $35 for the wooden structure the poor pup had travelled in.

Joey—I'd named him after my grandfather's Boston terrier—stumbled out of his cage and collapsed onto the living room floor, making no attempt to explore or even to get up. Euphoric, I crouched down to kiss and hug him.

John, relaxing with a Coke on the sofa, responded des-ultorily to my comments and questions. Yes, Joey must be exhausted after a full day's travel. But the reason he wasn't moving around was that he didn't know how to walk yet. "First time he's been out of his cage in ten months," John said.

I rocked back on my heels and stared. "I don't under-stand! Didn't they walk him? And I thought you said he was seven months old!"

John shook his head. "Oh, they fed him and every-thing, but they were waiting for someone to buy him. For ten months, according to his paperwork."

"You mean they wouldn't have let him out if nobody had?"

John shrugged. "Somebody did. *You* did."

Decades later, when I learned about puppy mills, I recalled this conversation and was thunderstruck. Joey— born in Kansas, the heartland of American puppy mills, raised with minimal expense and attention, plagued by deformed knees and congestive heart disease—had been the product of a puppy mill.

Since at the time I had no idea what a puppy mill even was, Joey's curious upbringing made no sense to me. And his "paperwork" was confounding: instead of the promised American Kennel Club certification, John handed over a Purina Dog Chow form with Joey's championship forebears pencilled in. But I had my dog, and that cancelled out any feeling that I'd been swindled.

A few years later, John resurfaced in a newspaper exposé. The reporter described how he'd placed classified ads for various dog breeds and how gullible would-be buyers had deposited half of the purchase price or more into his bank account. My hands trembled as I read. Dozens of people had fallen for this scam. Predictably, most had never seen their prepaid dogs. There was nothing in the story about the puppy mills for which John was an agent, probably because the reporter was as unaware of them as I was. I still had no idea that I'd unwittingly bought a mill dog, and that one day far in the future I'd share my home with other survivors.

Despite his wonky knees and weak heart, Joey learned to walk; but his gait was clumsy, and after half a city block, he would pant and wheeze. If I wanted a brisk outing, Joey had to stay home.

On the other hand, when I needed a confidant and companion, Joey was at my side. Long before I knew what dog rescue was, Joey rescued me. My marriage was unravelling just as I'd become pregnant, and I couldn't bear to tell anyone, even my family. When I rented a room at the YWCA, I confided in only two friends and, wordlessly, through emotion, in Joey.

Joey grasped the intensity if not the cause of my unhappiness, and he shared my exile. Because the Y didn't permit dogs, I moved him into my office: that way, Joey wouldn't be lonely and I'd have his company as I worked. No one suspected that late at night I'd go to the Y to sleep and then rush back early the next morning to walk my dog. In the evenings and on weekends I'd hug him and weep on his massive shoulder; he'd lean against me as if he understood my pain. Sometimes as I hugged him goodbye I'd surrender to his look of resignation and stay with him overnight, knowing I'd be exhausted the next day.

Joey also brought hilarity to my life. One morning, as he waddled along tony Sherbrooke Street, he squatted down and expelled a nylon foot from a discarded pantyhose he must have retrieved from the wastebasket and swallowed. I stepped on the foot and, as Joey kept walking, waited until the leg followed. As I tugged out the rest of the offending hosiery, Joey winced and then shuffled off, oblivious to the laughter behind him.

After months of counselling and negotiation I returned home, and Joey went with me. His role as my rescuer having ended, he resumed a pleasanter life as my dog. A month later my son, Ivan, arrived. Although Joey expressed his displeasure by pooping outside the nursery door, he soon accepted Ivan and before long embraced him as the other love of his life.

A year later, my husband and I separated and I relocated my little family to a country house in the Eastern Townships. The rural community was welcoming, and it seemed an idyllic place to raise a child. It was an easy commute to the Montreal college where I'd become a history professor. And, because the house was spacious and surrounded by nearly ten acres of rolling farmland, I could indulge my longing for more animals.

The first was a seven-week-old black-muzzled pup who bore a strong resemblance to his mostly German Shepherd Dog mother but showed traces of his black Lab father. When I picked him up for the first time and he began to whimper and struggle, I held him against me and cooed. That was it. I thanked his owner, a member of my local food co-op, and brought him home to Joey.

I named him Sir Thomas Tom, and we called him Tommy.

Nothing hinted at the dramatic influence Tommy would have on my life. Joey was my special dog, and would be until he died. Tommy acknowledged his seniority and tried to emulate him. Disdaining the woollen sock stuffed with a ticking alarm clock I'd been told would mimic his mother's heartbeat, he slept curled up against Joey instead.

By the time Suki joined our household, Tommy was a strong, confident dog who'd assumed the role of pack leader. Suki was a gift from a Montreal family who were guilt-stricken about her bored and lonely existence in their small backyard. She was four years old, an elegant Scotch collie, and the most intelligent dog of my acquaintance.

Dogs connect, bond, befriend, and fall in love, and from the first minute of their introduction, Tommy and Suki connected, bonded, befriended, and fell in love. As her people drove slowly away, one of the children hung out the car window wailing, "Suki! Suki!" But out in the meadow, cavorting with her new brother Tommy, Suki didn't even look back.

From early morning until they collapsed onto my bedroom carpet at night, Tommy and Suki were together. I discovered, too late, that they weren't just playing. At Tommy's behest, they had recruited neighbouring farm dogs to join them in cattle-chasing. As the cows grazed peacefully

Tommy would spur his pack into nipping at their heels and teats, terrifying them into flight. The dogs ran the tormented cattle until they were so exhausted and stressed that their milk production dried up.

Shaken and horrified, I sent abject apologies. I bought a metal chain and attached Tommy to the back of the house. Thanks to giant, professionally installed bolts, Tommy never escaped or harassed another cow. Suki had no need of restraint. She never strayed from Tommy's side.

Joey, who had adored and tried to kiss the cows from the first time he saw one, took no part in the other dogs' illicit raids. He stayed close to home, preferably inside the house. But one dark evening he wandered outside onto the shoulder of the road. An oncoming car hit him, flinging him into a ditch. I found him there, silent and shaking, immobilized by shock. But alive, still alive.

He spent the night at the veterinary clinic, bundled up in flannel under a heat lamp. By morning he was stable enough for me to drive him to the veterinary college in St. Hyacinthe, where Quebec vets refer their most urgent and most complicated cases. Joey, with a severely fractured jaw, was in that category.

During his surgeries—the first one failed—Joey's stoicism sustained him as he recovered from having a metal plate screwed into his broken bones. He soon charmed the staff, who rewarded him with affection and special treatment. If he felt abandoned, he didn't show it. He enjoyed attention, ate with relish, and gave no indication that he was in pain, though he must have been. "Life is what it is," Joey seemed to say, "and if you've got a biscuit in your pocket, so much the better."

But on a freezing morning in early December, while Joey was still in St. Hyacinthe, all of our lives changed forever. I was on the highway to Montreal, erect and watchful in the passenger seat, a box of exams at my feet. The road was treacherously icy. As a car appeared in the distance, ours skidded sideways on a patch of glare ice and then skated crazily across the highway, directly into the path of the oncoming car.

The impact was ferocious. Our car was crushed into pieces that spilled out onto the highway. The exams were drenched in blood. An ambulance arrived, extricated me from smashed glass and metal, and transported me to the local hospital. Although the driver was almost unscathed, my injuries were so extensive that the worried doctors arranged my transport to a state-of-the-art hospital in eastern Quebec.

In those first few hours, when my collapsed lungs were drowning in blood and I couldn't talk or breathe, couldn't move or feel my legs, a vision appeared to me: I was strapped into a wheelchair with Ivan and the dogs at my feet. I had a typewriter on my lap, and I was writing. I decided to live.

For over a month, I was the most interesting case in the hospital, strapped down in a quarantined ICU, a respirator rattling beside me night and day. Morphine, valium, and curare pumped through my veins. My body was broken and torn. I had permanent nerve damage, and my right leg was now slightly shorter than the left.

Months later, when I visited the doctor who had accompanied me in the ambulance, he leaned over my wheelchair and embraced me. "Madame," he said, his voice shaky with emotion, "you were tossed down into the gates of hell. I never expected to see you alive again."

During my hospitalization, Ivan's smart, no-nonsense, endlessly kind babysitter moved him into her house. And when Joey was released from St. Hyacinthe, she took him in, too. Tommy and Suki fared less well with another caretaker; they were erratically fed and watered, and confined to the basement.

One brilliant wintry afternoon I returned home by ambulance, and began to heal. Joey, old and patched with metal, kept me company, a broken dog with his broken human. Tommy and Suki were my personal trainers, my companions as I relearned the art of walking. And Ivan, by now in kindergarten, restored my sense of motherhood.

After nearly two years of convalescence, I took stock of my life: although my body was now crooked and faultily calibrated, I was still young and otherwise healthy, a strong engine in a damaged chassis. I was also impatient to plunge into whatever my second chance at life might offer.

There was one great sadness. Joey, who at ten years old had outlived most of his breed, was suffering from congestive heart failure. His last meal was a McDonald's hamburger on the way to the vet. I held him as he stopped breathing; it was such an easy passage. Afterward I wept, mourning this most contented and peaceable of dogs.

The day after Christmas, Ivan and I departed freezing Quebec for the excitement of a trip to Disney World and the Florida Keys, a gift from one of my brothers to celebrate my return to real life. Then Ivan returned to Montreal to his godmother's care while I travelled, alone, to fulfill my dream of visiting Haiti's magnificent Citadelle La Ferrière and the nearby ruins of the Sans-Souci Palace.

My four-day trip went spectacularly, gloriously awry. I spent it in Port-au-Prince sightseeing, mostly in the company of Joseph Namphy, a hotelier and environmentalist who proselytized about his reforestation project, serenaded me with baritone renditions of "My Way," and didn't laugh when I bought bread from street vendors and fed it to homeless dogs. After I returned home, he courted me with monthly visits and daily *billets doux* written on Le Plan Vert/The Green Plan letterhead. We married in May, and at the end of the school year, Ivan, Tommy, Suki, and I moved to Haiti.

Five years later, Haitian politics, Joe's family connections, and relentless violence brought a crashing end to our merged family, to Joe's businesses, and ultimately to our marriage. Ivan and I fled Haiti, but Tommy stayed behind—and in so doing, changed the trajectory of my life. If there is such a thing as rebirth, then I was reborn after I returned to Haiti to rescue him. Before that he'd been like all my other dogs, making my life simpler and better. But then, at the end of his life, my ailing old dog pulled me right into the heart of the mystery and magic of the shared world of dogs and humans. He became an ambassador for other dogs, and he led me to understand that I was meant to be a rescuer. It was a revelation that has guided me ever since.

This mission to rescue dogs was decades in the making. Now that I'm heading into the final chapters of my life, it's time to tell Tommy's story and the stories of those dogs who followed. It's a tribute and memorial to him and to them, and to all the rescuers I've met along the way. It's part of my unfinished business, and it began during the dangerous time when I returned to Haiti.

# PART 1

## I WAS (NOT) LEFT BEHIND

# ONE

## Sir Thomas Tom

It was August 1990. Port-au-Prince's Toussaint Louverture International Airport shimmered in the sunlight, undulating heat waves refracting the silver wings of the Air Canada jet. As I rushed toward the terminal building, the tarmac burned the soles of my sandalled feet. The very ground seemed to be urging me forward to the Rue Baussan in downtown Port-au-Prince, where my ailing dog Tommy was.

Until 1988, when I fled from it, Haiti had been my adopted homeland, where Joe and I were raising our sons, my Ivan and his Paul. Two things changed that. The first was a coup d'état that reinstalled Joe's brother, General Henri Namphy, as Haiti's president cum military dictator. The second was that leaked excerpts from my forthcoming book about the Duvaliers' corrupt, repressive reign unleashed torrents of abuse and threats against me and against Joe's businesses. Suddenly our lives had become intolerable, and temporarily removing myself from the fray seemed the only prudent course. But now I was back, pockets full of dog biscuits, frantic to embrace and reclaim the old dog I'd left behind two years before.

I hadn't meant to abandon him. I'd planned to return within a few months; by then, Joe and I predicted, the furor would have died down. I'd booked Paul's passage as well as Ivan's so that I could keep both boys safe in Montreal until the Haitian situation improved. But Paul didn't want to leave his father, and so only Ivan and I flew out, entrusting Tommy, along with our energetic little Shih Tzus Toussaint and Taffy, to Joe and Paul.

Haitian politics hijacked my plans. Another coup d'état sent Henri Namphy into exile in the Dominican Republic and precipitated violent attacks on his allies and family. Raging mobs smashed the Namphy family's houses. My mother-in-law's military guards stole her car and looted and gutted her modest house. Her feisty little dog, Puppy, was never seen again.

Rumours swirled that Henri's enemies planned to kill Joe, and one terrifying night he survived only by pleading for his life after gunmen accosted him. When wealthy industrialist Michael Madsen offered him refuge in his fortified home, I rejoiced, and urged him to take the dogs with him. Exhausted and sick at heart about his ruined fortunes, Henri's misery and humiliation, and the destruction of his mother's home, Joe asked me how I could think of dogs at such a time.

"They have nobody but you there to protect them," I responded evenly.

And so as Haiti convulsed and Joe's world teetered and crumbled, Tommy accompanied him up to Michael Madsen's palatial home to wait it out until calm was restored under General Prosper Avril, Haiti's new military dictator. But to avoid annoying his hosts, Joe left Toussaint and Taffy in the care of Claudette, our housekeeper, in a house that could at any time be attacked and invaded, and where the phone was no longer in service.

I accepted Joe's sense that arriving with three dogs would stretch his rescuers' tolerance past the breaking point, and if only one could go, it had to be Tommy, the dog who shared my breakfast, snoozed at my feet, and hopped into the backseat of my car for what he saw as joy rides throughout Port-au-Prince as I shuttled Ivan and Paul to the hotel swimming pool, to tennis and tae-kwan-do lessons, and to their friends' houses. Tommy was the dog of my heart, and Joe was right to choose him.

Up at their hillside estate, the Madsens' telephone still functioned, and so Joe and I were in constant contact. His situation remained precarious. His once-obsequious employer at the Hotel El Rancho fired him in a sarcastic, self-serving public announcement. Acquaintances shunned him and friends avoided him; only the Madsens had the courage to harbour him.

I listened to Joe's litany of grievances and offered sympathy and encouragement—until he accused Tommy of adding to his woes. Instead of showing gratitude, Joe complained, Tommy was a guest from hell, barking and whining and lunging at the end of his tether, irritating his hosts and frustrating Joe, who was tiring of apologizing for *my* dog's noisy protests.

I couldn't believe my ears. "What! Tommy's tied *outside*? Tommy's tied to a friggin' *mango tree*?"

"You and your damned dogs!" Joe said bitterly. The next time we spoke, he'd sent Tommy back to our unsafe premises on the Rue Baussan and showed no interest in finding out how he and the little dogs were faring there. Yet this was the man who for years had willingly if not joyously shared a home with my dogs as a *sine qua non* of my marrying him. "Love me, love my dogs," I had cautioned him early on, and he'd eagerly embraced dogs as part of our marital package.

Frantic weeks passed until our house had its phone service restored. When I spoke to Claudette, she told me that Tommy was missing me, and that even she, whom he'd always loved, couldn't comfort him or coax him to eat much. Worse, she was feeling so unwell herself that she'd asked her sister Josette to take over her housekeeping duties until she recovered.

When Joe finally left the Madsens and returned home, he proposed that we meet for a romantic weekend in Miami. I leapt at the suggestion. "And you could bring Tommy!" I exclaimed. That was the last I heard of the romantic weekend, though I did receive the occasional love letter, including one scrawled page that read in its entirety, "I Want You! I Need You! I Love You!"

I was trapped in Montreal, longing to return to Haiti but terrified to do so. I confided in Claudette, who was still on sick leave but visited the house and the dogs whenever she felt well enough. "Ah, Madame Elizabeth, please, *please* come as soon as it's safe, oui?" But when pressed to suggest just when that might be, Claudette burst into tears. "So much violence, so much danger," she said haltingly. "I don't know when it will all end. I don't even know if it will ever end."

Her despair was contagious. If it was too dangerous for me, it was also dangerous for my dogs. I had nightmares remembering the fury that followed the Duvaliers' escape to France in 1986. Vengeful hordes had even stoned the street dogs who'd staked out the paramilitary Tonton Macoute stations where they begged for scraps of food. In that poorest of nations, dogs were the lowest of the low and few wasted any pity on them. If things turned ugly again and gunmen once more attacked our house, Tommy, Toussaint, and Taffy wouldn't stand a chance. And Joe, it seemed to me, didn't give a damn.

I had to act. I had to bring them to Canada, beginning with Tommy. My first attempt, asking Joe to bring him to Miami, had failed. My second was to ask if he'd simply ship Tommy to Montreal or even to Miami, where friends had agreed to collect him and send him on to me. Although I chose my words carefully and willed myself to sound pleasant, Joe refused to cooperate. No, no! Tommy was fine where he was. And Joe had more important things to do than ship dogs from one continent to another.

Before this I'd been worried. Now worry was mushrooming into alarm. I'd assumed that Joe would be glad to be relieved of the dogs, especially Tommy, the biggest and oldest, and the one who was surely the saddest at my defection, as he must have interpreted it.

I tried a third time, with a detailed plan. I provided instructions on how to assemble Tommy's travel crate, then lying in two pieces in the courtyard. I quoted Air Canada schedules and assured Joe that I'd prepay Tommy's passage. I'd also phone Dr. Robert Joseph, our veterinarian, one of the very few in Port-au-Prince, to arrange the necessary vaccinations and paperwork. It would require very little of you, I pleaded, and would mean so much to me.

No, Joe snapped, No! And then, his voice rising to a bellow as his words fed his anger, he lobbed his problems at me like mini-grenades: Haiti is self-destructing and my businesses are failing; orders for our beaded wedding dresses have plunged! The tannery was attacked and has been shut down! Not to mention HANA—and here, speaking of his beloved, embryonic Haiti–U.S. airline project he'd proudly named Haiti National Airlines, Joe could hardly contain his rage. HANA is mired in financial woes and investor fury. The commercial plane owners have reneged on their agreement to lease us an aircraft. The fabric for the air hostesses' costumes was stolen *out of the house* and most of the girls have already quit. The pilots have vanished into thin air. Almost all my airport contacts have dropped me like a hot potato. All this, and you're browbeating me about a *dog*? So you can see that I have no time to invest in Tommy's travel plans. And aren't you coming back soon anyway? Then why make such a big production about bringing Tommy to Montreal?

I'd never been able to compete with HANA, but I had perfected the art of coexisting with her. In Joe's psyche she was much more than an airline or just another business; she was his greatest dream and ambition, the culmination of his life's trifectate goal: to become rich and famous, to accomplish this in Haiti, and to soar in public estimation above his brother Henri, a lieutenant general. And the more troubled HANA became, the more powerful a hold she had on my husband.

My marriage was in trouble, and so was old Tom. I renewed my efforts to rescue him. Joe, humiliated and embittered by HANA's plight, was obstinately uncooperative, but surely he wouldn't stand in the way of someone else's efforts? A kindly American-missionary airline pilot came to the rescue, offering to fly Tommy back to Florida, where he'd put him on a flight to Montreal. The plan was as simple as it was generous. What could go wrong?

I waited with nervous excitement for the pilot's post-flight phone call, but when it came, the news was not good. "Joe refused to let him go," he reported. "Yes, Tommy was right there and he looked all right, I guess, but unless I'd taken a machete and coup d'état-ed Joe, there wasn't a thing I could do."

I was growing desperate. Rachel Vincent, a young journalist of my acquaintance, was about to visit Haiti, and I begged her to go to my house on the Rue Baussan to check on Tommy and the Shih Tzus. A month later she handed me a photograph of a subdued, sad-faced Tommy lying passively on the kitchen floor. The photo had captured him well, she said. He was quiet and unexcited by her visit, friendly but distant. I knew then that something was seriously wrong with my dog.

On a bright June morning in the boardroom of the Montreal SPCA, where I was researching an article about pet therapy, I had an epiphany: I wasn't going to return to live in Haiti. This clarity brought me relief but also sadness. I loved Haiti even though it had become so unstable that neither Ivan nor I could be safe there. I missed Paul, I missed Joe as he'd once been, and I grieved for the end of our life together.

My decision was not unilateral. Joe was more committed to HANA than to our marriage. Despite myriad setbacks, including cost overruns and a gutting under-capitalization that had intensified since Henri's humiliating ouster, Joe was confident that HANA would take flight. I chose the security of my homeland while Joe accepted the dangers of his so that he could follow his dream of owning an airline.

Months before, he'd sent an emissary to Montreal with a briefcase full of documents and a request that I sign over my few shares of HANA so that Joe could sell them and stave off bankruptcy. I signed on the spot. By then, despite phone calls and amorous notes carelessly dashed off in oversized cursive, Joe had grown increasingly irascible and distant. My marriage, once so comfortable and solid, was collapsing. I couldn't even mourn. I had to concentrate all my energies on rebuilding my life in Montreal. Most urgently, I had to find a job.

Days after I made my decision, an unsolicited job offer dropped like manna from heaven and I became editor-in-chief of a thousand-page history book, *Chronicle of Canada*. After only a few days I began to bring Dolly, the young German Shepherd Dog I'd just adopted from the SPCA, to the office. I'd told Joe the truth about being unable to live without a dog. But Dolly didn't replace Tommy; she just expanded my heart.

Then a letter from my friend Yvonne Trimble in Port-au-Prince gave me a wrenching new perspective on events in Haiti. She hadn't wanted to tell me, she wrote, but Joe was now deeply involved with another woman. "*Your* husband is cheating on you in *my* house," she wrote, in a sour reference to Joe's mistress Mimi's recent purchase of the house that Yvonne and Joel, her husband, used to rent.

I was flabbergasted. I'd had no idea, no suspicions. How could I have, with Joe's admittedly intermittent romantic outbursts and declarations of love? But now I understood why he was never home when I phoned: "home" was Mimi's house. Until I had inadvertently facilitated their relationship by choosing to remain safe in Montreal, Joe had continued to betray both me and Mimi.

At first I was more astonished than angry. But then, as I attempted to make sense of this new development, I was struck by the urgency of its practical implications. With Joe's defection, who'd been looking after the dogs? A few weeks later, another letter answered that question.

"Elizabeth, you have to come back and do something," my stepson Paul pleaded. "Don't tell Joe that I'm writing, but I just dropped by the house and Tommy is in terrible condition. He's starving and looks sick and I'm scared that he's going to die. I contacted the Canadian Consulate and Embassy but they refused to do anything. You'd better come and get him. I don't know what else to do."

I wept and raged. Then I picked up the phone and made a series of calls to Haiti. One, to my friend Isidore who lived near our house, was a plea to send money to Josette to buy Tommy food. I'd soon be there, I said, and would repay him as soon as I arrived. Two weeks later I was standing, frantic with impatience, in the long lineup to clear Immigration and Customs in the chaos of Port-au-Prince's arrival terminal.

Nobody met me at the airport. A ruinous fuel shortage was forcing everyone to ration their supplies, and that included Yvonne and Joel. I crammed myself into a shared taxi for the hot, sweaty ride into the city. At the Rue Baussan, I slid out and began to pound at the gate barricading the house that used to be my home.

The massive gate creaked open and my old world reappeared. I hugged Josette and then rushed into the kitchen and flung myself onto the floor to hug my dog. Yvonne and Joel were already there, flushed with emotion. Tommy leaned into me as I buried my face in his fur. When I took his whitened face in my hands and caressed it, he smiled at me trustingly, as if he'd always known I'd come back for him.

As I lay there with Tommy in my arms, rocking back and forth, I felt the whisper of a pressure against my leg.

"Ti-Taffy! Little Taffy!" The matted, emaciated Shih Tzu wagged her tail hard, and I swept her up into my embrace.

I remembered the dog biscuits and fished them out of my pocket. Tommy sniffed at my offering and then laid his head back down on the cool floor, his tail gently waving. But Taffy began to eat, first nibbling and then wolfing down the food. "Joel, I *told* you she'd come with dog food," Yvonne exclaimed.

Minutes later I glanced around. "Where's Toussaint?"

Josette looked pained. "Toussaint is gone, Madame Elizabeth," she said. "Burglars broke into the house next door and Toussaint crawled out under the gate into the street and barked at them, so they shot and killed him."

"Oh, God! Poor, brave little Toussaint!"

"Ah, Madame!" Josette exclaimed. "Toussaint had courage, oui? He wanted to be like Tommy."

Tommy, hearing his name, lifted his head wearily. Pressed up against him, cuddled into his cavernous belly, Taffy was devouring a biscuit. Nearby, where we'd always fed the dogs, a cracked blue bowl was heaped with *ti-mi*— cooked millet—smeared with six raw egg yolks. "Monsieur Isidore sent me money to buy eggs for Tommy," Josette said. "But Tommy's sick. He hardly wants to eat." Looking down at her bare feet, she added, "Madame Elizabeth! Monsieur Joe hasn't paid us for months now, no money for food and supplies, no salaries. But I always give Tommy and Taffy any little thing I can find."

In this hungry country, Josette had kept my dogs alive; when Isidore had sent her money designated for dog food, she spent it all on what she considered life-saving eggs for Tommy. "Josette, *se bon moun ou ye*—you are a good person," I said shakily. "I'm taking the dogs up to Yvonne and Joel's house now, but tomorrow I'll be back, and I'll have money for you. We'll talk, and I'm longing to see Claudette!" I embraced her again and tears welled in her eyes. She stood, swaying against me, her body as flimsy as her fraying and faded cotton print housedress.

"Monsieur Joe brought *vagabonds* into the house, Madame. They took everything, and they still come here to sleep. But Claudette saved some of your things for you. She'll bring them tomorrow."

If only I'd known! I would have asked Yvonne and Joel to liberate the dogs from this cesspool of a house, and I would have sent them money for Josette. Yvonne read my mind. "If only we'd known," she murmured.

Joel, who'd gone to investigate the condition of the house, clattered back downstairs. "We need to leave right now," he said. "After dark the road's not safe."

"Haiti is much more dangerous than when you lived here," Josette added.

Once we'd started off toward Yvonne and Joel's mountainside home, Tommy and Taffy beside me in the backseat, Joel described the carnage in the house. The rooms upstairs were mouldering and filthy, grit covering the floor. The electricity and water had been cut off and there was an overpowering stench from unflushable toilets. The master bedroom had been pillaged.

Beside me, the dogs bounced from side to side as we groaned up the decrepit road, swerving to avoid craterous potholes and a stream of pedestrians and animals, mostly goats and mangy dogs. "It'd be a big waste to come all the way to Haiti to save one dog and then run over another one," Joel said, slamming on the brakes as we careened across the road.

I glanced over at Tommy and made him a promise. "Hey, old boy, I'll never, ever leave you again."

Yvonne nudged me. "He's sick, Elizabeth. He's a rack of bones and really weak. Wouldn't you be better leaving him here instead of putting him through all the stress of a long flight?"

I shook my head. "Tommy's going with me. Sick or not, I'm never leaving him again."

kept my promise to Josette to return to the house, but only because Joel had a business meeting downtown. Fuel was so scarce that he had to suction it out of his generator to keep his truck running. "If we'd met you at the airport, we wouldn't have had enough gas to get home again," he said apologetically for the third time.

The next day I paid overdue salaries, sent out for cleaning supplies, and had an emotional reunion with Claudette. She was wearing her best dress that had once been one of mine, with a shiny plastic belt cinching her minuscule waist and a length of blue cotton bound tightly around her head. In the two years since I'd last seen her she'd grown old and emaciated, her beautiful face gaunt and sculpted. What was wrong with her? "Ah," Claudette said, pointing upward, "le Bon Dieu alone knows because the doctor doesn't, and despite his prescriptions for all manner of pills and tonics, I can feel my life ebbing away."

"What can I do to help?"

"Nothing, Madame Elizabeth," she said tranquilly. "My life is in God's hands, oui?"

She and Josette were sitting across from me at the gashed but sturdy kitchen table, Claudette as theatrical as Josette was plain-spoken, her stories enhanced by pantomime and dramatic pauses. When I asked if they could explain why Monsieur Joe had refused to send Tommy to me in Canada, Claudette sighed deeply, raised her shoulders, and spread her hands outward. "At first, to make sure you would come back," she said. "Later, to punish you for going. To hurt you, because he knew how much you loved Tommy, oui?"

And what about Mimi? I asked. Tell me about Mimi. The sisters shifted uneasily. "She began to come here almost from the day you left," Claudette said softly. "At first we didn't know what to make of it."

"She got the worst of the bargain," Josette chimed in. "She took your husband but she left your dogs."

When we'd stopped laughing, I asked about the vaga-bonds who now slept in the house. Had any of them ever hurt the dogs?

The sisters reflected, and then said in unison, "No, no, they never hurt them." "Except," Claudette reminded Josette, "when Tommy attacked that bad element, you remember, that vagabond who sleeps in Ivan's room, in Ivan's bed? Monsieur Joe said Tommy had a bad temper and sent him to the vet for *piki*—shots?"

I sighed heavily. And what about the little dogs? How did they fare when I was gone?

"Ah! Well, after you left, Madame Elizabeth, Tommy allowed Toussaint and Taffy to sleep next to him, and you remember how Toussaint tried to imitate Tommy but Tommy would just growl at him? Well, Tommy started to appreciate Toussaint's company. They grew close, *pa vrè*— not so—Josette?"

"And after Toussaint died, Tommy and Taffy comforted each other," Josette added.

"Taffy is going to stay with Yvonne and Joel," I told them. "Yvonne loves Taffy. She's given her a good bath and groomed her, and Taffy is eating well and seems really happy."

The sisters nodded approval. "That's good, oui? Taffy deserves a nice home."

We spent the next hours scouring the house, a Herculean task. I also avenged Tommy for the "bad element" who'd provoked him to bite. Armed with a kitchen knife and a garden hose miraculously spared from theft, I marched into my son's bedroom. As Josette and Claudette applauded, I attached the hose to Ivan's cherished water bed and bled it dry. Then I slashed the rubberized mattress so that no one could ever again sleep on it.

Back at Yvonne and Joel's house, Tommy was tired and happy. But although we fed him home-cooked meals, he ate capriciously. Taffy, however, had rebounded from her months of privation and gobbled her food, then pranced happily around the house. And when she grew tired, she'd just snuggle against Tommy.

As the days passed, the issue of getting Tommy's veterinary travel documents was becoming urgent. Joel couldn't help. With his fuel supply dwindling, he'd cancelled all but non-essential travel. Finally, four days before I was scheduled to return to Montreal, my friend Max managed to rent a diesel jeep, an impressive feat in a country where diesel was now the only available fuel.

We loaded Tommy into the jeep, our mission being to find enough diesel to take him to the vet and home again. We drove from gas station to gas station, but the lines of frustrated, irate drivers were so long that, one after another, they ran out of fuel before we reached our turn at the pumps. Hours passed. Tommy, stuck in the broiling jeep with us, panted in the terrible heat. By now he'd emptied his water bowl, so I poured Max's bottled water into it and watched as Tommy lapped it up. "I hope you appreciate all this," I muttered. Tommy's face lit up, and with the slow motion of exhaustion, he wagged his tail.

Late in the afternoon, at yet another station, Max turned off the engine. "We're not going to make it to the pump," he said matter-of-factly. "When we need to move forward, I'll get out and push, and you steer." Then he cranked up the jazz playing on Radio Métropole.

We finally managed to buy five gallons of diesel. Then we began the steep ascent to the nearest vet. We were too late. The clinic door was shuttered for the night. Poor Tommy! In the silence of shared despondency I fought back panic as we climbed back up the treacherous mountain road with my undocumented dog.

The next day Joel came to the rescue. "I've gotten you an appointment with our vet for tomorrow morning," he announced. "I need to go to town anyway." Hallelujah!

The veterinary clinic was less than twenty-five yards from where Joel dropped us off, but it was almost more than Tommy could manage. Inside, he collapsed onto the floor, panting. I took a seat opposite a dark-suited man holding a plump black cocker spaniel on a red leather leash. The man started slightly as he noticed Tommy's head, which had become shrunken and pointy at the top where the bones joined together into a V.

"My ex-husband didn't take care of him," I volunteered, my anger at Joe's appalling neglect reignited by this stranger's evident horror. "But now he's going back to Canada with me."

The man forced his eyes away from Tommy. "My Bijou"—he pointed to his wriggling, healthy young spaniel—"is coming with me to West Africa, my next assignment."

"That's a tremendously long journey," I said, leaning forward to pet the spaniel. "Poor girl, you've got a long trip ahead of you."

The man smiled. "She does. But there's no alternative. I couldn't leave Bijou behind."

I swallowed. "No, you couldn't."

"Our dogs are lucky," he said kindly, gesturing with his open palm toward Bijou and Tommy.

"Very lucky," I murmured, understanding that he was referring to Haiti's piteous dogs and their relentless struggle for survival. Most people ignored them or chased them away. Sometimes someone would toss them a piece of bread or a chicken bone. But these skinny, four-legged scavengers might also be maimed or killed. I'd seen jeering children pelt a shrieking dog and then howl with mirth when its limbs snapped audibly or blood gushed from its battered body and the tormented creature dragged itself away. "Why do you do that?" I'd scream. "Because it's funny," they'd scream back at me. As Stan Goff lamented in his book *Hideous Dream: A Soldier's Memoir of the US Invasion of Haiti,* "[I]f there is really a cosmic justice that transcends death, the Somozas and Kissingers and Hitlers and Suhartos and Sharons and Ollie Norths will be reincarnated an appropriate number of times as a Haitian dog."

"*So* lucky," I said. Then I settled back into my chair to wait.

# TWO

## Tommy's World:
## An Enemy Within

The clinic was an oasis of peacefulness in a turbulent, suffering society, a clean and comfortable facility that offered its four-legged (or winged) patients much more sophisticated and comprehensive medical treatment than most Haitians could even dream of receiving. I'd visited the Hôpital Général several times while reporting for Reuters, and had nearly wept at the sight of strangers sharing bare mattresses in miserable wards so lacking in basic necessities that the patients' families were forced to bring in their own food and medical supplies. Your open wound needed stitching up? Then send someone to the pharmacy to buy needle, thread, and rubbing alcohol. You're hungry? Hopefully you have relatives to feed you.

The complexities of coexisting in this very different world extended to dogs. Where most struggled for mere survival, Tommy and our other dogs were pampered aristocrats.

I looked around the waiting room. Other than a uniquely Haitian hand-carved wall plaque, it looked like clinics everywhere in North America. Many of the clients who passed through its sturdy wooden doors were expatriates, and almost all their dogs looked like members of a different species from the hopeless curs out on the streets. Despite his decrepitude and his mixed lineage, even Tommy was recognizably "foreign," as Haitian passersby seldom failed to remark when we'd drive by in my Nissan Sunny.

I leaned back, closed my eyes, and in this brief reprieve from the turmoil outside, surrendered to reverie. How different our early years in Haiti had been, from the first moment Joe had welcomed us into Fo Pa Plus (No More Is Needed)—an idyllic chalet he'd rented in the mountains far above Port-au-Prince. The house was framed by bougain-villea and nestled against a rock-ledged garden that opened into a small fenced-in field where Tommy would chase butterflies. The air was fresh and cool. The patio over-looked the verdant valley that, by night, resounded with shouts and chanting as the vodoun priest presided over his weekly *cérémonies*. Streaming sunlight ushered in the day and shimmering sunset put our two boys to sleep. By the time Joe and I went to bed, the night sky would be inky black.

But from our first day in Haiti, our paradise also reflected the realities of life in that struggling country. Joe's car broke down on the day we arrived, and the men he hired to repair it robbed us instead. It was late when we finally arrived at Fo Pa Plus, and we were hungry. But Phany, Joe's housekeeper, had forgotten the groceries at the store; when Joe reproached her, she retorted angrily that it was quite normal to leave five bags of groceries at the cash register, and she did not appreciate being scolded.

Newly married and determined to be conciliatory, I defused their shouting match. Then, as Ivan whined and Joe grumbled, we dined on what I dug out of my purse: crushed packets of airline crackers, peppermints, a package of dried soup. Only Tommy did not go to bed hungry. I'd brought a plastic bag full of kibble, which he happily gobbled down. Phany, still sulking, watched him with narrowed eyes. I didn't realize it then, but the battle lines were already being drawn.

In desperately poor Haiti, the best that most dogs can expect is the occasional morsel of food in return for guarding the premises. Dogs seldom live inside houses, and only the luckiest may sleep in courtyards or on porches without being chased away. Few dogs are neutered, vaccinated, or vetted; if they fall ill, they endure or they die and another luckless mongrel takes their place.

In this sad world, what was Phany to make of this new canine arrival with his doting humans, his very own cushioned bed and neck scarf, dog dish and kibble, medicine and flea powder, veterinary records and travel documents, tagged collar and balls and Frisbees?

It didn't help that Suki, travelling on a separate flight, soon joined us. Severely groomed after a recent encounter with burrs, she leapt out of the car and flew through the field toward a joyous reunion with Tommy. With the canine couple together again, Tommy shed his sadness like a snakeskin and glowed. Suki's lush collie coat grew back in clouds of fuzz. And ever the thinker, she invented new games and pursuits for their daily activities.

They should have been sublimely happy. And yet: something was wrong. Once friendly and eager to welcome visitors, Tommy and now Suki were wary, Tommy aggressively so, of everyone except Joe, Ivan, Paul, and me. In the presence of Phany, her younger sister Judith, the local children, and the job- or favour-seekers who arrived in steady streams, Tommy growled, snarled, and snapped while the regal Suki bared her teeth and shrank back against her larger, more powerful companion.

I began to hear complaints: Tommy had chased a child, bitten a man who was repairing our stove, terrified a *marchande*—an itinerant peddler—when she came into our courtyard to sell the vegetables she carried in a giant basket on her head. These incidents always took place when I was in Port-au-Prince at the hotel Joe managed and where we had a room that I used as my study. Tommy was a problem, Phany declared. What was Madame Elizabeth going to do about it?

Joe was concerned; biting dogs could be costly, he said. But when he investigated, he discovered that the allegedly victimized repairman had no marks and admitted, after some thought, that Tommy had *seemed* menacing but hadn't actually attacked. In other words, the bitten man had not been bitten. "But you'll have to control your dogs," Joe warned me, "because these people will invent stories to try to get money out of me."

What, I wondered, had transformed Tommy and Suki into a two-dog pack of vigilantes? They were good dogs. They didn't need my control, they needed my help. The next day I summoned Phany and Judith to the dining room. "Something's upsetting my dogs, and it's got to stop." I paused. "Right away."

Young Judith looked worried but Phany went on the offensive. "In Haiti dogs don't live in people's houses," she said. "M'sieu Joe never had a dog before."

"But he does now. He also has a wife who's going to resolve this dog problem."

"Madame! Tommy doesn't like black people," Judith piped up, glancing at Phany for approval. "Just like Pipi doesn't like white people," she reminded me merrily. Pipi, a short-haired white dog, was celebrated in our Port-au-Prince suburb of Thomassin for biting white people, even those who, like me, tried to bribe him. He'd eat the treats we tossed him, then bare his teeth and attack.

I smiled grimly. "Tommy never had a problem with black people in Canada," I said. "He saw them all the time at my house." Judith had the grace to look abashed, and I continued. "But in *this* house, something's making Tommy and Suki unhappy. Someone must be taunting or even hurting them."

I ignored their sputters of denial. "I don't know who's doing it and I don't *want* to know. But it has to stop. So here's what I'm going to do. I'm going to let *you* deal with it, Phany. Whatever's happening, *you* stop it. You have one week. After that, if either Tommy or Suki hides away or snarls when you or your friends are around, I'm just going to fire everybody and clear the place out."

I never learned who had been tormenting my dogs. I continued to leave the house every morning, praying I was doing the right thing. I was. At the end of just one week, the dogs were already more relaxed. Within a month, they were back to normal. I have photos of a smiling Phany with Tommy and Suki hovering beside her on the porch. The *marchande* no longer hesitated before opening the gate into our courtyard. And I never again had to worry about an enemy within the house.

But outside our modest enclave, enemies abounded, even though Thomassin hadn't yet descended into the abyss that was swallowing Port-au-Prince. There, roiling shanty-towns spewed hunger and poverty, violence and despair, and proliferated like creeping vines that strangled interlopers and residents alike. Thomassin people were luckier: they planted small gardens, traded or sold produce and poultry, attended the religious services offered by *houngans,* pastors, or priests, and aimed to send at least some of their children to some sort of school for at least some of the time.

But in this rustic world, we and our "bourgeois" neighbours were like aliens from another planet. Thomassin was where we escaped the heat and chaos of Port-au-Prince, where we breathed in purer, cooler air and slept easily at night. It was where our children could safely traipse the paths from the main road where the *camionettes*—vans retrofitted to accommodate dozens of squashed, paying travellers—dropped them off after school.

And dogs: all the bourgeois houses had dogs, and these dogs guarded the premises until their people bolted the gates shut for the night. Even our rented chalet had come with a dog, an aggressive Doberman who briefly terrorized us and challenged Tommy; then she devoured a neighbour's kitten and Joe sent her away to a convent of nuns who prized her ferocity toward intruders.

As well, we bourgeois all enjoyed electricity, running water, indoor plumbing, cable for our colour televisions, computers, telephone landlines, private schools for our children, cars, passports with foreign visas, doctors and dentists, and solid houses with domestic helpers—along with escape plans for the ever-worrisome scenario of uprisings or attacks against us or our property.

The terrible time came when the real Haiti stormed our gates. Late one night, a gang of young men executed a simple plan: poison all the bourgeois dogs and then, as they died, rob the houses they were guarding. A total of twelve dogs died that night. The vet managed to save Tommy, but Suki had already died in my arms after dragging herself into the house. I had her autopsied and the vet found rat poison. Tommy was bereft. He looked everywhere for his mate until he finally understood that she'd vanished. His health languished, and not from the poison: his heart was broken and his spirit crushed. He no longer wanted to run and play, but kept close to my side and slept.

A young local vet diagnosed severe depression and recommended a series of vitamin B shots to help restore his depleted reserve. It was a treatment I now question, but at the time it seemed sensible and perhaps useful.

Suki's murder shattered me; Thomassin's natural beauty now left me cold. I felt exposed and vulnerable, sick with anxiety every minute I was away from home, leaving my boys and my dog hostage to hateful fortune. Joe told me I was overreacting, but I became obsessed with moving down to Port-au-Prince and leaving Thomassin behind.

And I found the perfect house on the Rue Baussan, directly opposite an imposing church, St. Louis Roi de France. The house had been designed for security, with towering stone walls and a driveway guarded by locking metal gates. And since our new neighbours were unlikely to throw poison into our yard, Tommy would be much safer.

Phany and Judith didn't come with us; I needed a fresh start in our new home. Joe happily hired Phany for a position at the hotel he managed where she'd have opportunities for advancement. In her place I hired Claudette, a Pentecostal Protestant who described in a lilting voice how much she loved dogs and cats, and even mimed rocking them in her arms. I loved her at first sight and laid out my priorities: the gate must *never* be left open; care first for the boys, then the dog, then the garden, with the house and its exigencies coming last of all.

Claudette, clapping her hands with joy, accepted the job and then, clapping again, asked how soon she could meet Tommy.

I don't know when Tommy stopped mourning Suki. Perhaps he never did. But in the bustle of our life in Port-au-Prince, he began to smile again. In the city he had much more human company. For one thing, I stopped accompanying Joe to the hotel; instead, I worked at home in an open-walled *galerie* that overlooked a jungle of a garden next door and faced the majestic church across the street. The boys came home for lunch and brought friends to play after school. The house rang with shouts of laughter, the thwack of soccer balls, the drone of cable television.

When Tommy wasn't in the study or in the backseat of my car, he was with Claudette in the kitchen. At eight years old, he was no longer a youngster. He was increasingly hard of hearing and slept much more than he used to. He had lost his zeal for romping. He had toothaches—Dr. Joseph extracted two rotten molars. And he was sometimes attacked by ticks that I learned how to tweeze out whole.

But life on the Rue Baussan was good, and more dogs soon joined us. They came to us in a curious way. In 1986, three years after we'd arrived in Haiti and when Henri Namphy first assumed its presidency as chief of a military junta, casual acquaintances declared themselves our great friends and demanded Joe's help in their business ventures. Strangers sought him out and begged favours. So many came knocking that Joe had chairs woven from banana leaves placed in our driveway to accommodate them. Foreigners also contacted him, ingratiating themselves in the hope that

Joe would provide introductions to high-ranked officials, especially to Henri. If fawning and flattering could be measured in liquid units, Joe and I would have drowned in them.

And yet, skeptical and wary as I was, I, too, benefited from Henri's position. Specifically, when former Duvalierists heard that I was researching a book about the Duvaliers, a surprising number of them subjected themselves to interviews with me. Although most of them clearly felt uncomfortable during these sessions, they expected their cooperation to win the approval of the powers that be and to offer a sort of redemption. Which was how I got to spend hours grilling some of the scariest of both François's (Papa Doc) and his successor Jean-Claude's (Baby Doc) officials and acolytes.

One of these, General Gérard Constant—Papa Doc's chief of staff, infamous for his complicity in the execution of fellow officers whom the president-for-life suspected of disloyalty—invited me into his home for a series of interviews. His confidences, reminiscences, and a few confessions were rambling, shocking, and often confusing, and I had to return again and again to the same lines of questioning.

Whereas most Duvalierists now painted themselves as secret dissidents and would-be conspirators, at my first meeting with Constant, this stern, imposing, powerfully built man left me queasy by declaring that he had deeply respected, admired, and even loved Papa Doc. But the dynamic between unrepentant Duvalierist and queasy interviewer changed at our second meeting when I stepped into a puddle in his living room. It was a puppy puddle, and General Constant was mortified. "Mireille raises puppies," he explained, "and"—shaking his head solemnly—"sometimes they make wee wee."

A man writhing with embarrassment over puppy pee is no longer formidable. A man fussily complaining as his wife arrives with a mop is even less so. Suddenly at ease, I bounced down onto the floor and began to play with the culprits, two fluffy little pups, the last of their litter. Only then did the general relax and, it seemed to me, become even freer with his darkest and most shameful recollections.

Several weeks later, the pups were still unadopted. Every time I approached the house I steeled myself to resist them. On my final visit, I carried one thousand *gourdes,* then worth five to the U.S. dollar. "What will happen to the pups if nobody adopts them?" I inquired of Mireille as I turned to leave. Her face lit up and she glanced quickly at her husband.

"I don't know. I hope someone will buy them."

I nodded. "Me too. They're good dogs."

As I expected, she wasn't going to let me go. "You wouldn't like a nice little dog?"

I smiled ruefully. "What would Joe say? We already have Tommy."

"But such small dogs," Mireille persisted.

"Let her be!" the general thundered. "Her husband doesn't want more dogs."

The conversation was going as predicted. "He probably doesn't," I agreed, "but the boys would be thrilled, and I happen to have some money with me." Mireille glanced at her husband; I had addressed the awkward issue of compensation.

"But we couldn't possibly ask you to pay," she said half-heartedly.

"You couldn't possibly get me to take the dogs without paying," I retorted, and opened my bulging purse.

"Well, well, then," General Constant boomed. "Mireille, prepare the receipt and say goodbye to these little ones. They've been much better behaved recently, by the way. Far fewer messes."

The receipt, in Mireille's painstaking handwriting, acknowledged payment and noted, in English, "For Two Puddell Dog." But there was no trace of poodle in the Shih Tzus I named Taffy and Toussaint, and who came to join Tommy on the Rue Baussan.

Toussaint and Taffy longed to play with Tommy, but Tommy remained aloof, a loner who'd lost his mate and made do with select human company. His sadness had burned away, but he'd aged rather than matured. Where he'd once been fiery and dynamic, he was now cranky and lethargic. But he seemed happy again, or at least at peace with his life.

He also retained enough of his machismo to resent young Toussaint, who wanted only to be his sidekick. And yet despite Tommy's surly indifference, the little Shih Tzu strutted and postured at a safe distance from his idol, aping his every move.

One evil night Toussaint proved his worth and Tommy got his comeuppance. In hardworking Haiti, where everyone is busy and even children bustle about, dogs, too, have to work. Tommy's job was to guard our house, and with it our lives.

Henri Namphy's two-year honeymoon with the Haitian people and the world media had ended in bloodshed and repression, and now we were reviled for our connection to him. Bootlickers spewed venom instead of spittle. Hangers-on weighed the costs and rewards of their unwanted loyalty. Acquaintances skittered away from chance encounters. Cautious and cowardly friends apologized and distanced themselves. Only a blessed few held firm; we commiserated with them and got through the ongoing nightmare.

We'd become sitting ducks for Henri's enemies, and for criminals. After all, who could or would protect us from attack, or take vengeance on our attackers? We had to hire armed security guards—ex-military or moonlighting soldiers who, to a man, succumbed to the overwhelming need to sleep on the job.

Joe fired them one after another, having exacted promises of wakefulness that each new guard breached in the dead—and deadliness—of night. One man prowled the house stripped to his clinging underpants, claiming that the coolness of near-nudity made him more vigilant. His successor, cleaning his gun, shot off his own toe. Another stole from the kitchen and our yardman caught him in the act. All of them slumbered and snored. I approached nighttime with dread and would lie awake until dawn, too terrified to sleep.

The only continuity in our Keystone Kops security arrangements was Tommy, who was ordered out to the driveway beside whichever incumbent guard sat nodding off on the banana-leaf chair formerly occupied by Joe's supplicants. "Dogs have to work, too," I told Tommy, patting his greying head.

Tommy's induction into security detail was no laughing matter. Our domestic staff, all of whom lived in during the week, were as vulnerable to attack as we were. They, too, were terrified, and disillusioned about our guards. But they trusted Tommy, and reassured each other that if he heard even the quietest invader, he'd bark and sound the alarm.

On the night of the worst attack, four men with Uzi machine guns scrabbled up and over our high walls. Tommy and the guard slept right through the commotion. If little Toussaint hadn't yelped a warning, we might all have been shot to death. Instead, Tommy woke up and barked ferociously, rousing the guard, who shot wildly at the intruders. He missed them by inches and kept firing until, screaming obscenities and threats, they clambered back over the wall and drove off down the Rue Baussan.

No one went back to bed that night except Tommy, who slunk off into the house and slept. Meanwhile Claudette and her cohorts huddled together, and the next morning delivered an ultimatum: replace our incompetent guard with a reliable one, or they'd quit en masse. They'd heard street talk about plans to eliminate us, and they preferred unemployed destitution to death on the job.

Joe, distraught and uncharacteristically glum, searched again for a reliable guard. He also hired a *boss maçon*—a mason foreman—who specialized in fortifying Port-au-Prince residences. Joe and I watched grimly as the crew hacked down our courtyard's luxuriant trees and then smashed scores of empty wine bottles into shards and cemented them along the perimeter of our stone wall. If the Uzi-toting gunmen returned, they'd slice open their hands trying to haul themselves over it.

It wasn't enough. Claudette delivered the bad news: *everyone knew* that another attack was planned; "bad elements" were cruising the streets and, come nightfall, another attack was certain. Unless Joe and I vacated the house, she and the other domestic staff would have to leave.

Joe, seldom angry and never silent, shook with mute rage. My overriding concern, however, was to plan our getaway. Two hotel owners who'd remained staunch friends agreed to harbour us for as long as we needed. But both categorically refused to accept dogs.

I explained to Claudette why I couldn't leave. Finally she and her colleagues agreed to a compromise: we would stave off attacks by leaving in the late afternoon and spending the night at a hotel, returning home in the morning. It was an arrangement that made her feel safe enough to remain in the house, looking after Tommy and the little dogs.

Our nocturnal retreats ended a month later, in late June, after the city shook from a deafening quarter-hour's thundering of cannons, grenades, and machine-gun fire— during which soldiers freed Henri from house arrest, stormed the palace, removed the civilian president, and pledged allegiance to their violently reinstated president, General Henri Namphy.

Joe was elated and hoarse from celebrating. I was relieved to be back home, but vastly uneasy about Henri's resurgence into illicit, army-fuelled power. Briefly, life returned to normal. Then a new crisis developed, as proofs of my book *Haiti: The Duvaliers and Their Legacy* began circulating and provoked an orgy of personal attacks against me. Macoutes and Duvalierists threatened my life and Joe's businesses. Slanderous articles appeared in newspapers. Joe's family cut off relations with me.

"But I only told the truth!" I protested.

"Fifty years too soon," my hostile in-laws retorted.

I felt as battered and helpless as a beaten puppy. I lost weight, and as my life became an intensifying nightmare, I couldn't sleep. My friends advised me to leave for a month or two until the fire had been extinguished. Claudette concurred, promising to care for the dogs until I returned. And so I packed, made lists, gave instructions. Remember to keep the dogs' water dish filled up. If they seem unwell, ask Joe to take them to Dr. Joseph. I'll be back by Christmas, to life as it used to be.

It was time to go. Joe waited at the front door, jingling his car keys. In the kitchen, Claudette sobbed and clutched her arms together, rocking up and down in grief. "I'll be back soon, Claudette," I murmured. "Oui, Madame Elizabeth," she whispered, racked by a fresh bout of tears. I embraced her and she clung to me, her face damp against mine. As Toussaint and Taffy danced excitedly around the kitchen and jumped up against my legs, I crouched down and ruffled their fur. After that I hugged and kissed Tommy, who stared at me with his knowing brown eyes. Then he turned to face the wall, waiting, with sad resignation, to be left behind.

# THREE

## Au Revoir, Haiti Chérie!

A polite summons roused me from my reverie. Tommy's turn had finally come. In the examination room, the vet ran his hands over Tommy's skeletal frame, lingering on the bony skull. Then, gently ruffling his just-shampooed fur, he remarked, "Our friend isn't feeling very well. He's weak." A short hesitation, and then: "You say you want him to fly back to Canada with you." I nodded silently. "Eh bien, what I'm thinking is, have you considered leaving him here until he's stronger? Because, Madame, I fear that our friend is so weak he may not survive the flight."

I looked into my old dog's trusting eyes and made my decision. "Then he's going to die trying," I said quietly.

The vet sighed. "Very well." He straightened, cast one last look at Tommy, and began to employ the tools of his trade: vaccines, syringed needles, cotton swabs. Tommy winced but made no attempt to escape. As the vet handed me the precious documents, he reached down and stroked Tommy's concave forehead. "Bon voyage, old friend," he murmured. "And good luck."

Two days later, Joel had scrounged up enough fuel to drive us to the airport. I hugged Taffy for the last time, and told her what a very good little girl she was. Then I slowly led Tommy to where Joel was waiting in the truck.

Tommy rode to the airport on my lap, cushioned by my flesh as we pounded over cratered roads littered with rocks and fallen trees, Joel veering to avoid meandering goats and dogs and people who darted out in front of traffic. Adding to the danger, most drivers coped with the fuel shortage by carrying containers of sloshing fuel in their trunks or backseats.

At the airport, Tommy and I shuffled across the broiling expanse of the parking lot and through the congested terminal. He collapsed every few yards and rested, his breathing raspy and uneven, his tongue elongated and drooling. Finally, I had to carry him.

*"Chen-ca mèg, li mèg anpil,"* a Haitian man shouted at me. That dog is skinny, he's really skinny. In a world of bone-thin dogs, gaunt and wasted Tommy stood out.

Inside, after I'd made Tommy as comfortable as I could in his plastic crate, I fastened the padlock that would keep him safely inside. Then, as I watched helplessly, airport personnel hoisted him onto a dolly and carted him off to be stowed with other baggage in the belly of the aircraft.

And I prayed silently that when they wheeled him back to me in Montreal, the vet's misgivings would have proven unfounded.


What was Tommy thinking, imprisoned in the belly of the plane? Was the loud throbbing of jet engines rhythmic and soothing? Did he understand that, in the incomprehensible ways of human beings, I was up in the air with him? Or was he even now dozing off, lulled by vibrations and profound exhaustion?

I myself couldn't sleep, brooding as I was on the violence that had uglified and terrorized our daily life and culminated in our fleeing from Haiti. When the plane landed in Montreal I disembarked with a sense of dread. How could such a frail old dog have survived the flight? The vet had warned me: our friend is weak. I pushed past other travellers and sprinted through Mirabel Airport's baggage department. Where was Tommy?

I heard a deep, assertive bark, Tommy's bark. I veered toward it and saw Tommy's crate on an untended trolley. Get me out of here! Tommy yelped. I'm coming! Thank God you're alive! I replied.

I fumbled with the padlock on Tommy's cage, released the latch, and opened the door just as Agent Christine of the Food Inspection Agency arrived. Tommy struggled to stand and then contented himself with delirious tail-wagging. I reached into the crate and lowered him out onto the floor. His legs were shaky and he collapsed. "He's old and tired from the flight," I said. "He needs food and water."

I handed over his veterinary paperwork. Agent Christine studied it closely, glancing from time to time at Tommy. "I've never seen a dog in worse shape," she observed.

"Chronic malnutrition, neglect, grief, and depression, and he's twelve years old," I said. "To make a long story short, blame my ex-husband."

Grimacing and shaking her head, Agent Christine felt Tommy's shrunken skull. "His paperwork indicates that he was vaccinated only three days ago. You realize that he has to be quarantined?"

Silently, I cursed the fuel shortage. But there was no question of circumventing quarantine. For the next twenty-seven days, Tommy would have to be confined to a cell at an approved veterinary clinic. I couldn't even take him to my own clinic, where I could have visited him every day.

Just as I was grappling with this news, Agent Christine informed me that the approved clinic was closed for the day. I was to keep Tommy away from all other animals and deliver him the next morning. Until then, Tommy (and any contagious bacteria he might harbour) could go home with me.

My friend Yves was waiting to drive me into the city. He lifted Tommy into the car and shook his head. "Sir Thomas Tom needs to see a vet." He paused. "And Joe should be shot."

Tommy lolled beside me, wheezing stale doggy breaths and wagging his tail in slow beats of contentment. Half an hour later I told him, "You're home, Tom! You're finally home!" Yves carried Tommy into the first elevator of his life and he rode trustingly up to the twelfth floor.

Ivan and Dolly greeted us at the door, Dolly the German Shepherd Dog bouncing up and down the stairs from the vestibule to the first floor of my split-level apartment. "A friend!" she seemed to squeal. "You've brought me a friend!"

But Tommy pawed with his wobbly legs at his new cushioned dog bed, turned his head sharply away from the food bowl and communal water dish, and ignored Dolly. Then, in a series of yellow-toothed growls, he set her straight. "This is *my* mom and *my* house," he snarled.

Dolly backed away and sat down. Tommy, his authority established, took a few shaky steps. Then, skinny legs buckling under him, he collapsed onto his cushion and fell asleep.

The next morning I deposited Tommy at the government-mandated veterinary clinic. At first the staff were so shocked at his gaunt, rickety body that they were reluctant to admit him, but their squeamishness quickly turned to compassion. "Poor boy! We'll look after him, don't you worry. When he leaves here, he'll be six or eight pounds fatter."

I begged to be allowed to accompany him to his kennel. Walking down the long lines of caged dogs—Were they all quarantined? I never knew—was like running the gauntlet. Tommy, once powerful and confident, had become a spindly, puny senior who walked haltingly. As the caged dogs barked and a few pawed their bars menacingly as he passed, Tommy shrank against me and trembled, suddenly fearful.

His barred, cement-floored kennel was devoid of comfort except for the blue bed that I'd asked permission to bring. Tommy was frightened and nervous, yet the law required me to leave him there. Tears ran down my cheeks as the kennel door swung shut behind him and my sick old dog whimpered and called out for me. As I walked away, his mewling grew fainter, a wavering riff of melancholy drowned out by more boisterous inmates.

The countdown began. The clinic's weekend holiday schedule shaved three days from Tommy's twenty-seven-day quarantine, and his night at home counted as well. Three weeks after I'd turned my back on him, his nightmare would be over and I'd bring him back home forever.

Tommy didn't know that. What he knew was that I'd reappeared in his kitchen refuge and swooped him up and saved him, as he'd always known I would. But after a few hours in what he understood was his new home, I'd tricked him into a car ride that led straight to solitary confinement in a canine prison.

And yet, with his limitless capacity for forgiveness, Tommy forgave me. On that clear September morning when Yves drove me to the kennel to bring him home,

Tommy smiled and shuffled beside me toward the exit—and liberation. "Tommy's going home!" a young kennel attendant called out to her colleague, and both young women wiped away tears.

The veterinarian shook my hand and gave me the release paperwork. He was concerned, though: Tommy had gained only two ounces since his arrival. The vet shook his head. "We tried to fatten him up," he said. "But two ounces? I'm perplexed. I just don't know why."

Tommy tried hard to jump into the car, rocking back and forth, panting with effort, but he was too weak. Yves scooped him up and placed him in the backseat. I climbed in beside him and embraced him, my tears falling onto his grey muzzle. Tommy panted even harder and gazed rapturously out of the window. Why was I crying? He, not I, was the one who'd been in prison. And now that he was free, why waste tears on what he wanted only to forget?

At the high-rise he'd visited only once, Tommy wagged his tail. Even the elevator didn't faze him, and he walked confidently to our apartment door where Ivan waited, arms outstretched, to embrace and carry him upstairs. Inside Tommy strutted from left to right, then sagged down onto his bed, tail still awag.

By nightfall, Tommy had accepted Dolly into his family circle. Now when she pranced and play-bowed, he smiled and twisted approvingly. On visits to the local dog park a short city block away, he sniffed and explored but often stopped to watch as Dolly leapt and darted like a canine ballerina.

"Whose dog is that?" someone inquired.

"Mine," I replied with a catch in my throat. "He's my dog."

# FOUR

## Tommy's Good Seasons

Tommy was well and truly home, the drama ended. *We'd made it!* Now real life loomed. My job as editor-in-chief of Chronicle Publications required such long hours that I'd been taking Dolly to the office with me so that she wouldn't pine alone in the apartment. But Tommy could scarcely make it around the block, much less the nearly three miles between downtown, where we lived, to Old Montreal, where Chronicle was located.

What to do? I had no car and Montreal public transport banned dogs; Dolly and I had an hour's walk to and from work. But Ivan, now fifteen, came to the rescue, promising to come straight home from school and care for him till I got home.

On that first Monday morning when I leashed Dolly and left the apartment with her, Tommy protested with shock and outrage—I could hear him right up until the elevator door closed. I'd left the radio playing to keep him company; the food dish was tempting with tidbits and the water dish pristine and full. He had toys and a cushion and Dolly's doorless crate. Uneasily, I set off for the office. That afternoon, Ivan telephoned to report that Tommy had been waiting near the door and thumped his tail when he appeared.

I shut my eyes and exhaled with relief.

"The only thing is, I don't think he ate much," Ivan added. "It looks as if he just nosed it. Maybe he's just getting used to being home. He still hasn't got much of an appetite."

Days later, this skinniest of dogs was still picking at his food. When I cooked for him, he'd hover excitedly around me. On the few occasions that he did gobble the food, I'd note the ingredients for his next meal. Sometimes that worked and he'd devour it. But it never lasted, and then he'd reject the same dish he'd loved the day before, sniffing it before turning away as if repelled. I devised different recipes to tempt him. And, for one or two days, Tommy would eat.

He developed crazes. At first, if I put ketchup on his food, he'd eat it. Next was HP Sauce; that lasted for a couple of weeks. Then came sardine oil, grated cheddar cheese, cottage cheese, and back to HP Sauce again—briefly—his favourite condiment.

He ate so erratically and so little that it was difficult to spot any thickening on his emaciated frame. But he was gaining strength, and loved to lurch around the dog park chasing squirrels. Slowly I increased his itinerary so that we'd walk the few blocks up to Sherbrooke Street. I didn't dare go far; Tommy was too big for me to carry if he tired out and collapsed. But he was building up muscle, and he loved to walk alongside Dolly, whom I restrained from pulling ahead of him.

Suddenly it struck me: this was Tommy's first experience of walking on a leash. As a younger dog in the Quebec countryside and in Haiti's Thomassin, he and Suki had roamed free in our fields and garden, and when we moved to downtown Port-au-Prince, Tommy had the run of our ample garden with its vegetable plots, apricot trees, and "Haitian kitchen," the outbuilding where traditional slow-cooking meals are prepared on braziers. In Haiti, nobody walks their dogs. I'd considered but abandoned that idea when I realized what some of the obstacles were, beginning with the homeless street dogs who might be perfectly friendly but had nothing to lose.

The first few times I snapped Tommy's leash onto his collar, he'd recoil slightly and shake himself as if to confirm he was attached to something. But he quickly decided that the leash was my way of binding myself to him, and as he walked, he'd continually glance back at me to make sure we were still yoked together.

He was as eager to greet people and other dogs as he was to sniff peed-on utility poles and foliage. At the dog park, Tommy stood with me on the periphery, watching intently as Dolly raced around with her younger canine friends. I wondered what he was thinking: was he nostalgic for the old days when he, too, ran like the wind and herded cows? Was he saddened to be forced to stand on the sidelines? But no, what I saw on his gnarled grey face was excitement and pride. "Look at my Dolly go!" he seemed to be saying. "What a dog!"

From the first day he was sprung from the quarantine kennel, Tommy hadn't hidden his admiration for his beautiful, energetic, agile, and confident canine pack member. Instead of jealously guarding me from her, he bathed in her reflected glory. Dolly's antics elevated his thrice-daily walks to the dog park from pit stops to special occasions.

Even so, on rare occasions Tommy did feel compelled to remind Dolly of his status as top dog. This almost always happened when she and I arrived home after a long day at the Chronicle office. Tommy would stand on his wobbly stick legs, barring the entrance to the living room, but as soon as Dolly play-bowed he'd relent and move aside.

It wasn't that Tommy had been alone until then. During Ivan's after-school hours they both enjoyed snacks, short walks, and long conversations, not to mention forbidden afternoon television that was shut off at the sound of my key in the lock. This boy and his dog—or was it this dog and his boy?—had grown up together, and were as comfortable with each other as the fleece blanket we snuggled around Tommy to warm his old bones.

But one October afternoon Ivan arrived home only to be assaulted by a stench as soon as the elevator door opened onto the twelfth floor. A stern Post-it from the superintendent was stuck to our door. Inside, Tommy lay on his bed, a clean oasis on the diarrhea-fouled floor. Ivan phoned me at work. I improvised solutions, and came home to a damp scrubbed floor and the sickly fragrance of air freshener. "He's pretty sick, Mom. You need to take him to the vet."

We borrowed a neighbour's car and headed for Dr. Hubert Jasmin's unfussy, welcoming clinic on the Rue Guy. When he saw Tommy, Dr. Jasmin frowned. "I'm worried," he said, stroking Tommy's skull. "When a dog gets to this stage, something's very wrong."

I still failed to grasp the gravity of the situation. "He's all bones," I agreed, "but he did have those two years with scarcely any food."

"But you rescued him nearly two months ago. He should have put on some weight." He lifted Tommy onto the examining table and gently ran his hands over him. He listened to his heart, palpated him, took his temperature, and drew blood samples. Then he sighed deeply. "Tommy has cancer," he said. "I can see the tumours without even having the test results back. Look!" With his hand he traced Tommy's spleen and liver. "He's too sick and too old to do a biopsy. There's nothing I can do anyway. This growth is slowly killing him."

I looked at Tommy and burst into tears. "What should I be doing for him?"

"Just what you're doing. His appetite is erratic because he's so sick. The diarrhea is related. I'll give you medication to control it, but it'll recur. You'll just have to live with it."

"How long does he have, Dr. Jasmin?"

"If I knew, I'd tell you."

At home I clung to Tommy and ranted. "It's so unfair! He finally made it home and now he's going to die!"

Ivan took the news calmly. "It's sad for us, but Tommy isn't sad. He just thinks he went for a nice car ride and now he's home again. And I'll help you, Mom. We're all in this together, even Dolly."

Especially Dolly, now Tommy's constant companion. The more Tommy struggled, the more he swelled visibly with pride as he watched Dolly, who continued to look up to him just as Toussaint and Taffy had. Ivan was right. We were all in it together.

The months rolled by. Even as he faltered and his health failed, Tommy's enthusiasm for life's simple pleasures was unchecked. But his growing tumours and queasy stomach kept his appetite capricious at best, and the flare-ups of diarrhea occurred more frequently. As winter chilled the air and snow covered the ground, he shivered miserably with no flesh to warm his old bones.

I bought him a bulky vintage Irish fisherman's sweater and transformed it into a winter coat. Its long sleeves even protected his front legs. After initial protests, he submitted as I tugged it onto him. He seemed to understand that it made him feel much warmer.

But this evidence of care didn't stop passersby from questioning Tommy's gauntness. "Why don't you fuckin' feed your fuckin' dog?" a young man once screamed at me.

One woman took her concerns further. She followed me home, discovered my name and apartment number, and then reported me to the SPCA for animal cruelty. A few days later the SPCA notified me that an inspector had visited my apartment but found no one home; would I kindly contact him and arrange a meeting? A meeting about what? Was this an aggressive campaign to solicit funds? Had someone in my building complained about the stink, swiftly scrubbed away and masked, on Tommy's bad days? More perplexed than apprehensive, I made an appointment for the following evening.

The inspector arrived and introduced himself. Dolly and Tommy, delighted to have company, wagged their tails. The inspector got right to the point. Someone had reported that I was starving my dog, and he'd come to investigate. "You'll appreciate, Madame, that the law requires us to look into all such reports."

I erupted into furious tears. Then, as the inspector listened attentively, I recounted Tommy's saga and produced his thick veterinary file. "Here!" I exclaimed, thrusting it at him. "You can ask Dr. Jasmin if he's been given all the care he needs. Here! Over a thousand dollars' worth already, and we're not finished because he'll get it until the moment he dies."

The inspector riffled through the papers. "I'm so sorry," he murmured. "You understand, I hope, that the SPCA *must* address complaints, even though, as in this case, they are entirely unfounded."

"Of course I understand. But why didn't the person who reported me just ask me why Tommy looks like this? He's always smiling and happy, and he's always with Dolly, the healthiest dog around. Shouldn't that be a tipoff that he has medical issues?"

"Everyone handles these things in their own way," the inspector said soothingly. "But yes, that would have been a better way to proceed."

Two days later, a woman approached me on the street. "I'm so sorry, I'm the one who reported you to the SPCA," she said. I gaped at her. "Someone told me afterward that your dog has cancer, but I'd already filed a complaint."

"But why didn't you just come up to me and say something?" I demanded.

She hung her head. "I guess I was so horrified by his condition that I acted without thinking." Beside me, warm in his heavy white sweater, Tommy panted and wagged his tail. Another friend! Perhaps she would bend down and scratch behind his ears!

A few days after that, Tommy's bowels exploded just after he'd stepped into the elevator. I was with my friend Lourdes, and we went into action. While Lourdes leaned against the elevator door to keep it open, I whisked Tommy back into the apartment and grabbed my cleaning supplies. As the door systematically slammed into Lourdes's back, I scoured and sniffed and scoured some more. Finally, notwithstanding its damp floor and overpowering artificial-lilac fragrance, we proclaimed the elevator odour-free and released it.

The stakes were high. Despite my best efforts I'd already had two complaints from the superintendent. I'd tried Pampers, cutting out a hole for Tommy's tail, but that was a dismal failure. My only defence was stockpiled paper towels, floor cleanser, and air freshener, combined with elbow grease and the fear of eviction. Tommy dreaded these uncontrollable discharges. Whenever his old body ambushed him with sudden spasms that literally spilled his guts, he tried to drag himself away from what was about to happen. Our joyous dog was ashamed; he'd hang his head and moan piteously.

We couldn't bear to see his humiliation, so we adopted a post-eruption routine of comfort and reassurance that he was still a very good dog, the best dog in the world, our beloved Sir Thomas Tom. Ivan, who had less stomach for cleaning up than I did, developed a repertoire of "jokes" to distract Tommy from my scrubbing and spraying; they were nonsense phrases he'd repeat in rollicking bursts of silliness that Tommy understood as comical and that made him forget his embarrassment. "Joke, Tommy?" Ivan would say. Tommy's ears would perk up and soon his face would be smiling once more.

Except when he was in the throes of pain, Tommy's joyous nature prevailed. Unlike me, he was oblivious to his not-so-slow deterioration; he asked only for more walks, more "jokes," more company, more popcorn and the treats he greedily demanded but couldn't finish, more dog park performances starring Dolly.

A few times Tommy also hunted, intrigued by chattering squirrels who chased each other from branch to branch as if they knew they had nothing to fear from the old creature staring fixedly up at them. They were right, but what concentration Tommy could summon to pounce, so closely missing one quivering fluff of a tail that its chastened owner fled up and squealed her displeasure from the tree-top. Tommy was as delighted as if he'd caught her—perhaps this scare was all he'd ever intended—and turned to me for the praise I rained down on him. "What a dog you are, Sir Thomas Tom, one of the truly great ones!"

By late spring, my employer was teetering on the edge of bankruptcy: I was never sure whether my paycheque would clear. *Chronicle of Canada* had been published months earlier and I was the sole remaining employee. Our Paris-based head office was in dire financial straits; the New York office had been shut down and the Australian was set to follow. Sitting alone with Dolly in my brick-walled office in Old Montreal, I researched, wrote, and edited the Canadian sections of *Chronicle of the Royals* for our London office. I also urgently searched for a new job.

Just weeks before Chronicle folded its operations, I accepted the position of dean of women at the University of Toronto's Trinity College. Ivan was ambivalent about the move; he was still missing Haiti and just settling into our new life in Montreal. And we'd be living in an apartment in a student residence, so what about the dogs? "The dogs were a condition of my acceptance," I assured him. "I described myself as a package deal that included you and the dogs." But by then we both knew we'd be bringing only one of them.

Toward the end of June, the cancer spread to Tommy's lungs. His breathing became so laboured that he'd gasp and collapse during even the shortest of walks. If he hadn't suffered before, he was suffering now. Tommy would not be coming with us to Toronto. His final journey would be across the Rainbow Bridge, that wondrous place next to heaven where good dogs wait peacefully to be reunited with their beloved humans.

I took Tommy for a last walk, short, halting, and infinitely satisfying, because he spotted a squirrel that accommodatingly dashed up a tree, sparing him the effort of trying to lunge at her. As she sat cursing from her safe, green-leafy perch, Tommy looked at me. "Good dog!" I said. "You sure showed her! Now she doesn't dare come down until we leave." Tommy wagged his tail and sagged to the ground for a brief rest. Then, in triumph, this dog of my heart slowly led me home.

I popped a last bowl of popcorn, the one foodstuff that had never lost its appeal, and Tommy ate a few morsels. Ivan told him some time-tested jokes, evoking feeble tail-wagging. Then Yves arrived and carried him downstairs for his last car ride. I refused to give in to tears; I didn't want to upset Tommy and darken his last day with my grief.

At the veterinary clinic, Tommy slipped away quietly and easily, slumped against me.

"He's gone," the vet said. I wept as he swathed Tommy from head to foot in a blanket.

"You'll receive his ashes by registered mail." I nodded mutely. Now I had all the time in the world to mourn, and as my life continued without him, to try to comprehend the finality of his death. What I didn't know, what I couldn't have imagined, was that Tommy's passing would affect my life—and the lives of so many others—in such profound and permanent ways.

# PART 2

# DOG DAYS ON HOSPITAL ROW

# FIVE

## Rerooting in Toronto

On July 1, 1991, Canada Day, I boarded a Via Rail train bound for Toronto and my new life as dean of women at Trinity College. I was alone. Ivan had a summer-long volunteer position, and since I was ruining his life by uprooting us once again (he said), he'd implored me to let him stay until fall so that he could at least enjoy another six weeks of happiness. Yves's family offered to take him in, and that settled the matter.

Nor could I bring Dolly. I'd just learned that the dean's residence was being renovated and that I'd be spending two or three weeks in the college's visitor's suite. It was an elegant, air-conditioned apartment that required a challenging trek up wide stairs and then narrow, winding staircases past offices and residence rooms. Walking Dolly in and out would impose her on dozens of people currently working and living in the stately and dog-free Trinity building.

Just as problematic was the apartment's thick wall-to-wall carpeting. Dolly was perfectly housetrained but cursed with an unfixable condition that caused mild incontinence. I couldn't begin my deanship with a leaky dog leaving faint trickles on that beautiful carpeting.

The day before I left Montreal, I loaded Dolly into Yves's dark blue Renault and we drove her out to a boarding kennel, a handsome facility at the end of an unpaved, tree-lined road. It housed dozens of dogs in large kennels, each with its own dog run; it was secure and well-monitored; and its owners were caring and knowledgeable. And so I left Dolly there, trying to convince myself that she'd enjoy this summer paradise.

I was a solitary figure as my turquoise and orange Beck taxi drew up to the imposing Trinity building and deposited me on the sidewalk. I reached the massive wooden double doors and pulled hard until one of them slowly opened, admitting me into the empty coolness of the marble-floored interior.

One of the custodial staff was waiting to escort me to my temporary home. Once inside, I explored the apartment and put away my belongings. I had very little with me. Most of my worldly goods were in storage and would be shipped when I moved into my permanent lodgings. I sank down onto the sofa and looked around. It was lonely in that cavernous building with its labyrinthine hallways and staircases. I closed my eyes and saw Tommy sprawled on the carpet at my feet. An instant later, the mirage evaporated.

July 2, my second day in the position I'd hold for the next thirteen years, was hotter, gearing up for an impending heat wave, and friendlier, with muted voices and laughter audible from nearby streets. Over at St. Hilda's, Trinity's women's college and then women-only residence where my apartment was being renovated, I settled into my new office. It was spacious and inviting, with upholstered armchairs, vintage bookcases, a large, modern desk, and a glassed-in wall that separated it from my assistant's office. I hadn't met her yet; she, like most others in the college, was vacationing.

I staved off loneliness by reminding myself that the shock of being uprooted would lessen as people began to drift back to the college and Dolly and Ivan rejoined me. I was excited about meeting my colleagues and students, and about the security and strange serenity of a college life modelled on Oxbridge, where deans, provosts, chaplains, and dons all live in residence.

But my heart was still in Montreal, where Ivan interrupted his excellent summer for a single weekend's visit to Toronto, and where Dolly was passing the time by flirting with a handsome dog in an adjacent kennel until I reappeared to bring her home.

That time soon came. I scheduled delivery of my belongings and joyfully informed the kennel that I'd be coming to collect her. Then I picked up my rental car and headed back to Montreal to reunite with my dog. The kennel was cool and breezy in the tree-shaded courtyard where Dolly jumped at me, whining with joy, knowing she was going home. After one mishap—I stopped for gas and left the keys in the ignition, locking Dolly in the car until a tow-truck driver opened the door—we drove peacefully through the muggy evening. It was nearly midnight when we reached St. Hilda's, where I hadn't yet spent a single night. I fished the shiny new door key from my handbag, and Dolly and I stumbled inside.

The apartment was hot and humid and smelled of cardboard. The movers had dumped my furniture and my eighty boxes of books into whatever space they could find, and I had nowhere to sit or to sleep. Somehow, despite my exhaustion, I made room for a single mattress on the floor. Then, loosening my clothes and shucking off my shoes, I lay down and closed my eyes. Dolly lay down beside me, sighed, and slept.

Dolly and I were home, and Ivan would soon join us. I'm a list-making packer, and within a few days I'd loaded my thousands of books into bookcases, all in order. I'd also lined my kitchen cupboards, stashed away dishes, pots, and pans, and taxied home a giant food order. A cheerful college maintenance man had carted away the detritus of moving, including my mountain of cardboard boxes. Furniture was dragged into position, electronics installed. The dean's suite was beginning to look and feel like home.

Ivan arrived in mid-August and, during Labour Day weekend, so did an influx of students. Soon the entire building and grounds rang with their voices and sang with their laughter, and my deanship began in earnest.

The month of September was frenetic, the learning curve steep. Trinity was a complex community that celebrated its traditions, the excellence of its students and the soaring successes of its alumni, and its special character as a community of scholars, identifiable by the academic gowns that made us unique on the University of Toronto campus and harked back to medieval university tradition. After two years at Chronicle—spent producing a masterful illustrated faux-journalistic history of Canada while staving off the company's catastrophic finances and sale to a new owner, whom I accompanied to the bank where he announced that his new acquisition couldn't repay its million-dollar debt—Trinity felt like the Rock of Gibraltar.

Three weeks after the opening of the school term, Tommy's ashes arrived by special delivery. They were in a small urn with a sympathy note attached at the neck with a blue ribbon. I was in my office and couldn't weep, but my hands shook as I cradled what was left of Tommy. How extra-ordinary that such a big dog could be reduced to such a modest container! But even in ashes, Tommy was a fiercely loving presence.

In my Trinity office, I had no dog for solace. Dolly had always accompanied me to the Chronicle office, but here, where my office was a two-minute stroll down a hallway from my apartment, she had to stay home. Unlike Chronicle's secure premises, St. Hilda's was an easily accessible space on the first floor of a bustling building that included class-rooms and swarms of students going in and out. Dolly had already escaped several times, rampaging solo through the city before she was caught; I once had to chase her through the university's vast campus until I nearly collapsed and she finally had the grace to come to me. Another time a student had walked into my office bent over so that she wouldn't let go of Dolly's collar. "I was at evensong," the student said, "and after a while became aware of a bit of commotion in the chapel, and a tinkling sound that kept getting louder. I turned around in my pew to look, and there was Dolly trotting up the centre aisle toward the altar. I sprang up and grabbed her, and brought her back to you!"

Dolly, unrepentant and incorrigible, fled at every opportunity, endangering herself and terrifying me. If I leashed her to a piece of furniture, she'd drag it behind her as she struggled along. Freedom! she'd insist. House arrest! I'd counter, and stopped bringing her to work. Now, sitting alone with Tommy's ashes, I realized how much Dolly must miss him too.

# SIX

# Trinity's Pet Therapy Program Is Born

A beloved dog's death is always a searing sorrow. Still, the consolation of a long period of mourning seemed a wasteful self-indulgence when other homeless dogs languished as I sat mired in grief. I first saw Rachel on a CityTV program featuring adoptable animals from the Toronto Humane Society. She was a scruffy, sight-impaired poodle cross with an enlarged heart, severe dental decay, and black fur streaked whitish by age. Two weeks later she hadn't yet been adopted—"We still have adorable little Rachel," the THS answering machine announced day after day—and so I took her home.

Rachel's past was her secret. But she was a clever little dog, perfectly housetrained, aware of her adorableness and keen to communicate her needs—and her rules. Despite her slight, fluffy body, little pointed nose, and cataract-clouded button eyes, Rachel was no passive lap dog. She demanded reciprocity and would cuddle only if she were petted. If I stopped stroking her to turn a page or pick up the phone, she would stiffen and, a minute later, push away from my now unwanted, unearned embrace.

I cannot pinpoint the moment I looked at Rachel and saw a therapy dog. I think the idea crept into my consciousness after I read an article about how Sharon Evans, an occupational therapist, had introduced a pet therapy program into Mount Sinai Hospital.

Years earlier, in Montreal, as part of my research for a *Gazette* story on that subject, I'd visited a hospital facility for severely autistic children where dogs played an important role. I spent a morning watching the children interact with a big dog, a Bouvier or a giant schnauzer, and what astonished me was that, to my uncomprehending eyes, *nothing happened*. That is, until the teacher working with the children interpreted that almost-nothingness as stunning progress. A little boy jerkily jabbing at a large, hairy black dog's fur was a miracle, she explained, because the child couldn't tolerate touching or being touched. Suddenly, after months of seeming indifference, he'd reached out and, in his own way, caressed the dog. "We were all so encouraged," the teacher explained. "His parents were overjoyed."

Suddenly I saw driblets of movement and communication and emotion throughout the room. "Here, we measure progress in millimetres," the teacher said. "And once we accept that standard, we're satisfied by the results." And the dogs? How important were the dogs? "Ah! Let's just say that we measure their contribution in leaps and bounds! The dogs are the catalysts that enable us to reach and teach these little ones."

I didn't delude myself that Rachel had those qualities, but for bedridden adults she seemed a perfect canine visitor. She was clever, cuddly, and obedient, and she craved human companionship. She knew what people wanted and how to make them give her what she wanted. She was so petite she could sit on a bed without disturbing its occupant. She was light enough to hold up so that she could be seen but not touched, and when she was upset, she just sulked and turned her back but never nipped. So I telephoned Sharon Evans, suggesting Rachel as a good addition to her program, and Sharon proposed that we meet for further discussion and to evaluate her.

Sharon was the key to what would develop into the Trinity–Mount Sinai Pet Therapy Program. Her mandate, to stimulate the long-term geriatric patients' hospital experience, had begun with exercise groups, games and music, and lobbying for brightly coloured walls decorated with paintings. She'd been aided by donations of a sound system and a baby grand piano for the once bleak lounge.

But Sharon wanted more for the patients, and so she began to mine the growing body of literature about fledgling pet therapy programs. Animal companionship relieved stress, lowered blood pressure, wiped away tears, and chased away sadness and despair, she read. The company of dogs allowed geriatric patients with deteriorating verbal skills to communicate. Pet therapy, Sharon concluded, would greatly benefit Mount Sinai patients.

It had taken her two years of research and writing letters and reports to convince the reluctant, germ-phobic hospital board to authorize her to establish and coordinate a program. She would screen the canine participants, verifying their veterinary records and vaccination status, and would request character and health references along with an annual TB test from the humans who would accompany them. Then both humans and dogs would register with the Volunteer Department.

Sharon finally had her pet therapy program. She began with friends' dogs, and, as people became aware of it, she added her acquaintances' and colleagues' dogs. Despite the occasional canine misfit, quickly retired—one gentle old basset hound would hide under hospital beds instead of comforting their occupants—the patients responded as Sharon had known they would. The fear that a dog would widdle or poop on the floor was never borne out, but just in case, she had a small trolley equipped with supplies for a thorough cleanup. Patients responded eagerly to the dogs and so did their visitors and staff, including doctors and nurses, who routinely swooped down for a bit of therapy-on-the-fly.

But Sharon had a problem: too few dogs. Serendipitously, I showed up with Rachel; soon she and I were strolling through the bright corridors of the hospital, visiting geriatric patients. Rachel was an obliging volunteer who greatly enjoyed her work, though she disliked the walk-ride-walk that preceded it, and in winter, despite her lined jacket and little boots, she had to be carried.

That summer I retreated to my friends' screened porch in the Quebec countryside to concentrate on my next book project. But my thoughts often turned to my experiences volunteering at Mount Sinai, and I realized that I had much more than my little dog to offer. I also had a unique group of university students. And by creating a program facilitated by dogs, I could build a bridge between them and Mount Sinai. I would trade with the gifts God had given me.

Before taking up my position at Trinity, where I also held the honorary title of dean of St. Hilda's College, I had delved into its historical background, which is how I came to read these poetic words of counsel and encouragement penned fourteen centuries earlier by the wise and practical abbess, Hilda of Whitby: *"Trade with the gifts God has given you. Being buffeted by trials, learn to laugh. Being reproved, give thanks. Having failed, determine to succeed."* Sound, comforting advice, and from the first moment I read it, I incorporated it into my way of thinking as a God-given gift.

By now I'd spent five years at Trinity. I had said farewell to five graduating classes and welcomed five new ones. I had lived and worked with the students. I sponsored the Latin American Society and attended its weekly Spanish Table luncheons. I played defence for the Saints, the Trinity women's ice hockey team. I counselled and chatted with students, including those who dropped into my office to pet my dogs. I wrote reams of reference letters, learning more about the students' personal histories, their academic achievements, their career goals, their hopes and dreams. Trinity had introduced me to a stellar pool of student talent, ambition, and energy, and what better use to make of these young people than to offer them a structured opportunity to volunteer at one of North America's premier research and teaching hospitals?

Mount Sinai Hospital is affiliated with the University of Toronto, and its nearby location on the section of University Avenue known as Hospital Row makes it easy for students to walk or cycle there, a crucial consideration because most volunteering is limited to daytime hours on weekdays. Volunteering was a growing passion at Trinity, and combining the realities of the hospital world with the magic of dogs would resonate with many students.

I began to visualize a pet therapy program in which these students took dogs, their own or other people's, to

Mount Sinai. Every single dog would be a willing participant in the program and love her work. The program would have dual goals: to allow patients to interact with a friendly, affectionate dog but also to use the dogs as vehicles to encourage and stimulate interaction with their student companions. My proposed model was unusual for such a program, but it made sense, and I believed I could make it work.

And so one scraggly old terrier with clouded blue eyes gave birth to the Trinity–Mount Sinai Pet Therapy Program. The program slowly grew and was accepted by Trinity's Junior Common Room as a student club. At Clubs Carnival, an Orientation Week event at which students sign up to join college clubs, Pet Therapy would acquire a long list of names—a list that would invariably shrink to manageable numbers as students realized that their schedules couldn't accommodate Mount Sinai's assigned time slots, and that attendance at an in-depth Infection Control presentation, TB tests, an immunization record form, and registration at Mount Sinai's Volunteer Department were all both compulsory and time-consuming.

We developed protocols for every stage of a visit. Groups of two or three students would accompany one dog. After picking up that dog in our lobby or at a student dogsitter's residence room, they'd record their departure time in the Pet Therapy logbook kept at the Portress's Lodge and sign out a little pouch that contained a collapsible water bowl, paper towelling, plastic poop bags, and doggy treats.

After entering via the hospital's back entrance, the students, wearing their Volunteer ID badges, would sign in at Volunteer Services. So did the dogs, whose Volunteer badges (in later years with photo ID) were pinned to their coats or to their bandanas. Then the students would summon a security guard to escort them upstairs to one of their assigned floors: geriatrics, orthopedics, or psychiatry, each of which had its own protocol for visitors.

All the wards enforced Mount Sinai's all-important rule of confidentiality. "Even if you see your teaching assistant doped up in the psych ward or your math professor strapped to a stretcher, you can't reveal a word to anyone. Lips zipped! What you see in the hospital remains in the hospital." We'd warn newcomers that anyone who violated confidentiality would be expelled from Pet Therapy. It never happened.

Less than a year before Dolly's heartbreakingly premature death from a just-diagnosed neurological disease, I adopted an old and deaf golden retriever whose passion for swimming had prompted Ursula Hart, director of Haven of the Heart Animal Sanctuary, to call her Marilyn Bell after Canada's revered long-distance swimmer. Marilyn Bell, who understood a few hand signals, spent her first weeks sniffing out her new lodgings and her new siblings, including cats Kate and Hortense, and revelling in lengthy walks in her new Queen's Park neighbourhood. But nighttime transformed her into a fearful dog who hid in my clothes closet.

Marilyn Bell's fearfulness ended suddenly, as if she'd shed it in the lonely closet, and one morning she woke up as the quintessential golden retriever: gentle, loving, and always up for a stroll. Months later, I decided to take her to Mount Sinai, and on her first visit Marilyn Bell made a small miracle.

At the nursing station where we stood waiting for the list of patients who'd requested visits, a nurse bent over a man slumped motionless in a wheelchair, a woman crouching beside him. I looked away, inadvertent witness to a private sadness. But Marilyn Bell, unburdened by such sensibilities, stared and panted and wagged her tail hopefully. The nurse noticed her and exclaimed, "Oh, look! Our pet therapy dog is here! Would you like to see her?"

If the wheelchair-bound patient had any reaction, I didn't see it, but the woman's face lit up as she leaned over her husband and said, cajolingly, "What a pretty dog! Shall we invite her over to visit?"

The nurse smiled at me and nodded, and I led Marilyn Bell over to the wheelchair. At closer range I saw that the man was middle-aged and as still as a stone. Yet he was trying to reach out for Marilyn, willing his lifeless arm to move toward the soft white furry face now so close to him. I held my breath and the two other women watched anxiously, but Marilyn, impervious to the drama, just panted and wagged harder in encouragement.

Then the miracle happened. The man compelled his arm to move and, slowly and shakily, it crept down onto Marilyn's head where it quivered as he tried to pet her. "Thank you!" his wife mouthed to me. "Thank you!"

The nurse had an idea. "Marilyn Bell looks thirsty," she said. "Would you like to give her a drink of water?"

The man nodded and the nurse carefully handed him a paper cone full of water. His fingers closed it around it and, slopping water, he lowered it down to Marilyn Bell, missing her mouth and jabbing the cup into her eye. Marilyn Bell did not wince or move away. She just sat there, a saintly presence in an old dog's body. And when the man managed to leak the remaining droplets into her mouth, she stuck out her tongue and lapped thirstily.

The man's wife blinked away tears as she thanked me once more. "That's the first time he's moved his arm since his stroke," she murmured. "I'm so happy!"

I do not recall the other patients we visited that day. I was too struck by the wondrousness of what I'd seen. Weeks earlier, that man had kissed his wife goodbye and headed out to work. The next time she saw him he lay motionless in intensive care, fighting for his life. But that afternoon, his longing to touch Marilyn Bell had overcome his bodily infirmity and eased him onto the path to recovery.

# SEVEN

## Pet Therapy Evolves

The satisfaction of offering solace was constant, and enrolment in Pet Therapy climbed. In 1997, Gillian Bowers, a first-year science student, joined us with Paddington, her family's seven-year-old sheltie. Gillian was practical and unflappable, a petite blonde dynamo who injected energy and organization into the program when she became its first coordinator.

She began with doggy uniforms, two beautifully sewn khaki-coloured coats trimmed with dark green tape, the word VOLUNTEER sewn on each side in dark green fabric letters. One coat was large enough for our bigger dogs, the other small enough for our little ones. The students noted with amusement how the dogs preened in their Volunteer coats, associating the coat with the hospital where they were treated as very special visitors.

I'd observed something similar at a Canadian Human Rights Foundation summer conference in Montreal, where I shared a residence room with a blind scholar and her golden retriever. During the day he was a diligent and happy service dog, but at night, when she removed his harness, he'd prance joyfully around and play, understanding that just as his uniform meant he was on duty, its removal freed him for recreation, relaxation, and even silliness.

The Pet Therapy coats had other unexpected consequences. Often the dogs' work began during the walk to
Mount Sinai, before they reached the hospital. Gillian, now
a mother of two and a speech pathologist in California,
laughed as she described Paddington's adventures. Garbed
in his Volunteer coat, he was often approached by curious
strangers who wanted—needed!—a quick hug and kiss.
"By the time we got to the hospital, Paddington had already
done tons of pet therapy and was pretty much pooped,"
Gillian recalled.

Under Gillian's stewardship the program was growing ever
larger, which also had consequences for me. We had a
roster of willing, sweet-natured dogs whose services we
needed for three hours at most. But what should we do
with the dogs whose people dropped them off at my office
on their way to work and returned for them only eight or
nine hours later?

One of these was a magnificent Scotch collie, the
family dog of Trinity resident student Jeremy Burman.
"You could drop an entire set of saucepans behind Casey,"
Jeremy said, "and he was so calm he'd scarcely notice." One
morning a week, Jeremy's mother would bring Casey to
the college. Casey was such a valuable asset to Pet Therapy
that, for want of an alternative, I kept him in my office. It
was a stop-gap measure that complicated my already complicated life and unnerved my assistant, who endured but
did not appreciate being pawed and licked as she worked,
but it kept Casey in the program. It also led the students
to create a new role for dog-loving resident students: Pet
Therapy dogsitters.

We wrote up the dogsitters' protocol and, with the consent of our very accommodating residence staff, I modified Trinity's (often-breached) rules banning dogs from residence rooms that cats, rabbits, guinea pigs, rats, hamsters, and birds already called home. Now, for a limited time, Casey and other dogs could relax comfortably and companionably with a student until it was time to don their uniform and badge and go off to volunteer at the hospital.

Resident student and Pet Therapy volunteer Vanessa Scott leapt at the opportunity to dogsit Casey, the "sweetest and calmest" of dogs. "He was a mop of a dog, with mounds of hair that got simply everywhere but was just perfect for plunging your hands into for scratchies," Vanessa recalled years later. "If anyone came to the door, Casey would bark and wag his tail so hard that his entire behind would waggle back and forth. He'd stick his nose into a stranger's hand, and had no aggression in him at all. He would never bite or growl. Casey was an excellent therapy dog."

Casey's transformation into a hospital therapy dog set me thinking. What about other wonderful family dogs in the wider Trinity community who spent their days at home alone, longing for walks, attention, and companionship— longing, in other words, for all that Trinity–Mount Sinai Pet Therapy had to offer, but whose humans, unlike Casey's, couldn't deliver and fetch them back home? If we could find students willing to pick dogs up and return them, would their humans agree to it?

I canvassed a few, and their responses were so enthusiastic that we invented a new Pet Therapy position: volunteers willing to pick up and drop off dogs by public transit. Thanks to these volunteer transporters, at least two more dogs enrolled as pet therapists. The first was Dixie Lee Ragtime, whose human was my friend Paulette Bourgeois, the renowned writer who gladdened the world with *Franklin the Turtle* and dozens of children's science books and novels. Dixie was a venerable eleven years old when he was inducted as a Pet Therapy volunteer. He was a sweet-tempered dog who'd helped raise Paulette's two children, Natalie and Gordon, and was now a loving and agreeable old fellow eager for whatever interesting adventures beckoned, including subway rides, shiny hospital corridors, and admiring humans.

Even in puppyhood, Dixie had known intuitively if one of his people was sick or just sad. If ever a dog were born to join a caring profession, it was Dixie. Not that he didn't have his faults—he had them in spades—but not a single one that made him any less empathetic. "He was my first dog," Paulette explained, "and because he was so sweet and so good, I never bothered to train him much. I didn't realize the implications."

The most concerning one was that Dixie became a chronic runaway, a captive to his obsessive desire for food. Dixie's disappearances became so common that his people developed an instant response. Paulette would grab two boxes of treats and start the car. Then, as she crawled along the city streets in search of the errant spaniel, Natalie and Gordon would sit on opposite sides of the backseat, hanging out the windows, rattling the treat boxes and shouting, "Yum, yum, Dixie, yum yum!" They found him every time. Happy and tired, he'd jump in the car and gobble treats all the way home.

At Mount Sinai, the dogs, including Dixie, weren't allowed to accept food even if patients pressed biscuits and other goodies on them, a rule that prevented dogs from begging, or accidentally nipping, or even favouring those patients who snuck them cookies. But edible rewards were just fine outside the hospital, and Dixie had earned his on the wards, cuddling the people he knew needed comforting.

Our other pickup dog was also an intuitive therapist, and she lived only blocks away from Trinity. When I heard that Father Mark Andrews, rector of St. Thomas's Anglican Church, was a dog-loving man with a young, easygoing golden retriever, I asked him if Molly had any aspirations to volunteer for Pet Therapy. He responded with a resounding yes.

Molly was born in 1999 in Galway, Ireland, and brought to the United States by American students with churchly connections. In June 2001, those connections led Molly to Father Mark, parish priest of Toronto's Church of St. Aidan's in the Beach, whose black Labrador retriever, Lancelot, had succumbed to spinal cancer. At first the quiet, sweet-natured dog seemed timid. But after Father Mark introduced her to the joys of swimming at his cottage, Molly shed her pampered city dog ways. "You couldn't keep her out of the water," Father Mark told me, "except for the hours she spent wandering the forest, playing incompetently but enthusiastically at hunting." Though she also chased balls, sticks, and logs, her favourite game was to dive for rocks and then clamber soaking wet out of the river to give them to her human. She was such a successful rock hunter that Father Mark built a low wall with her offerings. Although she was a beauty, "the Marilyn Monroe of dogs" with soft fur and huge long eyelashes, what Molly wanted was to be a stinky, dirty dog tramping in swamps.

Back in Toronto, life was different: as a priest's dog, Molly had duties to perform. Lancelot had always attended Wednesday's morning Eucharist service, lying quietly at the altar railing until the Agnus Dei roused him and he'd trot to the back of the chapel so that worshippers could line up at the rail to take Communion, after which he'd return to the railing. Molly, however, spent the entire service visiting parishioners and sitting on their laps.

Molly came into Trinity's life when Father Mark moved to St. Thomas's Church and we inducted her into Pet Therapy. It wasn't diving for rocks, but people were second best: Molly was always excited when the students arrived to take her to Mount Sinai, where she got all the attention and petting she craved and would come home worn out, relaxed, and happy.

More than a decade later, as we sipped Earl Grey tea in St. Thomas's rectory living room, Father Mark remembered our first meeting on the lawn outside St. Hilda's: "You stepped on Molly's foot." Ah! The famous evaluation process! Smiling, he cut me short as I launched into my explanation cum apology. "No, I understand completely. It was fine. Of course you had to do that."

Father Mark was right. Few of our dogs were certified by St. John's Ambulance, or any other recognized pet therapy organization, because we couldn't meet two of their core criteria. The first was that the dogs' human had to accompany them on visits, whereas our program relied on assigning students to visit with them. The second involved time commitments: at least a year. It was a sound practice but one our student-run program couldn't accommodate.

For seven or eight months of the year we'd provide a great service; then, just as the trees went into full bloom and the chill of winter faded into memory, our students would scatter until goldening September summoned them back.

"In a perfect world," Sharon Evans observed, "all your dogs would be certified and full-time and every dog and their human would be perfect therapists. But it isn't a perfect world, and all we can do is work with what we have, and do the very best we can with it."

Trinity–Mount Sinai Pet Therapy's core mission also differed from the goals of the certifying organizations. My first priority was that each dog enjoy his work and eagerly anticipate his next visit. A dog can be perfectly qualified for pet therapy yet fail to take pleasure in it. What's joyous for one dog may be tedious or frustrating for another, and so I was on the lookout for glum or frustrated dogs, and would retire them from the program.

And in our program, the dogs' overarching role was to stimulate conversation. I wanted our students to engage with patients and not just to offer them a happy dog to stroke and cuddle, though they were welcome to that if they wished. Sending two or three students with one dog made satisfying conversation and amusing banter even likelier. This was important for both patients and students, so many of whom dreamed of medical careers. "We'd talk about the dog, and other dogs, and other pets, and that would keep the conversation going," remembered Sarah Munroe, a Pet Therapy volunteer and coordinator who's now an emergency room physician and family doctor. "One woman always tried to give me gifts—money, rings—that I would politely refuse. I think she just wanted to give something back because she enjoyed seeing Sonia [the dog] so much.

And these experiences laid a foundation for my future training in medicine, where genuine communication forms the basis of everything I do. Pet therapy helped me to be comfortable talking to complete strangers—strangers who are unwell or injured and usually anxious—now something I do all day long when I work in the emergency department or my family practice."

Karen Fung, a periodontist, was so moved by her four years as Pet Therapy coordinator that she now calms her patients down—"Because nobody wants to see a periodontist!" she laughed—by regaling them with stories about Rachel and my other therapy dogs during their visits. "The dogs were like a conch," Karen told me. "They opened people up, they were vehicles to get them talking. And pet therapy changes people, including me."

Another former student, Zinta Zommers—a Rhodes Scholar and zoologist who now lives with her Great Dane, Zoe, in Nairobi—had a similar experience. "In the psychiatric ward, the dog was sometimes just an entry point into broader conversation. It certainly helped me learn to have conversations with many different people, for example at Oxford High Table dinners, where you often sit beside people ranging from scholars of ancient classics to playwrights and experts in animal cognition, and you can relate to them all."

Besides facilitating conversation, the student teams were insurance against any unexpected dog problems, anything from a slipped collar or harness to a growl or the unthinkable: a nip. Which brings me back to why I stepped on poor Molly's paw, and many other paws as well.

Certification programs have rigorous evaluations, and so I borrowed some of their tests for our own program.

Our annual dog quotient averaged six, one of them usually mine and at least one other a veteran like Molly. I preferred mature or older dogs; just like humans, those canine old-sters had life experience and coping skills, could usually be counted on not to jump up on or hump people, and were generally less wrigglesome. But even the worldliest dog was unlikely to have encountered the unique ambiance of a hospital, where patients hobble on crutches, shuffle along with walkers, and ride in wheelchairs or on stretchers, and staff workers push multi-shelved carts packed with every-thing from bedpans to cleaning supplies, not to mention the meal carts with their tantalizing food smells. To a dog, even hospital grub is fair game. So the trick is to expose the dog to a situation as close as possible to the reality—for example a crutch, wheelchair, or walker. For want of props other than a crutch, I improvised tests. One was to step gently on the dog's paws and observe her reaction. A dog who winced or cried slightly and withdrew her paw passed. A dog who growled or tried to nip me or the crutch did not. My tests were primitive but did the trick. And Molly, who didn't even flinch, was one of the best pet therapists we ever had.

Twice, in twelve years, our visits went awry—and our dogs passed gloriously. Emma Peacocke, a biology student who later earned a PhD in English literature, remembered that once, for no discernible reason, a woman smacked the visiting dog, startling but not alarming her. Emma, who hadn't seen the smack coming, went rigid with shock. But her fellow students "gently remonstrated with the cul-prit" and made sure there was a distance between her and her victim.

On another occasion, a younger man had been assigned to a bed in the geriatric ward because it had exactly the

right equipment to treat his condition. As the students chatted with him, Sarafima, their therapy dog, suddenly zeroed
in on his crotch and started to sniff hard, intrigued by his
catheter. At first the students were embarrassed, but they
quickly rallied and so did the patient, who just leaned over
and stroked Sarafima's head, admiring her elegant, elongated face. She smiled and wagged her tail at him, and the
human-to-human conversation resumed.

# EIGHT

## Solace and Hope

My beagle Russell was another superlative therapist. He'd been taken in by Ann and Pete Wilson, who foster dogs for Animal Alliance, and after Ann told me that he urgently needed a home, I adopted him. I had room in my apartment and my heart. My splendid and energetic Dolly had passed away, and nearly a year after that, Marilyn Bell, our gentle, loving therapist, had succumbed to the bone cancer that destroyed her spinal column.

Russell was a feisty middle-aged dog notable for two things: his severely deformed front legs and his passion for special female dogs. If ever a dog could fall in love, Russell was that dog. He'd also loved his mother, and after she was snared in a wildlife trap and died, he'd fallen into a deep depression. His disgruntled owner, likely the one who'd stomped on and broken his puppy legs, declared Russell useless and announced he was going to shoot him. A concerned neighbour whisked Russell to safety in the form of Ann and Pete, who thought I might be just the right human for this grieving dog.

The day I brought him home, Russell scraped his paws bloody as he struggled along the unfamiliar pavement. At the entrance to the dean's suite, he limped up to Rachel and nipped her face, drawing blood. But afterward he fell in love with her, and soon she was snuggled contentedly against him in their shared basket.

At first, Russell was not therapy material; if anything, to judge by his obsession with Rachel, he needed his own therapist. But as he calmed down and settled into life with other dogs, cats, and a loving, non-abusive human, he flowered. Instead of scuffling along, grating his paws on the pavement, he tried to lift them high as if he were a Lipizzaner-beagle hybrid. He was no longer visibly surprised and confused by affectionate handling, and when I petted or cuddled him, he'd pant with pleasure. He also stopped hesitating when other humans approached him, as they often did, drawn to him because of his awkward gait and his striking handsomeness; as he listened to them, his strong, emotional character would win them over.

"What a great pet therapist Russell would make!" my students and I would say. Except that Russell couldn't walk all the way to Mount Sinai, much less both ways. The problem of transporting him and other elderly dogs between Trinity and the hospital was something that stood out in Zinta Zommers's memory. "So many of the dogs were themselves previously injured that they had difficulties walking. I remember trying to coax—beg!—Russell to keep walking so that we could get to the hospital on time. But he refused, and so we'd struggle to lift him into his cart and wheel him across campus and down University Avenue. Sitting there in the cart, wearing his Pet Therapy uniform and staring out into the traffic as he rode, he looked like a king surveying his kingdom. We'd always get weird looks from the bankers and hospital staff outside on their lunch breaks."

One year we used a Jamaican alumna's donation, made in gratitude for the work we were doing, to buy Muttluk dog booties in three different sizes. It took a few frustrating minutes to boot-up all four legs, but the Muttluks protected the dogs' sensitive pads and were an efficient solution to the city's excessive sidewalk salting that made the dogs' walk to and from the hospital a misery. Except that Muttluks couldn't solve the problem of Russell's deformed legs, which worsened so much in winter that he had to be taxied to the hospital. Getting there was no problem because we always specified that one passenger would be canine. But hailing a cab from the dozen lined up in front of Mount Sinai was another story. Once seven in a row shook their heads when they saw Russell, until I gave up and flagged a passing cabbie, a breach of taxi protocol that I felt was entirely justifiable.

Unlike its queues of taxi drivers, Mount Sinai Hospital had no qualms about the enthusiastic, expressive beagle who limped happily from one patient to the next, drawing them out and lightening their burdens. In 1999, to my delight, Russell was honoured at the Volunteer Recognition ceremony. When he was called up on stage to accept his award—a Mount Sinai pin and a ribbon-festooned bag of gourmet dog cookies—I helped him up the steps. And then, dapper in his Volunteer coat and pleased as ever to be the centre of attention, Russell stood on that large stage looking out at an audience of hundreds of well-dressed fellow volunteers and well-wishers. As they applauded, he gazed at them delightedly: "You like me! You really like me!" Then he began a regal walk-around, to the right and the left, looking graciously out at his admirers until I gently pulled him away and the laughter subsided.

When Gillian Bowers graduated, she passed her torch to Zinta Zommers and Karen Fung, who shared it for the next four years. Both had dogs at home, but Zinta's black and grey Pipars (Latvian for Pepper) was by then too rickety to enjoy or even endure the hard work demanded of our Pet Therapy dogs, and Karen's young beige "schnoodle" Coco lived outside of Toronto. So Zinta and Karen worked with Casey and Russell, in addition to handling complex scheduling and further developing the program.

Each year, about thirty-five to forty-five students, ninety percent female, would visit the hospital with five or six dogs, three of whom did most of the visits. Schedules for the visits were created after resolving such scenarios as this one: on Thursday, five students were available, four for the afternoon shift, one for the morning when at least one more was needed; Rosie and a miniature schnauzer were available for the afternoon, but only if the schnauzer could be picked up at his house; three of the students much preferred the psychiatric ward but the nursing station on the geriatric ward reported five patient requests for visits; and the psychiatric ward favoured large dogs but only a smaller one was available.

Sarah Monroe said wryly, "I remember how difficult it was to coordinate those schedules with the dogs and the hospital. Getting two or three students and a dog on a particular day, and then sorting out which ward they'd go to, was surprisingly challenging."

My fat and feisty cat Kate's passing was the sole cloud on what was otherwise a new decade shiny with promise. After the eight years of research and writing it took me to

complete my book *A History of Celibacy,* it became a surprise
bestseller and began its peregrinations across the world in
seventeen more editions and translations. It was the first in a
trilogy on historical intimate relationships, and I was hard at
work on the next one. I'd also decided that at the end of my
five-year renewal as dean of women, I would retire to fulfill
my life's dream of being a full-time writer. I bought a little
house that would be a perfect retreat, with a sunny study for
me and a nearby parkette for the dogs. Until then, I wanted
to refine the Trinity–Mount Sinai Pet Therapy Program so
that even if it didn't survive my retirement in 2004, its record of solace and hope would be a proud legacy for both
the college and the hospital.

In June 2000, the week her first grandchild was born,
Sharon Evans retired to devote herself to what quickly grew
into a pack of grandchildren, and Joanne Fine-Schwebel
and Lesli Herman of the Volunteer Service Department
continued to support and supervise us. Sharon had been
our program's strongest in-house advocate and facilitator,
helping us develop and expand it—and by the time she
left, the hospital had recognized our program as a unique
and substantial contribution to its overall pet therapy offerings. Sharon wasn't surprised: "I knew Mount Sinai would
continue to support such an excellent program with such
exceptional volunteers—and I'm talking about the dogs as
well as the students!"

Our therapy dogs served the psychiatric patients especially
well. The psychiatry ward, a student favourite (though I
preferred the challenges and wisdom of geriatric patients),
was quite different from all the others. Its patients were

ambulatory and usually hospitalized for short periods of time, and most were young or middle-aged. We didn't visit individual rooms; instead, the Pet Therapy team waited in the common room, where patients interested in engaging with the dogs joined them.

Casey the collie, my office buddy and a patient favourite, would simply sit and wait for people to approach him and his dogsitter Vanessa. Most patients greeted him as "Lassie," and as they'd pet him, they'd talk about the dogs in their own lives, past and present. Claire Hicks, now a lawyer, recalled that Marley, her black Labrador–border collie cross, had similar experiences. Like Casey, Marley was an emotionally intuitive dog who'd stand even straighter and more proudly when Claire would fasten on her Pet Therapy coat. In the psychiatric ward, she gave patients kisses and lapped water from cups they offered her. Marley sensed their goodwill and responded with outpourings of love. She also trusted them, and would never interject herself between them and Claire as she usually did with strangers. A cautious dog—Claire once interrupted a robbery in her apartment and found Marley hiding behind the sofa— Marley was supremely comfortable in her role as a therapist.

So was Serendipity, Jessica Langer's bichon mix. When Jess, now CEO of a digital marketing agency and a professor of marketing, was a first-year student struggling to adjust to residence life, I suggested that she join Pet Therapy and bring Seri, one of her parents' pack of three dogs. Seri was, Jess said, "a kind and always friendly dog, usually bubbly but calm when she needed to be. She just brought positive energy into a room." I'd already met Seri, and after I tested her, she and Jess began their visits to Mount Sinai. On the psychiatry ward, Jess felt "an air of real sadness—until Seri came into the room. It wasn't as simple as flipping a switch. What Seri did was bring a kind of peace, a kind of pure joy that had been absent and was now present. She didn't solve anyone's problems or take away anyone's illness. What she did was shine a light into a dark place. She brought—not hope, really, but rather an intensely in-the-moment, present happiness."

As Pet Therapy expanded, a student's special circumstances also gave us a resident dog. When she came to Toronto for university, New Brunswicker Kathryn "Kes" Smith had left the aforementioned Sarafima with her parents. But an unexpected career change left them unable to care for her, and so the beautiful and clever Dalmatian came to live with Kes in residence, where she was quickly adopted by the whole floor. Emma Peacocke recalled that Sarafima "soaked up" attention from nurses, doctors, and patients. Many visits were almost wordless as people caressed Sarafima and spoke to her in low, soothing voices while other patients formed knots as they waited to visit with her. She also excelled at dispelling the gloomy tension when patients' family members had run out of things to say to their hospitalized loved one; they'd turn to Sarafima for comfort.

Scientists tell us that the blissful, calming effect people experience through physical contact with a friendly dog—an experience that's at the heart of pet therapy—is rooted in neurochemistry and is the result of oxytocin, "the cuddle hormone," surging through the veins of both cuddled dog and cuddling human. Oxytocin explains how humans transformed wolves into "man's best friend," creating relationships essential for our mutual well-being. We are indeed *Made for Each Other*, as Meg Daley Olmert titled her book describing the evolution of the human–animal bond.

Love plays a starring role in those relationships; as Jess Langer told me, she places it at the very root of this dynamic. "Our love for dogs—and theirs for us—is so deep, but the relationship is so very simple. And that uncomplicated love is the foundation of why pet therapy works. It's what so many of us crave and so few of us get, especially in our darker times. Not to say that human love can't be unconditional, but it's never uncomplicated. The love of a dog is simple. That's why it's so important."

That uncomplicated love between patients and our small pack of therapy dogs made our program so strong and valued that in 2002, Mount Sinai again recognized our work and honoured Karen Fung with a special award for coordinating the program.

Rachel, whom I had retired at the age of sixteen, was weary, and even the shortest visits exhausted her. A year later, a massive stroke ended her life. Russell, devastated, looked everywhere for her. At the hospital, he couldn't concentrate. A few weeks later I introduced him to Rosie, a cheerful old dachshund who'd been dumped outside a rural Humane Society. Russell immediately attached himself to her, cuddling and licking her, even refusing to eat if she wasn't around. Soon, I was taking Rosie to Mount Sinai.

Her tenure was short but brilliant, and she won Pet Therapy's Top Volunteer award for 2002–2003. After befriending a senior patient with a terminal condition, she would sit quietly cuddling him while he stroked her, closing his eyes as he did so. One day I received a request from the Volunteer Department: would Rosie agree to be photographed for an article about Mount Sinai? Well yes, she would. I carried Rosie to where her friend waited, and then watched as they were photographed together, the dying man smiling serenely as he leaned against her soft, squashy body.

Meanwhile, I was becoming known for my connection with old dogs; a rescue contacted me about Pumpkin, who became my third dog. Pumpkin was in urgent need of secret placement and palliative care. She was a failed hunting dog who'd been banished to an enclosed backyard, where she and another rejected beagle were fed erratically and sheltered only by a collapsed lean-to. After years outside, the other beagle froze to death. Attempts at intervention had only worsened the situation, and the local Animal Control declined to prosecute. Finally, on Halloween night, a heartsick neighbour took action. Disguising himself and mingling outside with other costumed trick-or-treaters in the carnival atmosphere, he liberated Pumpkin and whisked her away to safety.

This happiest of fat old dogs had a cancerous eye. After it was removed, she was given a prognosis of six to eighteen months. The vet also diagnosed a diseased liver. Yet despite medical crises and chronic pain, Pumpkin was a shining spirit who sprinkled her magical dream-dust everywhere she pattered.

After a cardiac scare, I began to spend weekends at my house rather than at St. Hilda's. These weekends began with a chaotic trek—with Rosie resting comfortably in a carry-bag on my aching shoulder, Pumpkin walking, and Russell in a stop-and-start protest as his aching legs rebelled. I had to carry him as far as I could before releasing him and resuming our ungainly struggle toward the subway, then the streetcar, and finally the short walk leading to peace in our very own paradise, the coolness of our high-ceilinged Victorian row house.

Monday mornings the college beckoned, but thanks to Henri Pilon, Trinity's archivist and a friend and neighbour, my dogs and I returned in the luxury of a car. It was never simple. Pumpkin and Rosie would wait excitedly on the street corner until Henri's car appeared, but Russell was one of those rare dogs who hate cars and are violently carsick. I'd open the back door, my arms full of dachshund and old towels, and lay them down on the backseat. I'd heave Pumpkin up on the towel, then finally turn to Russell, already frothing at the mouth and whining in a soprano protest. I'd lug and lift while he bucked away until I finally settled him, yelping now, on my lap. Then, trying to act as if everything were normal, I'd chat with Henri while Russell gagged. On our first two Mondays, he threw up all over me and the back of the front seat.

Henri, tight-lipped but saintly, accepted my abject apologies and didn't ask that I make other arrangements. After that, Russell got no breakfast until we reached Trinity, and I began to travel with an arsenal of paper towels and upholstery-cleaning products to supplement the heap of bath towels.

In his panic Russell would also shed profusely, ejecting his fur like a porcupine its quills so that it layered the entire backseat. One night, Henri informed me, he'd driven friends to the opera and one of them had emerged with her backside coated with beagle fur. She wasn't a dog person, he said, and she was not pleased. So I added a hair-removal roller to my supplies, and now whisked as well as rubbed down the car before Henri drove off to descend into the catacombs that were then Trinity's archives.

Few friends would be as forbearing, but Henri's cat Pablo, a temperamental warrior who made the whimpering, upchucking Russell look like a canine wimp, had seasoned him. Whenever Pablo's whims went unindulged— for example, if Henri tried to stand up, which meant dislodging Pablo from his lap—Pablo would snarl and attack. Henri always kept a bottle of hydrogen peroxide, a tube of Polysporin, and sterile pads at the ready. "He's a wonderful cat," Henri would say in Pablo's defence, "but he's got a temper." One fine evening, Russell and I visited Henri's house for a glass of wine. When I inquired about the gauze wound around his hand, Henri shrugged it off. "Pablo was mad at me. But that happens only one percent of the time."

I looked at the blood oozing from the bandage. "That's a pretty big one percent, my friend."

Russell, understanding all, refrained from comment.

# NINE

## The Long Farewell

When my next book was published in 2003, the historian Margaret Macmillan hosted its launch party in the stately and enormous Provost's Lodge, where the only dog was a splendid porcelain Cavalier King Charles spaniel perched on the hearth. For days after the launch I was euphoric, but it also marked the countdown to my leaving Trinity, and I had to make decisions. Specifically, I gave Mount Sinai notice that next year I'd no longer be available to run the Pet Therapy program. The Volunteer Department supervisor's response was unequivocal. "No. No, you can't leave, you just can't." And that was that.

I agreed to oversee the program for one more year, later extended to a second, and began to prepare for my withdrawal. To start, I needed to enlist more good dogs. My Russell and Rosie had both retired, and worse, death was in the air. I just wasn't sure whom it would carry off first. Russell had been diagnosed with adrenal Cushing's disease, and despite powerful medication, was losing weight and was too tired to work. Rosie, the merriest of dogs, was fighting a losing battle against what the vet called "a metabolic catastrophe."

Rosie died just after the emergency clinic vet had phoned to report that she was improving. I was stunned and heartbroken—just weeks ago she'd been her perky little self, responding well (I thought) to her medications and to her pleasant life. I couldn't fully grasp that she was gone, and longed for time to properly grieve. But once again that struck me as wasteful, given that I had space in my life and house for another orphan. And so, far too soon, I welcomed a new dog into our family, another dachshund.

But if I'd fantasized about reclaiming at least a shadowy tranche of Rosie, I failed spectacularly. Alice was nothing like sturdy, honey-brown Rosie in either looks or personality. She was a petite reddish dog with a long, thin nose, and after seven years as a breeder in a Missouri puppy mill, she'd caught the first lucky break of her miserable existence. Instead of being killed when her fertility faltered, she was signed over to Dachshund Rescue of North America, and later, Canadian Dachshund Rescue, and the chance for a real life.

Alice arrived swaddled in a hand-knit, dark green wool coat, fearful and silent. Holding her was like holding a board with a pounding heart. When I embraced her she stiffened; when I stroked her, she cringed. Finally, I set her down on the floor and watched as she scurried toward Russell, who was staring at her with glazed eyes. A second later, he nuzzled her. Then the two of them crawled into his grey Drop'n'Flop bed and snuggled.

In Missouri, Alice had been repeatedly bred. She was too tiny to deliver naturally, and so the millers performed amateur Caesarian sections that left clumsy gashes across her belly. One of them must have kicked her in the head, because her skull was dented. The ulcerated iris of her right eye, afflicted with the genetic disease microphalmia, had ulcerated into muck. It was so strikingly tiny that CDR had listed her as "Alice (Small Eye)." I promptly renamed her Alice Blue Gown.

Alice disliked walking, and not just because she'd never walked. She had luxating patellas—floating kneecaps—a common affliction in puppy mill dogs. She also had a collapsing trachea and a chest infection, which caused a vicious cough that kept both of us awake at night. When she was strong enough, I took her in for dental surgery that removed all but seven of her rotted teeth and left her tongue lolling out through the gaps. It also cured her cough.

Slowly, despite her medical problems, Alice shed her mill-dog terror and adjusted to her new life of creature comforts, affection, and companionship. She was Russell's great love; the ultimate underdog, she melted into his embraces. The cats, too, favoured her, and Hortense, my graceful little tortoiseshell, twice offered her the gift of a mutilated mouse. The only way Alice resembled Rosie was in her preferred mode of transportation: in the crook of my elbow.

After years of providing stellar canine therapists—Rachel! Russell! Marilyn Bell! Rosie!—I had run out of suitable dogs. Alice's rescuers had hoped she might develop that aptitude, but disappointingly, she was too resolutely needy and contented with Russell's doting to follow in Rosie's paw prints.

Luckily, a huge brown dog joined the program and was soon a popular and eager member of our therapy team. Sonia, Trinity student Chana Hoffmitz's ten-year-old Labrador retriever–border collie–Newfoundland dog, was eighty pounds of portly, long wavy-haired sweetness with a large ribcage and stubby little legs. "Sonia was a natural caretaker," Chana remembered. "My mother used to take her to see sick or elderly shut-ins in the neighbourhood, and she loved those visits." When Chana would get out Sonia's Volunteer badge and bandana—she was too large for the biggest Volunteer coat—Sonia would quiver with excitement. She loved being in the hospital, and before doing her rounds, she'd go behind the desk at the nursing station to bestow kisses on the nurses and to enjoy their caresses. One blustery day Sonia arrived at the hospital soaking wet and too soggy to visit patients. After Chana towelled her dry, the Volunteer Department came to the rescue and wrapped her in a robin's egg blue Volunteer labcoat with the sleeves rolled up around her legs, a happy clownish canine whose hospital visit prompted gales of laughter everywhere she went.

Although I'd remain as the official Trinity supervisor of the program and continue to oversee its operation, my deanship was drawing to a close. The Trinity community made leaving the college a joyous event, marked by parties and receptions; my official photographic portrait, with Alice on the windowsill behind me, was framed and hung among my predecessors on the walls of Melinda Seaman Dining Hall. Photographer John Loper had tried very hard to find a pose that included Russell and Pumpkin. At first I hugged them on my lap but they wriggled and squirmed and fell off, forcing John to spend half an hour dabbing at my academic gown with Scotch tape as he removed hundreds of beagle hairs. By then we were both so exhausted that I gladly accepted his compromise suggestion of Alice on the windowsill.

My final party in the dining hall included two breath-takingly thoughtful gifts. On behalf of the college, Provost Margaret Macmillan announced that the Dean's Reception Room, a splendid Victorian sitting room complete with a grand piano, had been renamed the Abbott Room. The St. Hilda's Alumnae Association presented me with a pair of bookends in the shape of dogs with chain collars bearing engraved tags, one reading *Saint* and the other *Hilda's*. They knew me, those women!

So did another community: dog rescuers urgently seeking a home for Old Olive, a fourteen-year-old beagle mix who'd strayed from home and, with her companion, a young Jack Russell, had landed in the Kingston Humane Society. On Christmas Eve their owner came to fetch them but balked at paying the $75 fine for Olive. As she cried out to him in her kennel, he walked away with the Jack Russell and left Old Olive to her fate.

For a week Olive languished in the shelter until I responded to an emailed plea and agreed to adopt her. Then, Dora Sesler—owner and president of the international talent-management agency Sesler and at the time a volunteer dog transporter who would become an important part of my future Serbian dog rescue mission—braved a January snowstorm to bring her to me in Toronto. Olive arrived confused and shaking with anxiety. Her head was permanently atilt from a bout of vestibular disease. She drank extraordinary amounts of water, ate with gusto, and was stone-deaf to everything but sharp hand-clapping or loud, high-pitched tones. But she quickly summed up her new living situation, stopped shaking, and began to shine.

For three years, this most excellent of dogs revelled in life. Olive was smart and self-confident, and quickly learned hand signals: Come here! We're going for a walk! In a house full of accidents—Pumpkin's kidneys were failing and Alice was casual about where she eliminated—Olive was fastidiously clean. She loved toys, especially another dog's, but rather than fight for them she'd wait till the coast was clear and then snatch and run away, carrying her purloined treasure in her mouth.

Despite her tilted head, Olive could retrieve tennis balls in the living room. But at first she couldn't navigate stairs. On the tenth day she taught herself how to do it, and from then on took each step slowly and carefully, thinking her way up and down. She tolerated the cats but only if they sidled up to her sideways, away from her face. In the park she was a frisky, roll-in-the-snow tail-wagger who play-bowed to other dogs, even the puppies. She had a crush on an unneutered young Lab, who reciprocated her feelings. Whenever Olive arrived, Johnny would drop his red ball and lope over to play.

If Pumpkin was the happiest and sweetest of dogs, Olive was the dog fulfilled, the successful model and inspiration to dogs who'd never before seen such confidence and exuberance. My other dogs adored and admired her. Had either she or Pumpkin come into my life years earlier, before their health problems became too overwhelming, I would have enrolled them into our Pet Therapy program.

The travails of aging were also affecting Sonia and Molly. Sonia's hospital visits had become too exhausting to continue. For years I'd limited all dogs' actual ward time to forty-five minutes, which was as much as I thought they would enjoy considering the time they spent walking to, from, and inside the hospital. Sonia's veterinary diagnosis was devastating: she had metastasizing cancer. In the summer of 2005, Chana bade her old friend farewell.

Molly, too, struggled with the physical demands of her job. Despite her youth, she'd developed painful hips; although glucosamine helped, Father Mark began to drive her either to or from the hospital. Years later, as we reminisced about Molly's life and work at Mount Sinai, Argos, who'd succeeded her as Father Mark's rescue dog, pranced happily around the rectory living room, diverting our attention. A once-emaciated, now lean and energetic Labrador retriever mix, Argos brought me a Kong that I threw and he retrieved, leaping onto the sofa to drop it next to me. During tea, he perched on an armchair and watched us hopefully.

I asked if Argos also went to church, as Molly and Lancelot had. Father Mark responded with something that resembled a harrumph, and launched into a tale of Argos's most spectacular churchly disaster. Argos had been hanging out of a third-floor rectory window, peering into the nearby church during evensong and barking incessantly. That evening the congregational hymn was "Let All Mortal Flesh Keep Silence," throughout which organist John Tuttle wove "How much is that doggie in the window? I do hope that doggie's for sale" for the sake of the appreciative congregation.

And had Father Mark named this blatantly pagan dog for Ulysses' Argos, I quipped? For a minute Father Mark sat lost in thought. Then, his voice soft, he told me this story. Upon returning home from an annual theological seminar in Savannah, where he'd studied *The Odyssey*, he was greeted by a recumbent and ailing Molly, who wagged her tail but couldn't lift herself off the floor. When she died at the veterinary clinic he'd rushed her to, Father Mark knew that she, too, was an Argos, an ever-loyal dog who'd resisted death until she had a last glimpse of her beloved human. And so, in remembrance of Molly's fidelity and concern for his well-being, he named the next dog he took into his house and heart Argos.

When the Trinity–Mount Sinai Pet Therapy Program came to a final halt after I really and truly withdrew from it, I considered it not a failure but a necessary ending. For a dozen years I had traded with the gifts God had given me: capable students bursting with enthusiasm and good ideas, a pack of some of the most joyful and empathetic dogs anyone could hope to see patter into their hospital room, and a great and welcoming hospital willing to induct us into its vulnerable human heartland.

I'd always been aware that the program could survive my departure only if another university officer were willing and interested in taking it over. Given the amount of work and responsibility involved, to say nothing of the passion for dogs that drove me, I'd already accepted the likelihood of that not happening. It did not, and our program died.

But the hundreds of visits we made with our eager dogs, the patients encouraged and the students enriched and the dogs cheered, did not die with it. The awards we won were not forgotten. Our goals were not invalidated. We mattered, and we were missed, and other people and other dogs would have to take up where we left off.

Mount Sinai worked hard to make that happen by inviting people with dogs certified as pet therapists to visit the hospital. "Socially isolated patients often benefit from our visiting dogs and their owners," its website advises. "These specially selected pets enhance a homelike quality, and bring comfort and diversion to patients and their families." Fifteen years after she retired, the dream I shared with Sharon Evans—of offering Mount Sinai's patients the solace of loving dogs—lives on.

1 - Margaret Marshall Saunders's story of this abused dog, Beautiful Joe, urged rescuers to advocate for dogs and tell their stories.

2 - Here I am with my infant son, Ivan, and our English bulldog, Joey, who was my confidant and companion.

3 - Here I am in my Port-au-Prince kitchen before bathing Toussaint (on chair), with Taffy (in my hand) and Tommy (at my feet).

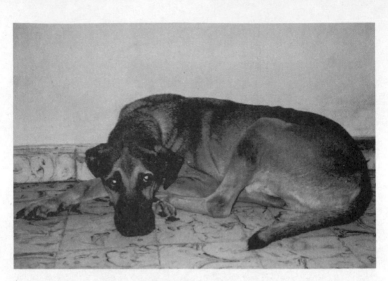

4 - Tommy, lonely and neglected in Port-au-Prince, waited for me to rescue him. The photographer could not overcome his sadness.

5 - Though suffering from terminal cancer, Tommy spent his last nine months in comfort and safety with his family.

6 - Casey, regal and empathetic, was an excellent therapy dog.

7 - Marley, emotionally intuitive, loved her role as a hospital therapy dog.

8 - Russell was a feisty beagle with deformed legs and a passion for female dogs, especially the self-possessed old poodle/terrier Rachel.

9 - Deputy Sheriff/Dog Warden Gary Kronk prosecuted Bonzi's owner for cruelty and neglect, and let Bonzi ride in the cab, the first dog he brought in that got to ride gunshot.

10 - Florida inmate dog trainer Glendale Edwards hugs Nabisco, who has completed his training program and will now leave the prison.

11 - Cathy Leistikow, shelter manager, gave Bonzi special privileges and grieved when he was adopted so far away.

# PART 3

# BONZI IN PRISON AND OTHER KARMIC IRONIES

# TEN

# The Beagle and His Bossman

He was born in 2003 in Madison County, Ohio, a mostly beagle pup whose protuberant eyes and smallish size hinted at chihuahua ancestry. As he matured, so did the high chihuahua-esque pitch of his howls. Mostly, the little dog looked and acted like a blue-tick beagle driven by a quiveringly sensitive nose. He also had a short, waggy tail that was a barometer of his emotions—he was a deeply emotional dog!—and a way of cocking his head inquisitively as he considered territory, objects, and most importantly, the humans he was genetically predisposed to love.

His name was not yet Bonzi, so let's just call him Little Guy. Little Guy lived on a rural property not too far from the Ohio Prison for Men. He was not the only dog. When he was about a year old, his owner—we'll call him Bossman—acquired two female chow-retriever puppies. Little Guy loved them! Alas, his love was unrequited: Bossman almost never let him play with the pups, and if Deputy Sheriff–Dog Warden Kronk hadn't rescued them when he did, they could not have survived much longer.

The thing is, Bossman kept the girls locked in a windowless metal garden shed, a filthy, unventilated den. And with his scattershot approach to feeding and watering them, the incarcerated puppies just had to hope that today was a day he'd toss them some kibble and replenish their water bucket.

Inside the house, in the mudroom, Little Guy also hoped. But if Bossman didn't appear, Little Guy hunted. It was slim pickings: a mouldy pizza crust, unshelled peanuts, a mouse cadaver. Then his beagle instincts would take over and he'd shake his prey wildly to make sure it was dead before he devoured it.

Mostly Little Guy dreamed of Bossman, who'd fling open the mudroom door and shout for him, dump kibble from a big cardboard sack into a gritty bowl, and splash water into a plastic pan. Sometimes he'd even scratch behind Little Guy's ears, fondling them. But Bossman would also curse when he found the pee Little Guy had tried to hide in corners and in the filthy rug when he had nowhere else to release his bursting bladder. And it was Bossman who, that one time, gave Little Guy a terrible beating and stomped on his stumpy front legs. When the right leg snapped, Little Guy shrieked out his agony and shrank into a huddle, trying to fend off Bossman's wrath as it fell on his small, defenceless body.

Which is how Little Guy came to have a right front leg that was noticeably deformed—it had been severely fractured and left to heal on its own, curving into a sort of V shape with a sharp bone sticking out at the elbow and a puffily enlarged paw turning outward and so tender to the touch that Little Guy would wince and growl in protest when anyone attempted to examine it or to clip his nails.

After that attack, Bossman removed Little Guy from the house and chained him next to a wooden box beside the driveway. How Little Guy wanted to run! How he longed to plunge his hound's nose into the soil and into the air to breathe in the swirling scents that led to thrilling hunting prospects. He strained so furiously against the chain around his neck that he damaged his trachea until it collapsed and would remain, for his lifetime, a fragile, treacherous organ. But try as he might, he could not break free.

Little Guy did not give in to despair or even sadness. Thanks to his sunny nature and his happiness whenever he got to play and run and head-butt and just scamper around, he gladly forgot everything except the joy of existence. That didn't change even after the arrival of the great big muscular and oh-so-testy pit bull.

A half-hour's drive away from Little Guy, in a mop closet in the Ohio Prison for Men's cell block A, two blue-garbed inmates huddled around a washtub holding another squirming beagle. Water gushed and gargled out as hot as it ever got there, hitting the chilled air and creating pufflets of steam that softened the profiles of the two men.

They were Jacob Browning, a veteran dog trainer, and Elijah Tibbs, a rookie in the Second Chance at Life and Love dog-training program, a collaboration between the Ohio Prison for Men and the Humane Society of Madison County. Fifty-two inmates in two cell blocks—minimum security B with unlocked cubicles and medium security A with locked cells—trained homeless shelter dogs to be obedient and respectful family members. The dogs usually spent three months in the prison, trained according to the *Second Chance Canine Program Training Manual,* written by the program aide, inmate Shane Livingston.

On this day in 2004, Jake and Elijah were bathing a dog who'd just come into the prison. "It's okay, Lola," Jake said soothingly and then, to his companion, "Some of them have never been bathed before and it's real stressful for them. They think we're drowning them. There's a few I've had to muzzle—Yes girl! Good girl!—but here's a trick that usually relaxes them." The beagle shook herself and Jake removed his glasses, wiping droplets of water from the lenses before resuming the bath.

Elijah Tibbs chuckled. "Why not just leash her to the pipe and use both hands?"

"Because here's a better way than tying her up," Jake said, sliding his right hand under the dog's breastbone. "All's I do is use my fingers to keep her still. See how she sort of melts into my hand? And then bathing's her easy, isn't it, Lola?"

Elijah wrinkled his nose. "That water's nasty! Dang! That's one dirty dog."

Jake was rhythmically soaping the beagle, now settled down on her haunches in the washtub. "Now listen up: the first guy who bathes, feeds, and plays with her will be the guy that dog attaches herself to for as long as she's in the program. Isn't that right, girl?" He began to rinse until the scummy suds ran clear, and then he turned off the faucet. The beagle, shivering now, shook herself briskly, drizzling water on both men.

Jake draped a towel over her and rubbed her dry. Then he took a fresh towel and buffed the last damp spots. "One more thing before you take her out to the yard. Don't even *think* about bathing a dog in the showers."

Elijah's eyes widened. "No shit! The guys would either riot or kill me."

Jake handed him the leash. "It's freezing out, so just take her for a quick piss. Then I'll show you how to brush her out."

Afterward, Elijah stood just outside the open cell as Jake ushered Lola into her new home, a large metal crate that jutted out almost directly across from the steel, lidless toilet bolted at the entrance to the cell Jake shared with trainer Garvin Schwein. The bunk beds, flush against the outside wall, and a sink, wardrobe, and tiny desk completed the furnishings. Unlike other inmates, forbidden for security reasons from moving their bunk beds, dog trainers could move theirs to better accommodate their dog crates, even if that interfered with the patrolling guards' sightline. The only problem was, Jake and Garvin couldn't figure out a more efficient layout for their ten-by-twelve-foot cell.

But they had a dog. In the tense, dangerous, testosterone-fuelled world of Ohio Prison's nearly two thousand inmates, they had the comfort, the responsibility, and the privilege of living with a dog. For Jake, already incarcerated for a decade and facing an indeterminate life sentence, the canine program fulfilled the promise of its name: Second Chance at Life and Love. Corny as it sounded, that was just how it felt to him.

Even before his trial, Jake had felt the gradual extinction of the outside world as family and friends recoiled at his crime and abandoned him. Few convicts mentioned the brute facts about prison—its beatings, rapes, and coercion—to their loved ones, who were already worried enough about what went on there. But even if he'd wanted to, Jake had no visitors to unburden himself to. In the hell of prison he walked alone, shrouded in loneliness.

That is, until Second Chance, when he got a dog to live with and to love, a little creature whose life was also in shambles and who also needed that proverbial second chance. As did young Elijah Tibbs, who'd served three years of his twenty-year sentence and—if Second Chance wasn't axed, as some great (and not so great) programs were— would walk out a free man certified as a journeyman dog trainer. He'd be barely forty, still young enough for a shot at a real life. Which was why Jake Browning had agreed to show him how to bathe a dog in the mop closet.

Now, standing a few feet outside the open cell because inmates were forbidden to visit each other's cells, Elijah was relieved to see Jake's cellie disappearing into the recreation room. Good, because the guy was a jerk and the other guys had told him that when program coordinator Shane Livingston and the correctional officers the inmates called COs weren't around, Garvin Schwein would sometimes manhandle the dog he was supposed to be training. Elijah had even ventured to ask Shane about it. What if you saw some asshole messing with a dog? You couldn't snitch, so what the fuck were you supposed to do?

Shane, keeping his voice down, had set him straight. Talk to that asshole man to man, and if it happens a second time, men to man. If there were a third time, you could only hope that nobody saw you when you roughed the guy up, or that a decent CO would overlook this rough justice.

Elijah had nodded. Shane always made so much sense about things. For that matter, so did Jake, a peaceable, soft-spoken guy who read almost as many books as Shane for Chrissakes, and never had a bad word to say about anyone. It was weird that he celled with a hurricane of a man like Schwein. Maybe it was because they were the only two guys in Second Chance who actually liked training hounds.

"See, Elijah," Jake was saying now, "I'd bet anything this girl's a failed hunter. Watch this." He took out a stuffed pony that had been in the box of dog paraphernalia the Humane Society had brought in for the trainers. At first Lola shrank from it; she had no idea what a toy was. When Jake cajoled her, dangling the pony far enough away to intrigue but not alarm her, she sniffed at it tentatively, prepared to withdraw to the safety of her crate if it attacked her.

"See, Elijah?" he said. "Notice how she reacts to the toy?"

"She's cautious? Or she doesn't like ponies?"

Jake grinned. "How would you describe it in your journal?" As Elijah looked at him blankly he added, "It's the kind of information that'll help interpret her behaviour and build up a profile for her."

The younger man grimaced. "That's the one part that's real tough to get used to. All the observations and stuff we got to keep track of."

"Let me show you something." Without moving from where he sat on the lower bunk, Jake reached up to a narrow shelf for a thick folder and passed it to Elijah, still slouched outside his cell. Elijah riffled through the cards, notepaper, and photographs, all featuring dogs who were usually accompanied by smiling people. "*This* is why we keep daily journals," Jake said. "To help our dog's new family understand everything about him. His behaviour and body language, his likes and dislikes, because you know that dogs have those, just like people. And so the new family can follow our training methodology and maybe"—he crossed his fingers—"keep on with it after they adopt him."

He pointed to a glossy photo of a pudgy greying beagle posing open-mouthed beside two squatting children, then tapped his heart. "My first. He's the one made me love beagles. He's turned me into the Beagle Guy." He swallowed hard. "Jack. They kept his name. And they send Christmas cards with his photo. At least they did, for a while."

"Maybe this Christmas …" Elijah's voice trailed off. Then he said, "Christmas inside the fences is so fucked up! Do we at least get to keep our dogs?"

Eddy Stackhouse, who'd sauntered up and was leaning against the wall beside Elijah, answered the question. "If they don't get adopted, the shelter's happy for us to keep them. They have enough problems getting staff to work over Christmas."

"Too bad they don't trust us to take over," Jake said. "How about I volunteer to wear a ball and chain so I can't escape? And at night they can lock me into a cage with a bowl of kibble."

"Sounds like a plan. I'll write up a request," said Shane Livingston, stepping inside the cell and balancing himself gingerly on the lidless toilet. "I actually came looking for you, Eddy, to give you a heads-up about Tracy. Tracy's going to an adoption fair this weekend." Then, at Eddy's stricken expression, "Sorry, dude. I just spoke to Sarge"— Sergeant Basil Whyte, Second Chance's unit coordinator—"and Betty called him with a list for this year's last adoption fair. You know the shelter stops adopting out a couple of weeks before Christmas." (Betty Peyton, director of the Humane Society of Madison County, also coordinated the prison's Second Chance training program.)

"But Tracy's not ready yet. I've got so much more work to do with her!"

"Maybe nobody will adopt her and Monday morning she'll be back. But at least you'll know that whichever way it goes, it wasn't a Christmas impulse thing."

Eddy pushed against the wall, heaving himself upright. "Okay, I'm going," he muttered. Back in his cell, he held Tracy in his arms and didn't try to stanch the tears. Later, as he dutifully recorded the day's observations and activities in his journal, he thought but did not write: "Today my heart was torn apart."

# ELEVEN

## The Saddest Season

Ohioans joked that on Christmas Eve in 2004, as Santa Claus was guiding his team across the countryside delivering toys, he overshot the state of Ohio because it was entirely buried in snow. This is apocryphal, because many good little boys and girls found gifts under their Christmas trees, and it must have been Santa who left those crumbs on the cookie plates left out for him. But what's true is that by Christmas Eve, blizzards had buried northern Ohio under record amounts of snow, and southern Ohio hadn't recovered from terrible ice storms. Sleet and freezing rain pounded the state. Transformers exploded; trees and power lines snapped and fell.

That terrible winter, nearly half a million Ohioans celebrated Christmas Eve with neither power nor heat. Meteorologists measured the snow in feet. A few days after Christmas, Governor Bob Taft declared a state of emergency. Nearly sixty counties were so devastated that they qualified for federal disaster assistance. For millions of Ohioans, the Christmas of 2004 lives on as a bitter memory; a few even saw it as a foretaste of an apocalyptic future.

The little beagle with the crooked legs survived Christmas because Bossman unlocked his chain and carried the frigid dog to the shed where he tossed him inside with the puppies. For days before, Little Guy had huddled hopelessly in his box, so cold and weak that he could hardly summon the strength to nip at the icicles that were his only sustenance. He couldn't see the road, but he could hear the puppies, even over the roaring wind. They howled and sometimes they barked. They also banged up against the metal walls of the shed, making a sort of tinny sound that Little Guy found comforting because it kept him in contact. Now he, too, was inside, and when he thawed out a bit, he joined the girls slamming around, trying to get out, trying to attract attention.

Bossman always fed and watered them haphazardly. But this time he'd gone away again, and when he wasn't there at all it was even worse, and now they were nearly frozen and the thirst had become terrible and the hunger had intensified into a snarling, all-consuming stomach gnawing.

That's how Little Guy spent the Christmas of 2004, in the dark and miserable shed where time passed interminably as the wind wailed and snow pounded down onto the tin roof, and he was so cold and frightened, even with his little friends to cuddle against and warm himself. Inside the shed it was so dark and silent that he couldn't even conjure up Bossman, whom he longed for to come and save them.

For Little Guy loved Bossman! What else could you call it? When Bossman picked up a stick (or, as sometimes happened, a tennis ball) and threw it, sometimes even removing his chain so that he could run free on his crooked little legs, Little Guy fetched it with the enthusiasm of a retriever in the happy knowledge that, for these moments at least, Bossman was pleased with him, and he wanted nothing more than to please Bossman, which fetching seemed to do. "Good dog," he sometimes said, "good boy." And hearing those words, Little Guy felt the ineffable pleasure of knowing that, for this beautiful instant, all was right with his world.

But now nothing was right. The cold and the hunger and the thirst had weakened and drained him, leaving him limp and shaky as hallucinatory kibble and glugging water appeared then receded before him as he struggled to pull himself toward them. Beside him, the girls were all but silent except for occasional moans and high-pitched keening that were all they could dredge up to convey their misery. As Christmas came and finally went, the dogs knew only that death was lurking in their cold and wretched hovel.

U p in Toronto, I was elated at the prospect of celebrating the 2004 Christmas season in my own house and not, as for the preceding thirteen years, the dean's apartment. "Most people don't wake up every morning and marvel that they've slept under their own roof, but I do, and it still seems miraculous," I wrote in that year's Christmas letter.

My only sadness was that two months earlier, Russell, my crippled old beagle, had died. He'd lost his footing on the stairs, and the fall broke his back and paralyzed him. He was already in failing health, and he lost hope. The next day at the veterinary clinic, with the X-ray of his shattered spine pinned onto a screen behind him, I held him and wept as his eyes closed forever.

My dachshund Alice, the Missouri puppy mill survivor, grieved even more than I did. I'd lost the feistiest and
most profoundly emotional dog I'd ever met, but Alice had
lost her champion. She'd loved Russell with all her heart,
and for a full week after he died, she stopped eating. She
resumed only after Pumpkin, my elderly, one-eyed beagle,
stepped in and began to cuddle her, doing her best to take
Russell's place.

By the time my son, now a university student in
Montreal, arrived home on Christmas Eve, the dogs and
I were healing and happy. We hunkered down inside
and celebrated together, warm despite the snowy bluster
and howling winds outside. Just after New Year's Eve, as I
kissed Ivan goodbye, he held me by the shoulders and asked
me to make him a promise. Two dogs were enough, he said,
and much as I'd loved Russell, I must never again burden
myself with a third. "Please, Mom, *promise* me you won't go
out and get another dog."

I promised, and at that moment, I meant it. Little did
I know that events unfolding in the Ohio Prison for Men,
which I'd never heard of, were about to make mincemeat
out of that New Year's resolution.

Christmas in any prison is the saddest day of the year, and the
Ohio Prison for Men was no exception. In 2004, a few for-
lorn decorations reminded the residents of their Christmases
outside the fence. Some of the old-timers recalled their
early years inside, when Christmas looked like Christmas,
and included a dressed tree. At the same time, Christmas
remained an official holiday, and the holiday schedule was in
place: no visits, no phone calls, no work. Two days earlier, as

the inmates filed out of the chow hall after lunch, the guards had handed each one his traditional bag of Christmas goodies. This year the meagreness of its offerings—one mini candy cane, two mini candy bars, a calendar featuring a Biblical quotation for every day of the year—reflected the preoccupations of the world outside the fence: a shrinking economy, a growing disdain for incarcerated citizens, and the resurgence of emphasizing punishment over rehabilitation.

The four dog-trainer buddies had carried their bags back to the range. Elijah, the youngest, opened his first, peering inside then bursting into guffaws. Eddy pulled out the calendar and flipped through it. "This will be useful," he said. "And inspirational." Jake shrugged and grinned. "Guess I'll save mine for Christmas. I want to be surprised." Shane tore the crinkled wrapper off the candy cane and popped it into his mouth. Outside the fence, he would have crushed it underfoot as an insult. After a decade inside, he was glad to have anything at all.

Christmas was a vacation day except for the dog trainers, who were always on duty. That year the prison was colder than usual, and during the terrible storm its power supply had shut down for two days, leaving the inmates without heat or radio or television. By Christmas Eve electricity had been restored, but the men, fully clothed with their winter coats piled on top of their blankets, still had to brush dripping icicles from the wall behind their bunk beds.

The next day the quartet of trainers joined the single file of inmates hungry for Christmas dinner. A paper cut-out of Santa Claus lent the dining hall a modestly festive air. The men picked up one of the small metal trays and walked down the serving line, where at each serving station an inmate server scooped a helping into it. As always, the

Christmas meal consisted of turkey, stuffing, mashed potatoes, vegetables, warm buttered buns, and a sliver of pie. On their way out, they'd be handed their bagged supper: four pieces of white bread, two slices of processed cheese, and an apple.

The trainers found an empty table, square and bolted to the floor, and seated themselves. From habit, they attacked their meal, scraping every morsel from the modest compartments before the guard monitoring the chow hall could order them to "hurry it up," to pick up their trays in order to make room for the next rotation of inmates. Eddy ate without concealing his enjoyment. "Good!" he enunciated, pointing at his full mouth. "Maybe even better than last year."

Shane, shaking his head in disbelief, dipped his bun into a smear of gravy and then, with practised sleight of hand, slipped it into the pocket of his denims. "Let's see what Sadie thinks," he guffawed. Sadie, his current dog-in-training, was a border collie mix with four puppies who were great favourites of the staff and the trainers, an object of the general population's bemusement, and Shane's pride and joy.

"If it don't make her sick, Sadie's gonna get fat," Elijah said. "I also seen that CO sneaking her treats."

"The dunderhead wants to adopt her," Shane muttered. "He's already spoken to Betty. I tried to explain to him that I can't train her properly if he keeps spoiling her. If it weren't for Betty, he'd have taken her home for Christmas. She convinced him that Sadie needs the whole ninety days to be properly trained and to wean her pups."

The rules, prominently posted in the cell block, were clear: "Dogs are *not* allowed to have people food. Staff are *not* allowed to give the dogs people food. Only animal trainers and animal caretakers are allowed to handle the dogs." They were sensible rules, rooted in experience, but it was so tempting—and so easy—to ignore them that everyone did, including the COs. Even the strictest of them did not hesitate to pet an appealing dog or slip her a hunk of sandwich or cheese, and that was especially true of those keen to adopt one of the dogs. But it was what it was. The power dynamics of the prison did not allow the trainers to complain.

And really, Shane tried to convince himself, there was nothing to complain about, though he was driven to cement Sadie's loyalty to him with tidbits just as delicious as those of the CO who would soon adopt her into his comfortable life outside the fence. After all, the officer would then reward Shane with a steady stream of anecdotal updates and the occasional cute photo (with wife and children obscured or cut out), and even seek advice. In the end, what more could a trainer ask for?

Eddy Stackhouse, his tray wiped clean of Christmas, had an answer to that question. "Guys, I promise you all this: if I ever get out of this dump, I'm not going to leave the dog I'm training behind. I'm going to adopt that dog and take it with me." His jaw set hard. "And they're gonna let me."

Christmas at the local Humane Society's shelter was no more or less fun for the dogs and cats than any other day, but it was a sombre day for the staff members assigned to care for them at the sacrifice of family reunions and dinners. The shelter consisted of a block structure with kennels and outdoor dog pens, and two dilapidated trailers that housed cats, offices, and a feline sick bay. Everybody complained that it was grossly inadequate and longed for the day they could move into warmer, more spacious quarters.

That Christmas, as Betty Peyton pulled up in her Dodge Daytona for a quick inspection before heading out to her family's dinner, she noticed a familiar vehicle parked beside her. "Gary Kronk! Don't you know it's Christmas?" she exclaimed as she entered the shabby building where the deputy sheriff stood chatting with Cathy Leistikow, the shelter manager.

"That's why I'm here," Gary said. "I wanted to make sure the animals were having a good Christmas too." He grinned. "Didn't want them to think I'd forgotten them."

"They'd never think that, Gary," Cathy said. And, to Betty, "Didn't I tell you he's just the best volunteer ever?"

"They don't come better," Betty agreed. "But we don't want to get you into trouble with Liz and the girls. They must be waiting on you for Christmas dinner!"

"That they are," said the dimpled, silver-haired deputy sheriff, pulling on his gloves. "Merry Christmas, ladies, and see you tomorrow."

"I'm hearing some very interesting rumours," Betty said as soon as Gary had gone.

"Tell me," Cathy said, briskly folding clean bedding for the cats' cages.

Betty pulled a pile of clean rumpled towels and tattered blankets toward her and began to smooth them into piles.

"Seems the county is thinking about restructuring the dog warden duties and shifting them to the sheriff's jurisdiction. The talk is, they'd offer Gary the position.

That way he'd still be a uniformed deputy sheriff and on call for backup or emergencies, but mostly he'd work as dog warden."

Cathy nodded approvingly. "It'd give the position clout, especially driving around in a marked pickup. I guess they'd install kennels in the pickup?"

"And a computer in the cab. See, that way he could build up a database of all the county's registered dogs. And driving around like that, he could also spot the unregistered ones and get their owners to register them."

"Yes! And folks would take the dog warden more seriously if he's also a uniformed deputy sheriff packing a pistol."

"You bet. People need to be more responsible. The law about registering dogs is there for good reason."

"Well, let's cross our fingers that the rumours are true. Because having Gary Kronk as dog warden would be the best Christmas present the dogs of Madison County could have."

# TWELVE

## The Beagle Meets the Deputy Sheriff

Spring had sprung in that May of 2005, its cold snaps and spring snowstorms taunting echoes of the long, brutal winter. But Deputy Sheriff Gary Kronk, who'd just been appointed dog warden as well, wasn't thinking about the weather as he pulled up into a driveway on an isolated rural road and jumped out of his vehicle. As he strode up the driveway clutching his catchpole like a spear, a large white male pit bull glared and growled at him from the porch. Gary was so focused on the pit bull that he barely noticed the small beagle chained to an improvised kennel. As he approached the house, he shouted out repeatedly for the pit bull's owner. He'd been directed to this run-down rented property after responding to an urgent call from a neighbouring home.

"You need to get right out here," the caller had shouted. "Damned pit bull won't let me outta my house!"

Twenty minutes later Gary had arrived at the caller's house, set back on the same rural road. He'd manoeuvred his 1998 Dodge pickup truck into the driveway, grabbed his catchpole, and then raced toward the porch. But instead of an infuriated pit bull, a man holding a cell phone greeted him at the foot of the stairs.

"It's run off! Thataway," the man said, pointing down the road. "Other side of the road, three places over, you can't miss it, big white pittie." He relayed his story quickly, in hoarse bursts: that morning, as he opened his front door on his way to work, he was startled to hear a deep growling that erupted into savage howling. He stepped out onto his front porch to investigate and then jumped back inside as he saw the powerful dog that usually guarded or prowled a nearby property and was now crouched in attack position.

At first the man had spoken calmly, trying to reassure the animal that all was well. But that only provoked it to lunge furiously at him and snap at where his hand would have been had he not withdrawn it and slammed the door shut. Then he braced himself against the doorframe, which shuddered as the attacking animal lunged against it time and time again. "It wouldn't let me out the door," the man had told Gary Kronk, "and finally I had to phone you."

Soon it would be Gary's turn to call for backup. The closer he advanced toward the house, still ordering the human occupant to come outside, the more aroused the pit bull became. He hadn't yet set foot on the porch stairs when the animal flew at him, snarling and baring his teeth. Gary warded him off with his catchpole and, without taking his eyes off him, backed away from the house. As soon as he could safely reach for his cell phone, he contacted the sheriff's office for help.

Within ten minutes, a brand-new Ford Crown Victoria roared up the driveway as another officer responded to Gary's appeal. He'd barely turned off his engine before eighty pounds of raging canine attacked the vehicle, tearing at the bumper with his teeth and, in minutes, causing more than $700 damage.

At the height of the action, a passing school bus driver stopped to inquire why two sheriff's department vehicles were parked, lights flashing, in the driveway of this nondescript house. The incensed pit bull had a new target. As the driver moved to open the bus door, the dog threw himself against it, trying to get inside. Gary leapt into his truck and pulled up beside the bus, shouting at the driver to drive away and not turn back.

But the country road was busy that day. Just as the school bus sped off, a jeep appeared, piloted by a man on his way to visit a friend half a mile away. At the sight of the sideless vehicle, the pit bull dashed onto the road and ran after it. The driver, unaware of the danger, pulled up at the house that had been his destination. The frenzied dog jumped at him, and terrified, the man began to shriek. Hearing the commotion, the homeowner raced outside, shotgun in his hand. "Shoot him!" Gary and his colleague bawled at him from up the road.

Two shots resounded, wounding but not killing the dog, who limped back up the road toward home. As it approached them, one of the deputy sheriffs readied his gun and pulled the trigger. Which one? Telling the story years later, Gary will only say, "He got shot."

Afterward, Gary turned his attention to another witness: the little beagle barking frantically and pulling against his chain as he heard what he couldn't see: his fellow canine's death by bullet. "I'll get back to you, little fellow," Gary said. "First I have business to do."

After he'd interviewed neighbours drawn to the scene by the gunfire, and lifted the dead pit bull into the back of his truck, Gary walked back up to where the beagle was staked to the right of the driveway. The doghouse had been improvised from a box, and lacked bedding or straw. Gary also found no sign of food and water bowls, but he knew from the neighbours' accounts that they often stopped by to feed him. The dog's owner, they had all agreed, was negligent even when he was at home. And quite some time ago, days or maybe even weeks, he'd driven off and left the pit bull and the beagle to fend for themselves. Now only the beagle remained, an outside dog kept alive by the kindness of strangers.

Gary bent down and petted the beagle, who strained to lean into his leg. He might be a rookie dog warden, but it didn't take years of experience to know that this was blatant cruelty. He inhaled deeply and stood up, shaking his head. He wanted nothing more than to scoop up the little dog and carry him away to safety, but as dog warden, he had to follow the proper legal procedures. As soon as he gathered all the evidence and prepared the necessary documentation, he would prosecute the perpetrator in court. If only he could let the little guy know that the daily nightmare of his life was about to end.

Two days later, Deputy Sheriff–Dog Warden Gary Kronk had finished his investigation and was legally equipped to seize him. He'd prepared the paperwork to charge the owner with cruelty and obtained an arrest warrant. This would be his first ever cruelty charge, and he'd worked painstakingly to make sure it would be successful.

Gary Kronk, whose association with the sheriff's office dated from 1979, was a trained and certified officer. For thirty-seven years he'd also been a full-time employee of Invensys Climate Controls, formerly Ranco, until it shut down its Ohio operations and began to manufacture heat pump valves in China. But instead of struggling to find another job—the fate of so many of the 220 other laid-off employees—Gary had been installed as a deputy sheriff. Soon after, his duties had been expanded to include the position of dog warden.

In 2005, this was an unusual arrangement. He was the only Ohio dog warden whose vehicle, a black pickup truck, was emblazoned with SHERIFF and the sheriff's departmental badge in imposing gold lettering. Gary also wore the departmental uniform and carried both a radio and a gun, making him the best equipped dog warden in Ohio when it came to responding to calls that came in from all over the county alerting him to stray, lost, injured, or abused dogs. He would rev his pickup, chase them down, and then transport them to the Humane Society of Madison County's shelter.

Being dog warden was the best job in the world, Gary always said, though he was probably the only one without any dogs at home, because he and Liz only had cats. People called him the guardian angel of the county's dogs, and that's what he'd become to Little Guy, whom he was about to legally seize.

For the second time that week, Gary pulled up into Bossman's driveway and parked next to the beagle. Little Guy greeted him excitedly, barking and prancing and wagging his stubby tail. Tools in hand, Gary fastened a leash around his neck and was about to prise open the chain when he suddenly straightened up and cocked his head. From the metal shed came the distinct sounds of whimpering, interspersed with an occasional bark. Damn! How many dogs had this s.o.b. abandoned here?

As he approached the shed, Gary could hear faint movements and the whimpering intensified. The door was padlocked shut but he wasted no time in breaking it open. He slid a tension wrench into the keyhole, pushing it down with his left index finger until he felt the pins underneath and forced them down. Then he removed the pick, turned the wrench, and pulled gently, opening the now unresistant padlock.

In the dark interior, he was greeted by the stench of feces and urine so overpowering that he grabbed at his handkerchief, pressing it tightly over his nose as he gasped for air. With his left hand, he shone a flashlight. The white light captured two cowering puppies, whimpering more loudly now and huddling together in terror. "Nasty, nasty place," he said later. Now, despite the nastiness, he had to act fast. He reached down and picked up both of the quivering dogs and then stepped outside into the welcoming sunshine.

Once the two dogs were securely leashed, Kronk returned inside, holding his flashlight aloft. He searched methodically, making one last check before he stepped back out, sure now that there were no other dogs. After he gently nudged the puppies into one of the cages bolted into the back of the pickup, he returned to liberate the now-howling beagle. Minutes later, he carried Little Guy out to the pickup where, ignoring his brand-new rule about transporting dogs, he heaved him onto the passenger seat in the cab and headed into London to deliver his precious cargo.

"What a cutie!" Cathy exclaimed half an hour later as Gary appeared with a small beagle who had huge protuberant eyes and a high-pitched, chihuahua-like bark emitted in short, frenetic spurts of what seemed to be happiness because he accompanied them with a furious waving of his tail, waggling it like a metronome keeping time to a brisk polka.

"Come here, little fellow!" Cathy exclaimed.

Little Guy slunk cautiously forward toward this new human. Gary handed her the leash. "Got two more out back. Puppies, and in even worse shape than this little guy. This one was outside, and sometimes the neighbours fed him. The pups were stuck inside a shed and nobody knew they were there. Just luck I happened to hear them."

The shelter staff went into action, bathing and towel-drying, feeding and watering. Only once was there resistance, when Little Guy yelped in protest and nipped warningly when his carer tried to soap his front legs. "Whoa! He doesn't want anyone touching those crazy legs," the carer exclaimed, gingerly rinsing them instead. "Must be they hurt you bad, eh boy?" Little Guy remained tense and defensive, until he realized that his legs were no longer in danger. Only then did he relax and allow himself to sink into the oblivion of sleep on his Kuranda bed. In the cage beside him, so did the girls, clinging to each other so tightly that they seemed to be one furry heap.

When Gary Kronk dropped by the next day to visit them, Cathy told him that she and Betty had given them all names. The black-faced puppy was Velvet. Her sister was

Twinkle. And the beagle? "Ah, the boy!" Cathy laughed. "We're calling him Bonzi Billy Beagle, the Bonzi after Fonzi on *Happy Days* because he's such a chipper little guy, and Billy Beagle because that's just a perfect name for him."

"He *is* a chipper little fella." Gary smiled, leaning down to pet the dog he'd just rescued. Bonzi responded with frenzied tail wags, butting his head against Gary's hand. Yet despite his insistence on being petted, the little dog leaned into the side of his cage, vigilant against possible attack.

"How're they all doing? Did I get them out in time?"

"They're coming along good. Real skinny and still shy and very concerned about food, and the boy won't let us touch his legs. But as far as we can tell, the girls are very loving with each other and with the boy. But none of them," she added, "has had a good life."

Gary nodded. No, they had not had a good life, and he was doing everything he could to make sure the law held their owner accountable for animal cruelty, neglect, and endangerment. Through the bars of his cage Bonzi clawed at Gary with his grotesquely shaped right paw. Gary bent down to give him a farewell pat. "You are my first cruelty case," he told the little beagle. "And by God, we're going to win it."

# THIRTEEN

## Strike One, Strike Two ...

The man we've called Bossman did not cooperate with the law. Although a bailiff served the warrant for his arrest, he failed to appear at the courthouse on the date appointed. Gary also discovered that he'd never returned to the rented house where he'd left his dogs.

Legally, Bossman had forfeited ownership of his abandoned, neglected, endangered, untagged dogs, who'd become wards of the Humane Society. After nearly two months of nutritious and plentiful food, they were fattening and fluffing up, healing and forgetting and becoming the playful pups they should always have been. They'd been examined, tested for heartworm, vaccinated, dewormed, and neutered. Their temperament tests confirmed that Velvet and Twinkle were timidly friendly with humans and just plain scared of cats, while Bonzi loved people, cats, and puppies, but sometimes picked fights he could not win with bigger, tougher, scarier dogs. The shelter staff already knew that he liked nothing better than to groom kittens.

The dogs were healthy and happy. It was time to find them real homes, Betty and Cathy agreed. Betty took the puppies to an adoption fair, and that afternoon Velvet went home with her new family. Two weeks later, after their references had been approved, Twinkle left the shelter with her excited humans.

Bonzi did not fare so well. Gary Kronk visited him every day, and the shelter staff treated him as their mascot, but the beagle with the odd legs did not appeal to shelter visitors. "He looks old," some said, misidentifying his blue-tick colouring for the grey of seniority. "He's ugly," said others, mystifying Cathy and Betty, who invariably described him as "adorable." "With those legs, can he even walk?"

One day Bonzi's luck changed, or so it seemed, and he went home with a woman who swore that she was in no way intimated by his boisterous ways. But when Gary visited Bonzi at his new residence—that's how deeply attached he was to the little dog—he was disturbed to see what he considered chaotic living conditions. He urged the woman to contact Betty at the shelter, and he reported his findings to her. The adoption, a failure, needed to be terminated.

Strike one, and then another bit of luck. A family visited the shelter and applied to adopt him. Children! Bonzi loved children as much as he loved puppies and kittens. But two weeks later his family returned him. He was not good with the children, the mother complained, and whenever they were around, he hid under the bed.

Strike two, although everyone suspected that the children must have been provoking him, and Bonzi came back home to the shelter where he resumed his privileged life. Gary Kronk continued his morning visits and Cathy allowed Bonzi to spend the day in the shelter office. Bonzi had insinuated himself into her heart and enjoyed favourite-son status.

But Bonzi did not sit quietly in the office. He was exuberant and continually underfoot and, despite his handicap, sometimes managed to jump over the gate barring the office's open door. Then, without looking back, he would tear down the corridor to the cat room until Cathy or another staff member chased him down and dragged him back to the office.

Bonzi loved cats! Whenever the staff opened the cat cages to clean them he'd try to climb inside, and he'd do the same whenever they opened the door to the cat play-pen room. The staff accommodated him by housing all the dog-friendly cats in the bottom cages so that he could reach them. He had a special yen for kittens; if a kitten carrier were opened, he'd scramble in and begin to groom the little creatures. "That Bonzi!" Cathy would exclaim. "He's a real mother hen with kittens."

Yet happy though Bonzi was in the shelter, safe, warm, and nourished, indulged by the staff, he still spent every night locked alone in a cage, waiting for sunrise and the arrival of the shelter staff's early birds. The boy needed a home and a family of his own, Cathy and Betty lamented. The best way to make that happen was to send him to the prison for three months of the intensive training that would smooth over his rough edges and teach him the skills he needed for an adoption to succeed as his first two had not.

Meanwhile, after a second arrest warrant for Bossman was issued, he surprised everyone by surreptitiously showing up at court and pleading guilty to the charges in return for a suspended jail sentence. Bossman had a conviction for animal abuse. Deputy Sheriff–Dog Warden Gary Kronk had won his first animal cruelty case. Velvet and Twinkle had been adopted, and Bonzi remained safe in the hands of the Humane Society. It was an auspicious start to Gary Kronk's new position as dog warden and for Bonzi's upcoming transfer to the Ohio Prison for Men's Second Chance canine training program.

At the entryway just inside the Ohio Prison for Men's minimum-security cell block, five inmate trainers in "state blues" stood waiting for their dogs. Nearly an hour earlier, an official had alerted them to prepare for the arrival of a vanload of Humane Society orphans. But the scheduled arrival was delayed, and the trainers passed the time chatting and shuffling from foot to foot.

At last a correctional officer pushed open the door, and he and Betty propelled a pack of five excited dogs into the entryway. The dogs, all young hounds straining against their leashes, were handed over to their designated trainers, along with manila envelopes containing their paperwork.

Next the trainers led their charges across the cell block to the cubicles that would be their homes for the next three months. It was lunchtime, the usual time for delivering new dogs, and the scores of inmates lined up to get into the chow hall provided a large audience. As the men whistled and catcalled—"What kind of a dog is that?" "Damn, that's a fine-looking dog!"—the trainers, flattered by association, stood taller as they walked.

Except for Perry Fielding, Bonzi's trainer, who had to endure a different kind of commentary: "Hey! Your dog is bowlegged! How come they stuck you with a broken-down mutt like that?"

Each dog was introduced to his cell and his trainer's cellie, who would be his secondary trainer. When, as sometimes happened, the cellie already had a dog, the incoming dog would meet her new canine cellie. The next part of the dog's initiation was a visit to the yard for a pee and poop pit stop. The Second Chance training manual spelled it out: the best way to begin housetraining was to take the new-comer to the "dog yard," the only part of the field where dogs were permitted.

This restriction was rigorously enforced. To allow the dogs to roam farther onto adjacent fields on the prison cam-pus was a cardinal sin. The prison staff had the right to patrol and to cross from one cell block to another unhindered by either errant dogs or their poop, and non-trainer inmates demanded the same courtesy. The same was true inside the cell block, where trainers had to be diligent about cleanli-ness and about barking. Though their cells were all side by side, they shared their cell block with non-trainers. Most of these men welcomed or at least tolerated the dogs, but a few resented or disliked them. In the tense atmosphere of the prison, the slightest slip-up could provoke complaints. It could even risk cancelling Second Chance.

This was Bonzi Billy Beagle's brave new world, and on that balmy summer afternoon he bounded into it on his crooked little legs and flung back his head and howled delightedly as this new human friend rushed him outside to where he could run and play with the other dogs who were just as unruly as he was. But the new friend tugged roughly at his leash, and after a while Bonzi sensed that this outing was not the joyous one he had anticipated. He tried one last time to salvage the moment, lunging so sud-denly at another dog, an old acquaintance from the shel-ter, that the new friend nearly stumbled but then steadied himself and firmly reeled in the leash until Bonzi sat at his feet. Bonzi capitulated. He still had vivid flashbacks to Bossman, and he knew that his safest response was a cautionary yelp and a quick nip followed by a humble shrinking into the ground.

It was not a promising start to his Second Chance—which was really his third and last chance. This was only Day One. It was later, two weeks into the three-month program, that it became apparent that Bonzi's luck had run out.

I t was the yard that did him in, that great expanse of manicured grassland so full of possibility for a little dog. For most of his life Bonzi had stared out at a rolling field with only passing vehicles to break the monotony. Sometimes there'd been activity behind him, when Bossman either released the pit bull or the big dog burst out of the door and loped wherever he loped, agitating whomever he felt like agitating, including, on some scary occasions, the small beagle chained to a box.

Bonzi had learned to defend himself from noisy cars and trucks by barking terrifyingly and lunging at them, and he'd been rewarded by seeing them beat a satisfying retreat up the road. The pit bull had required a more nuanced approach. Whenever that powerful creature loomed near him, Bonzi would whine in protest and then, adopting his highest-pitched squeal, warn that although he might look like a pushover, he'd give as good as he got.

An infinity of lonely hours bolted to his dog box, watching the road and fending off the pit bull, had ingrained these responses into Bonzi's brain. His nights in his cage in the shelter and his pleasant days in Cathy's office had dulled but not eradicated them. His sojourns in his two (unsuccessful) adoptive homes had been dogless and so brief that it was almost as if they hadn't happened. People came, cooed, and carted him away to unfamiliar places full of noise and food, and then they stopped cooing and suddenly he was back in Cathy's office, pilfering treats and sneaking into the kittens' crates to lick them because he could not find puppies.

Now he was in another place full of noise and people and other dogs, with a vast flat grassland he longed to play in, and where he was crated in the tiny cubicle his two humans shared with him. When he heard other dogs in nearby cubicles, he cocked his head, howled his greetings, and did not understand his humans' consternation when he was so happy to hear his canine friends vocalizing their responses.

The yard also posed its problems. Even before the doors opened onto the fragrance of freshly mowed grass, Bonzi was transformed. His ears perked up, floppy and Dumbo-esque, and he bounded and pranced, tugging at his leash as he hurtled toward the other dogs. When he was released to play, he flung himself into the scrum and then raced around, chasing the faster dogs, propelling himself left and right and stopping only when the other dogs obeyed their trainers' commands to return to them. Then, rasping for breath, Bonzi would trail them back and flop down in front of his own trainer.

In his two weeks in the program, Perry had documented all this behaviour. "There's no such thing as a stubborn dog," the manual insisted, "only a dog you haven't figured out how to motivate. Though there *is* such a thing as a stubborn trainer!"

"The guy who wrote this hasn't met Bonzi," Perry grumbled. His cellie and co-trainer grinned and chucked the beagle under the chin. "Dude, you ain't gonna get the best of us," he said.

Without raising his head, Bonzi wagged his tail very hard.

Two weeks after he leapt into his new life as a canine trainee in the Ohio Prison for Men, Bonzi and the other dogs were outside in the yard. After their potty break the trainers unleashed them, calling out "Play time! Play time!"

Bonzi needed no encouragement. He raced away toward his play buddies and began to play-bow to initiate his favourite game of chase. A boxer mix obliged, and Bonzi scurried after the bigger dog, pumping his bowed front legs in a rhythmic scooping motion as he pounded along.

Suddenly Bonzi veered away from the boxer and headed across the yard to where a heavy-set correctional officer was cycling toward the Recreation Hall.

"Oh shit!" Perry said, and started to run flat-out across the field. But the "yard dog," the nickname for correctional staff posted to yard duty, who routinely cycled to their assigned areas in the prison, was oblivious to the infuriated little dog and pedalled straight ahead. "Oh *shit*!" Perry repeated, sprinting even faster to avert what was about to happen.

He was too late. Bonzi, in a barrage of fury, had already lunged, screeching out his shrillest bark as he snapped at the yard dog's boot. Startled and angry, the correctional officer kicked out and temporarily dislodged his attacker. Bonzi attacked again, this time unbalancing his target, who crashed onto the grass, still clutching his handlebars.

Bonzi, instantly docile, sniffed curiously at the enraged correctional officer as if wondering what he was doing on the ground. As Perry jogged up to the scene of the crime, the officer, swearing profusely, heaved himself to his feet and was pulling his bike up. Their exchange, loud and furious on the one hand, subdued and apologetic on the other, was brief. Bonzi sat quietly, watching the humans battle it out.

Then the glowering yard dog brushed himself off and, still muttering warningly, rode away on his bicycle. Perry looked down at the little beagle. "Don't look so fuckin' innocent," he growled. "Because of you I'm probably gonna get kicked out of the program." Bonzi stared up, his dark eyes exuding compassion. Then, leashed up again, he trotted peaceably back to their cell.

That afternoon Betty received a telephone call from the prison. "Oh no," she exclaimed, "he didn't! Oh! He did?" She sighed deeply, twice. "I'll get right out there," she said. "Yes, right away. I'm sorry," she added before ringing off. "That Bonzi!"

Betty was calm as she headed out to the prison, steering with her left hand and snacking on peanut-buttered crackers with her right. "That Bonzi!" When she'd eaten she picked up her cell phone. "George? Sorry, I won't be home for dinner. I'm on my way back to the prison to pick up the beagle. Yes, the crippled one, Gary Kronk's cruelty case. How come? 'Cause the little bugger's got himself kicked out of the program!"

An hour later, after a tense meeting with the Second Chance coordinator and a sullen Perry, who was about to be reassigned to maintenance, Betty and Bonzi were on their way back to the shelter. Cathy had stayed late to welcome the recalcitrant hound, and when he saw her Bonzi jumped up, squealing delightedly as he pawed at her hands. "Hard to stay mad at you, Bonz," Cathy said. "But this time you've really messed up." Bonzi wagged his tail.

Betty chuckled. "Yep. All those guys inside longing to get out, but Bonzi can't even last a month inside before they chuck *him* out."

"Chasing bicycles? Chasing cars or joggers or running children? It's called predatory aggression and it's natural in dogs. Don't forget that they were predators for thousands of years before we domesticated them," Shane Livingston said to Betty as they sat across from each other at the trestle table in the centre of cell block A. "In herding dogs it's common, but not in pet dogs. Not in beagles! It's a serious issue that needs to be tackled." God Almighty, he thought, is this dame really going to sneak a dog kicked out of cell block B into cell block A?

"How?" Betty asked. "What do you suggest would stop a little bugger like that right in his tracks? How would you fix it, Livingston?"

"I wrote a section about it in the manual," Shane reminded her. Damn! She was the one who had encouraged him to write it, she was the one who brought him mountains of training books and articles, and she was definitely the one who made it mandatory reading for all Second Chance trainers.

But Betty said calmly, "It's been a while since I've had the time to look at it. Refresh my memory, please."

"Back in a sec," Shane said. "My copy's in my cell." Minutes later he handed Betty a much-thumbed *Second Chance Canine Program Training Manual,* by Shane Livingston, journeyman animal trainer. Betty began to read at the opened page.

"I see lots of ways to deal with predatory aggression here," she said after a while. "You just have to decide which one is best for the individual dog's temperament."

"That's right. Though in prison," he said, deliberately, "you're more limited than you would be outside. For example, you can't ask prison staff to stop what they're doing if a dog is chasing their bikes or the Gators they use to deliver mail and supplies. If they did stop and stay still it would probably short-circuit the predatory aggression, but that's the job of the dog trainers, not the yard dog or mail lady."

Betty didn't blink or even pretend to be surprised. "So then what would *you* do? How would you *fix* it?"

Shane shrugged. "Sometimes the best solution is management. Just accept that you can never let your dog run free off leash. Whatever he does, he's on a leash that you're at the other end of. That pretty much guarantees no aggressive incidents. Because if there are any, you're liable for the dog's bad behaviour and you risk being sued. Meaning, the victimized staff member would sue the prison. Remember: follow the money."

"And the prison would immediately shut down the entire dog-training program," Betty said.

Shane could hear the suppressed alarm in her voice. "Right. Don't forget, when anything happens, the prison staff blames the trainer. *Always.* Which is why I highlighted personal responsibility as a cornerstone quality for a great trainer. Meaning: a guy who doesn't make excuses for himself or for his dog's behaviour." He sighed and added, "A guy like Jake Browning."

"The Beagle Guy." Betty nodded. Then she pushed herself up and said briskly, "Switchover time. I'll be back with the next batch in a day or two."

Shane watched her leave. Cell block B was a world away from cell block A, and except for the worst sort of bad luck—a correctional officer reassigned from B to A, for example—she could pull it off with no one the wiser. She just needed to enrol the damned beagle with a new number. Shane held his head in his hands. Nobody must find out. He owed it to all the dogs to help her succeed in this crazy scheme, though it was clear that she had no intention of elaborating on the details of what had happened other than some beagle's trainer had been sloppy and his dog had done something he shouldn't have, something drastic, to judge from Betty's concern. But she wasn't the confiding type. She held her cards close to her chest, which was one of the reasons Shane trusted her. Anyway, it didn't matter. Whatever had happened was water under the bridge. A trainer must have let his dog screw up badly, and now that dog was doing penance back at the Humane Society shelter.

The drone of male voices was punctuated by excited barking as trainers led several dogs to the entryway to be handed over to the correctional officers, who would escort them outside to the Humane Society van. Shane remained where he was. He wasn't one of those trainers who mourned the loss of each dog. He had enrolled in and now helped run the program because he loved dogs. After six unforgiving years in another facility, his transfer to the Ohio Prison for Men and its dog-training cell block had seemed an extraordinary stroke of luck. The dogs, he said, were down on their luck, just like he was, and were looking for another chance, just like he was. And so he welcomed each newcomer into his cell and his life as a new best friend, and he lived vicariously through them, wanting no other life than theirs. Their tribulations were his tribulations, their joys were his joys, and, in the end, their triumphs were his triumphs.

The greatest triumph of all wasn't when a dog sat or heeled on command, but when he walked confidently out of the prison and into his new adoptive family's arms. Shane refused to sink into depression when that happened. After all, the once-unlucky dog was getting a reprieve, and as the program logo proclaimed, that vaunted second chance at life and love. His own efforts as a trainer played no small part in this metamorphosis, and that was what Shane held on to.

Other trainers were not as stoic. As each rotation of dogs finished their training, the cell block quivered with the pain of the impending separation. There was one last bath in the mop closet. But most of the leave-taking took place in the trainer's heart and soul. Some men could not bear to see their dog trot outside and disappear forever. These trainers said their goodbyes inside, and then handed their leashes over to another trainer or an inmate volunteer "canine caretaker" as the dog headed out of the cell block.

Eddy Stackhouse's grief each time a dog graduated from Second Chance was legendary. Three years earlier, he'd been transferred out of the "end of the road" prison known as Lucasville, where he'd pretty much given up on life until a religious epiphany inspired the courage and will to resist the beatings and rapes that had all but destroyed him during his first years of incarceration. As he walked into the Ohio Prison for Men, Eddy saw the first dog he'd laid eyes on since his final days outside the fences, when he was still a drunk, stoned, empty-souled teenager.

That dog, a Rottweiler mix named Mystic, was a revelation. Eddy knelt on the ground and petted her all over, and Mystic reciprocated, wagging her tail and licking his hand as he smiled for the first time in years. In that instant Eddy knew that he was meant to be a dog trainer. He approached Cassius Cheeks, Mystic's trainer. Cassius, also a born-again Christian, listened to his urgent plea. Afterward, he allowed Eddy to take Mystic out into the yard for leashed walks, and taught him how to brush and groom her.

But Eddy's application to enrol in Second Chance was stalled. The program was so popular that trainers seldom left voluntarily, and openings depended on an incumbent trainer's winning parole or transferring to another institution. Finally Cassius Cheeks interceded with the program coordinator, praising Stackhouse's potential and suggesting that another dog-training cell be opened to accommodate him. No! Impossible. And so Cassius, by now committed to his protégé's dream, resigned his position as a dog trainer in favour of Eddy. The next day Eddy became Mystic's trainer and Cassius was assigned to the Chapel of All Faiths as a clerk and transferred to a different cell block.

He had made an enormous sacrifice. As in other prisons, Second Chance dog trainers enjoyed status and privileges. They lived side by side, a small community of men who worked together at an intense job that separated them from the general inmate population. In prison, no man was ever completely safe, but the dog trainers were safer than other inmates. They had all succeeded in avoiding disciplinary infractions for at least six months prior to applying to the program. They had all completed their secondary education. And in a mind-altering world of prescription drugs, they were all drug-free, and, because they were constantly tested, they could not afford to slip.

The program also allowed them to earn accreditation as apprentice dog trainers by crediting them with six and a half hours per day for a total of four thousand hours of experience. When they were finally freed, they would be journeymen trainers, members of an honourable profession able to earn a decent living.

Best of all, they got to live with a dog, and there wasn't a man in the program who didn't see that as the supreme benefit. They also learned, as if by osmosis, that observing how dogs perceive and make their way in the world is a transformative process. The anger, guilt, and shame that had been stamped into their psyches would begin to fade away as they looked into their own souls and felt redemption.

Eddy Stackhouse's journey was no different, and that included the pain of losing beloved dogs. Mystic was the first. She changed Eddy's life and he changed hers. By October 18, 2002—he never forgot that painful date—she'd become such a well-trained, confident, trusting dog that the Humane Society agreed to send her to a "meet and greet" with a family who had applied to adopt her. Eddy's heart was shattered, and he feared that Mystic's was, too. But he'd prepared her well for her second chance at life and love, and he had no choice but to hand her over and escape back to his cell to grieve.

He'd lost the first friend he'd had in twenty-two years, and the only one who loved him. To assuage his sorrow, Eddy had incorporated his own ritual into the Second Chance's prescribed exit procedure: he would glance meditatively around his cell for the last vestiges of the dog's presence, a stray toy or a tattered towel. Then he would meticulously scrub the cell, the cage, and the feeding and water bowls. Finally, as if he were burying a memory, he would fold the dog's blanket and smooth it down into a locker. Then he would sit in silence on his bed, waiting until calmness conquered his inner turmoil.

By the summer of 2005, the cycle of loss and renewal was as familiar as the clanging of bars when Ohio Prison released its residents to confront another morning. The day before, five dogs had trustingly trotted alongside their trainers to be handed over to strangers who walked them over unknown lawns and then locked them into cages for a van ride to their new lives. Today, also at lunchtime, that same van had pulled up in the prison parking lot and the same strangers had unloaded seven more dogs about to embrace their Second Chance. And inside the prison they could not leave, a gaggle of inmate dog trainers lounged by the entryway, waiting with suppressed excitement for their new companions.

Eddy was standing with his good friend Jake Browning, whose pain at losing each dog was like the man himself: slow burning and patient. "So, Beagle Man," Eddy greeted him, "any inside info on what dogs Betty's sending us?"

Jake flung his hands out to the side and shook his head. "Not really. Sarge mentioned that she's bringing me a beagle but no other details." He clapped Stackhouse on the shoulder. "Hey, Eddy, the good news is that by chow time, we'll both be in love!"

Shane Livingston had more practical concerns. "Damn! Can't anyone ever be on time?" he grumbled, glancing at his watch. "We've been here since they called us at noon."

A loud creaking thud interrupted the bantering. To a man they straightened up, stopped talking, and watched as the door that confined them to cell block A inched open and the first of seven shiny noses appeared. Several chaotic minutes later, the Humane Society workers nodded hasty good-byes and disappeared. Sergeant Whyte, the Second Chance unit coordinator, stood beside Shane, consulting a clipboard with its list of dogs identified by number and name, and by the number and name of their assigned inmate trainers.

"Okay, that wraps it up," the sergeant said. "Oh, Livingston, that's a nice husky you've got this time." Shane, smiling slightly, waited. "My daughter's been making noises about getting a dog for the kids. And, you know, after that movie *Snow Dogs,* she's got her heart set on a husky."

"If Bob seems a good fit for little kids, I'll do everything I can to get him properly trained, okay, Sarge?"

"Okay." Sergeant Whyte leaned over and broke one of Second Chance's cardinal rules—"Prison staff will not pet, play with, or feed or give treats to the dogs in training"—by scratching briskly behind Bob's silky ears. "Hey, Livingston? Thanks."

Shane sighed. "Sure thing, Sarge. Now we're off to the mop closet."

Sergeant Whyte gave Bob a last quick chin chuck. Shane tugged once at his leash and Bob looked up at him expectantly, then followed his new human across the range.

Before they reached the mop closet, Shane encountered a group of men crouched down around a beagle. The little dog sat panting, his huge dark eyes searching each man's face, one after another. "Would you look at his legs!" "Geez, effing dog's crippled. How're you supposed to train a dog like that?"

"Same way you train any other dog," Jake Browning, the beagle's trainer, said laconically. "You're training his personality and habits, not his physique. Anyway, he's the dog Betty hooked me up with, and I'm going to do my best with him." He glanced up at Shane, who towered above him.

Shane knew at once who this tail-wagging little troublemaker was. "You need any help with him, just say the word. Uh, what's his name?"

A slight smile creased Jake's worried face. "Bonzi Billy Beagle." Other trainers tittered.

"Great name," Shane said. "Hey, Bonzi Billy Beagle, meet Bob. Bob, say hi to Bonzi Billy Beagle."

# FOURTEEN

## Bonzi Is Redeemed

Jake Browning sat on the lower bunk in his cell (Garvin Schwein had taken the top bunk) and patted the mattress, inviting Bonzi Billy Beagle to jump up—if he could. Second Chance protocol forbade this—"Dogs are *not* allowed on beds or chairs"—but sometimes you could make exceptions, and this was one most of the guys made. Bonzi wagged his tail and gazed intently into Jake's eyes, and yet he did not jump up. Ah! That had been the test. With those crazy legs, he *couldn't* jump. Jake leaned over, grasped Bonzi around the waist, lifted him onto the narrow cot, and then leaned back and waited.

Bonzi had never felt the soft comfort of a bed. Bossman kept his bedroom door closed, and during his short-lived sojourn in cell block B, Perry Fielding had confined him to his crate, as per the rules. And so now he sat motionless, exactly where Jake had placed him, and waited for what might happen. What he knew was: Bossman, who was fast receding in his memory, wasn't here and so he could relax. After a while he sighed and his eyelids fluttered until they closed completely and he slept. Watching him, Jake saw the gentle rise and fall of his chest and his rhythmic breathing punctuated by put-puts of snores.

"I took one look at this twisted little beagle and my heart ached for him," Jake wrote years later in a handwritten memoir titled *Bonzi: My Crooked Leg Little Buddy*. "I felt pity and sadness as I noticed his paw turned at an awkward angle and his other front leg bowed like an old cowboy's. How can this little guy walk? I wondered. Does it hurt every time he takes a step? At the time, I had no idea that this was a 'rescued' dog or that he had special circumstances. I just knew that here was a broken animal. (Oh, was I wrong!)"

In 2005, Jacob Browning was a once-broken man whom Second Chance was mending. He no longer despaired at the advent of his second decade in prison. What mattered was his tenure as a dog trainer, and, since his transfer to Ohio Prison for Men in 2001, the only anniversary he bothered to mark was his acceptance into Second Chance.

In offering him the job of training—and loving—one homeless dog after another, Second Chance had brought renewed meaning and purpose to a dreary, pointless existence riddled with guilt, hopelessness, and raging regrets. The dogs looked to him to teach them the skills on which their future success and happiness depended. They were as diverse as his fellow inmates, but the same training rules of association and motivation—the principle at the core of the Second Chance training philosophy—applied to all.

What this meant in practice was no striking, yanking, yelling, or choking. ("There is *zero tolerance* of any inmate teasing or playing aggressively with the dogs" was the manual's first rule.) Instead, you were supposed to observe and reflect: What does your dog like, and what does she dislike? Figure this out and use the information wisely, and in a timely fashion—which the manual defined as no more than one second after she's done something—to establish consequence and motivation.

Jake's copy of the manual was well-thumbed and marked up, as any bible should be. His growing expertise was supplemented by Shane's seminars, pep talks, and one-on-one confabs, sometimes squeezed in Jake's cell—legally, because as program aide, Shane was permitted into other trainers' cells—or, more often, huddled together out in the range. This, added to his determination, dedication, and patience—Shane also saw passion—had transformed Jake into a sensitive and successful trainer, one of the bedrocks of the program.

Some of the men resented the time they had to spend on journalling. Not Jake! If you weren't committed to keeping careful records, how could you really be a full-fledged trainer? So, even when he was tired or still hungry after another puny supper of processed slop, he'd push his gawky, old-fashioned glasses firmly on his nose and, in the waning light of the cell block, record his observations of that day's doggy performances.

What was striking about Bonzi was not how his training progressed—he was usually receptive to Jake's tactics—but his extracurricular activities, which Jake found endlessly surprising. What this little dog with the messed-up legs liked most in the world was to run—and run and run. He refused to play rough and tumble with the other dogs, and he showed no interest in toys. What obsessed him was chasing other dogs, and even then only his special friends.

Those dogs, Jake believed, seemed to understand that this funny-looking little beagle didn't want to play, he just wanted to chase them until the trainers ended the game.

The trainers became accustomed to Bonzi and his unlikely antics, but inmates who weren't part of the Second Chance program were another story. Weeks after Bonzi's arrival, some of them would stop Jake and ask, "What's wrong with your dog? Why are his legs mangled? Hey, man, you should carry him!" Then, as Bonzi scampered along, heeling on his left side, Jake would respond with his habitual answer: "All I know is, he's happy."

Jake was happy, too. As soon as he'd seen Bonzi's legs, his cellie had lost all interest in the dog they were both supposed to be training. So instead of being Bonzi's primary trainer with Garvin assisting whenever he felt like it, Jake was Bonzi's only trainer, and Bonzi was Jake's very own dog. Even during their long nighttimes locked into their cell, Garvin ignored the little dog.

Jake knew for a fact that for Bonzi there were none of the special secret training sessions out behind the hill where inmates were forbidden to go, where Garvin "trained" some of their larger, more robust hounds by dominating and intimidating them into obedience, teaching them tricks that, Shane insisted, added nothing to their adoptability because they performed them out of fear. Garvin taught Bonzi only one thing: to twirl, dancing around on his back legs as he shook his two bowed front legs together in what resembled a prayer. And he taught him in the cell, easily, because (Jake was sure) Bonzi already knew how to twirl, as if he'd taught himself that awkward swaying, and Garvin merely gave him the cues to do it.

Time passed, with only squabbling prison politics, friendly chit-chat, and the occasional rainstorm to distinguish one day from another. (Shane was the odd man out: he was a voracious reader who ate up the prison's Buddhist study holdings and the one book a month his family sent, all that was allowed.) Each day by 6:30 A.M. all the trainers had crawled out or hopped down from their bunks, flung on casual clothes, and opened the crate to release and leash up their dogs. From most of the thirteen dog cells there also resounded hoarse "Shhs" as trainers urgently shushed dogs whining or barking in eager anticipation of their early morning pit stop, oblivious to the scores of inmates who were still asleep.

After they returned to the cell, the dogs were crated while their trainers bathed, dressed in the requisite state blues, and then, when the call came, filed out to line up for entry into the chow hall for breakfast. Afterward, from 8:00 to 10:00 A.M., they worked with the dogs out in the yard, walking them and teaching or practising the essential commands: Come! Sit! Stay! Heel!

At 11:30 the dogs were taken outside for another potty break, and after their trainers had returned from lunch, they spent an hour or two in the yard socializing with other dogs and running through their commands. When they weren't working with the dogs, the trainers were discussing them and gossiping. More than once Shane Livingston had erupted, accusing them of running a sewing circle instead of a network of professional dog trainers, which elicited a muttered "Livingston's a fuckin' dick" before the men resumed the tittle-tattle: who had requested a move into a new cell to get away from his cellie, who in the program was fucking up, who was about to be fired.

"The only thing two trainers can agree on is that the third one is doing a piss-poor job of it," Shane snapped at them. Jake, who pretty much stayed above the fray by keeping his mouth shut, had been unable to refrain from laughing.

Later, shooting the breeze with his trio of best buddies, Shane grinned as they rehashed and applauded his earlier *bons mots,* but he soon shepherded the conversation into the serious topic of the nature of dog training. The problem was, he confided to Jake, Eddy, and Elijah, that to be any good at it, a man had to make an emotional investment. "And that," Shane said, "boils down to giving a shit. All of a sudden you're part of something larger, and you begin to believe that you're making a difference."

Eddy nodded. "Because of the dogs."

"Absolutely because of the dogs. Because they exist only in the moment and are a great barometric reading of a man's personality, yet they accept you as you are." A rustling murmur among his friends. "This is what I know: dogs are more than symbols of redemption, as we're always hearing. They're our means of redemption."

He paused and then resumed, the words tumbling out: "These dogs, these creatures that are without guile or duplicity, that bond with you almost spiritually and, Please Don't Anybody Roll Their Eyes, are healers, true healers."

Nobody rolled their eyes and Shane continued. "Because dogs are intuitive! They just know. They can see beneath the surface of people, and gradually they awaken the empathy and the compassion that was buried deep inside us. And that's why and that's how they redeem us."

But redemption was also hard work, and when the clock struck 4:30 P.M. and the trainers took the dogs out for another pit stop, most of them were tired. Their dinner had been a sorry, rushed, too-early event that left them hungry for the ramen noodles they would heat up later on if any of them had any left from their last prison supply catalogue order. Meanwhile, they had to groom their dogs, write up their daily journal, and then take the dogs outside for a final potty break before the 9:30 lock-up. (The correctional officers made exceptions for puppies and for dogs with diarrhea, and, if a trainer requested it, they would unlock his cell and accompany man and dog out into the yard.)

This schedule suited Bonzi as well as any other. He'd grown to love Jake, his latest human, and he was easy enough to train despite a streak of impenetrable stubbornness that was at odds with his usual passivity. What sort of experience had he had with the humans in his previous life? Jake wondered. Why did he stare so fixedly into your eyes as if peering right through to your soul? Why did he flatten himself onto his belly when something—an inmate's raised voice, a yard fight before it was quickly broken up—suddenly caught his attention? Why did he stiffen whenever Garvin took notice of him? But except for these descents into extreme wariness, the small beagle with the funny walk was always happy.

He was at his happiest at night, when Jake lifted him onto his bed. Bonzi would waste no time. He'd burrow under the covers, sigh deeply, and fall into a deep sleep. "I think he was looking for comfort and acceptance," Jake mused in his memoir, but he was also talking about himself, and the comfort and acceptance he felt with the little beagle nestled so trustingly against his leg.

# FIFTEEN

## The Dog You Deserve

On Day 85 of the current canine rotation, the Second Chance dog trainers gathered for a town hall at the trestle table in their section of the cell block. Except that, unlike true town halls, this one was impromptu, unauthorized, restricted to dog trainers, and presided over by Shane Livingston. "Guys, we're comin' down the home stretch. Five days to go so our dogs can really strut their stuff when Betty comes for them." A long silence, so noticeable on the always-buzzing range that other inmates who were clustered outside their cells glanced over at them.

Eddy Stackhouse looked stricken. Jake Browning visibly blanched, and his eyes, magnified behind his glasses, looked just like Bonzi's, bulging and dark and moist. Shane was focused on the final days of training. "Guys, we all have five days of hard work ahead of us," he was saying. "Are your journals in good shape? And can your dog really do all the things you claim to have taught him? You know, the stuff that'll help get him adopted and that will definitely help him *stay* adopted and not get returned to the shelter. The stuff that Betty says some of you fudge in your journals so that she's embarrassed at PetSmart adoption fairs when the dogs actually don't know their commands?"

That caught their attention, jostled them away from the fray. First and foremost they were trainers, committed to preparing their dogs for a much better life than they would otherwise be likely to have. Suddenly Eddy Stackhouse stood up. "Remember that old saying, 'Every trainer ends up with the dog he deserves'?"

"The Australian Royal Air Force Dog Training's motto," Shane said. "I dearly love that maxim."

"Me too," Eddy said. "And I'm so happy that I deserved Dixie, because she's a sweetheart. Things worked out real well for me with her. And for her, because she's a model pup now and her new family will love her."

Jake Browning, palms pressing against the table, raised himself up slightly but did not stand. "And look at Bonzi. That dog's one bundle of joy and pretty easy to train. I just treat him like the dog he thinks he is—easiest way to deal with a little dog with a big dog attitude."

"Hey, Beagle Guy," a trainer chimed in, "all you need is biscuits to train that crazy pup."

"Biscuits are always good, but he's just a good little dog, a happy dog." Jake lowered himself back down. "We love him," he said.

"Damn right!" his cellie Garvin Schwein called out. "And you should see him twirl."

Ninety-three days after they arrived, seven dogs had been readied to return to the world outside the fences. Their trainers had bathed them, brushed them, and taken them on their last run out in the dog yards. The day was so deceptively sunny and warm that it seemed as if summer had never ended. Afterward, the men hunkered down in their cells for a few last moments of communion with their dogs. In his cell, Jacob Browning was alone with Bonzi. Garvin had already said a perfunctory farewell—"Hey, little man, give 'em hell out there, you hear?"—before sauntering out onto the range where a few non-trainers had congregated.

Jake, holding Bonzi, felt the little beagle relax against him. "I'm gonna miss you, little buddy. Now you be good out there, you listen to what your family tells you." He hugged Bonzi closer to him. "You're going out to people who'll love you. I'm real happy for you. But I'm gonna miss you. You're a special little guy."

The call came just after noon. The time had come. Jake fastened Bonzi's leash for the last time, and then they walked out together across the cell block the man might never leave and the beagle would never see again. Bonzi heeled without being told, and only briefly lost his focus when they reached the dog Dixie, already waiting at the door with Eddy and Elijah. Dixie, more subdued than Bonzi, wagged her tail in greeting but did not respond to Bonzi's play-bowing. The men stood together in silent misery.

The outside door opened. In the excitement that verged on pandemonium of what seemed to be a new adventure, the dogs whined and a few barked, until all the trainers had surrendered their leashes to these new people who were urging the dogs along in an unfamiliar group walk. Jake stood staring as Bonzi trotted away alongside a stranger, looking back and balking as he realized he was leaving Jake, and then scurrying to keep up with his friend Dixie, walking steadily straight ahead of him.

Jake watched until the unwieldy procession was out of sight. What was going through Bonzi's mind as he stopped to look back at him? How could the little guy even guess that this was for the best, that only by leaving his beloved human could he ever find a family to cherish and care for him forever? But if it was hard for Jake to focus on that, how much harder for the little dog to understand that he wasn't being abandoned yet again?

"Well, I just said goodbye to my little buddy," he said afterward to Elijah Tibbs and Eddy Stackhouse. "He did well, though I really could have used a couple more weeks to work with him." He took off his misted glasses and wiped them methodically on his blue shirt. "I'm going to miss him."

Images flashed through his mind of Bonzi out in the dog yard, chasing his uncatchable buddies until he could scarcely breathe, twirling as soon as he caught sight of Garvin, even before Garvin asked him to, and most poignantly, burrowing under the covers to snuggle against Jake's legs. If only he could also have taught Bonzi what this all meant, what it was preparing him for, the good life outside these fences. He'd be confused; he wouldn't understand at first why Jake had handed him over to someone else, betraying his love and trust. But soon, when he was adopted, everything would fall into place and restore his faith in Jake, the first human who had truly loved him.

Back in the Humane Society shelter, Bonzi was feeling everything Jake had imagined he would. This was the third time he'd been taken from a home and locked back into a cage in this familiar place that his ninety-three days with Jake had bleached out of his memory. He'd been so happy, so warm and content, so eager to play and to learn, to sit and to heel and to twirl, and then at night to lie quietly nestled against his human. Now, in a room echoing with other caged dogs, he retreated into himself and slept, soundlessly and sadly.

In the morning, before the shelter staff had taken him out to potty or poured kibble into his empty bowl, he had a visitor: Deputy Sheriff–Dog Warden Gary Kronk. Bonzi sat up straight and wagged his tail. "So you sailed through the program this time, Bonzi!" Gary greeted him. "This time you got honourably discharged."

Bonzi wagged harder at the familiar face. "Glad to see you're going to get your second chance on the adoption floor." Bonzi waited, panting slightly. Then, as the uniformed man crouched down to scratch his ears through the bars, he tilted his head back so that the busy fingers could find just the right spots.

At first shelter manager Cathy and director Betty were so hopeful. Who could resist this little scamp of a beagle, so enthusiastic, so playful, so energetic and now housebroken, obedience-trained, and flawed only by a propensity to chase moving objects? But dog-seeking visitors to the shelter looked and passed Bonzi by. Why? Cathy shook her head as she contemplated Betty's question. "'Ugly and too old' kind of headed the list," she said as Betty ranted in frustration.

On the day Betty escorted the latest pack of Second Chance graduates, including the Shih Tzu who had followed Bonzi as Jake's prison dog, back to the shelter, their training completed, Bonzi was still there, roaming contentedly during the day as the office mascot, incarcerated during the night and holidays. Gary Kronk stopped by to see him almost daily. Cathy and Betty indulged him. But after that entire rotation of new dogs—Bonzi now played with

Jake's perfectly trained Shih Tzu in the dog yard—the staff were checking references and making final decisions about adoptions. They already had several promising applications for the Shih Tzu, and the demand for the other prison dogs was brisk. But for Bonzi, who sometimes twirled gratuitously and plunked himself down in a sitting position whenever asked, no applications at all. "Poor fellow," Cathy said. "Looks like he'll be spending Christmas with us this year."

"Well, maybe not," Betty said, one cold December afternoon. "Guess what? Yesterday I got an emailed application for Bonzi, and I'm going to start checking out the lady's references right now. That's the first thing on my to-do list for today."

"Hey! That's great! I'd love to meet her."

"Hmm," Betty said. "See, Cathy, the thing is, this lady lives up in Canada."

# PART 4

# BONZi IN FREEDOM:
# GO NORTH, YOUNG DOG!

# SIXTEEN

# The Dogs of Hurricane Katrina and Petfinder

In late August 2005, as Bonzi Billy Beagle was settling into his cozy, comfortable life with Jake Browning in the Ohio Prison for Men, a catastrophe in slow motion was unfolding nearly a thousand miles away in the southern state of Louisiana.

Hurricane Katrina killed at least 1833 people and transformed southeast Louisiana into a submerged wasteland. As animals drowned or starved to death by the hundreds of thousands, the now disgraced Michael Brown, director of the Federal Emergency Management Agency (FEMA), dismissed desperate appeals to help surviving dogs and cats, saying, "They are not our concern." (Brown was removed from his position that September.)

The fate of one dog encapsulated the horror of post-Katrina New Orleans. Little Snowball was waiting in the rain alongside his boy, a three- or four-year-old African American whose family was lined up to flee the fouled and chaotic Superdome on a convoy of buses bound for the relative safety of Houston's Astrodome.

But before they boarded, a policeman confiscated their dog. No pets were allowed on the bus. As Snowball was snatched away, the child cried "Snowball! Snowball!" until he vomited. Snowball became the focal point of an immense international effort to find and return him to his grieving little boy. Despite a huge reward, Snowball vanished in the war zone of downtown New Orleans.

In Toronto, grieving for Snowball and countless other animal victims, I developed an early morning ritual. I logged into NOLA.com, the New Orleans website, and then, as Canada Friend, into Pet Forum, a virtual community of animal lovers, advocates, and rescuers that included displaced New Orleaners frantic about the pets they'd left behind. Pet Forum members shared in the minutiae of an army of rescuers who headed down to New Orleans and its devastated environs in vehicles stuffed full of supplies for the hungry, thirsty, exhausted, traumatized animals they would be caring for. If I could have overcome my physical limitations, I would have signed up as a foot soldier in that army.

Even as the nightmare of Katrina faded from public notice, animal rescuers continued their work. One of their most difficult problems was the near-impossibility of reuniting rescued animals with their owners. Petfinder, the digital tool for rehoming adoptable pets, responded to the crisis. With financing from Maddie's Fund, a family foundation dedicated to ensuring that "no adoptable pet is euthanized for lack of a home," Petfinder was redesigned and transformed into a vast database that was exactly what the rescuing community needed: a way to reunite lost pets with their people.

Petfinder literally saved lives. The Animal Emergency Response Network of animal welfare organizations relied on it, and so did Katrina victims, who used it to post pleas to rescue the pets they'd been forced to leave behind. Petfinder was searchable by geographical location, breed, age, and special needs, and potential adopters could specify whether they already had dogs, cats, or children. It could link each entry to a rescue, a Humane Society, a pet insurance offer, or an animal training service. Petfinder was an algorithm of hope, digital technology at the service of humans and animals in need, an immense virtual community dedicated to dogs, cats, and other companion animals.

But like any digital system manned by humans, Petfinder sometimes made mistakes. It made a mistake in late 2005, when I turned to it in my quest for a nice little beagle to go walking with me through the streets of Toronto. And by making that mistake, one miscued keystroke, it catapulted young Bonzi Billy Beagle into my life.

greeted each day by poring over NOLA's Pet Forum, but after I logged out, I shed my Canada Friend persona and resumed working on my latest book project. As a writer, I spend long hours in my study or at my dining room table, mapping out my book, composing, revising, polishing. That's after I've finished my research, conducted over the years in libraries, online, and in books and articles, often in tandem with writing another book.

And of course I am alone, because writing is by nature a solitary pursuit, though my dogs and cats are always with me, snuggled into dog beds and an armchair. But this life-inside-my-head, this endless consultation with my interior self, is too powerful to confine to a small room, or even to a whole house. It thrives on movement, on lengthy strides and changing scenery, on surging chest and heaving lungs: it thrives, in other words, on long walks that loosen mental cobwebs and spur new patterns and thoughts.

Walking is such a crucial element in my writing life that I can truly say "I write, therefore I walk." And when I walk, I greatly enjoy the company of a dog who likes walking just as much as I do.

But by the fall of 2005, all three of my dogs had withdrawn their walking services. Piloting them any farther than the neighbourhood park, which was no walk at all, was out of the question. Because of her luxating patellas or "trick knees," Alice had always disliked walking and inveigled me to carry her. But lugging around a portly little dachshund is no way to free the spirit to write a book in your head; your forearm and elbow begin to throb, and before long your only thoughts are about getting Alice home before your entire arm falls off.

Pumpkin, once an avid walking companion though she stopped to investigate every tree trunk and blade of grass, was in failing health and happy just to sleep her days away. Old Olive, who'd been an immensely satisfying walking companion, had slowed down so drastically that I didn't dare take her more than a block or two away in case she collapsed and I had to somehow transport her back to the house. The decline had been caused by two attacks of vestibular, or "old dog," disease, a temporary, stroke-mimicking syndrome in which the dog's head tilts, her eyes roll or "dance," she loses balance and circles or falls, and is nauseated by food. By the time she recovered, Olive had lost her capacity for sustained walking and began to look and act like the very old dog she was. And so when I went outside to walk away the puzzles and the mazes in my head, I walked alone.

By November, I made a decision. Even though I already had three dogs, the maximum permitted by Toronto's city bylaws, and though I had long ago pledged to rescue only needy senior dogs, I needed to break both the law and my self-promise, and adopt a younger dog who loved to walk— because I *could not* write books without a dog to walk with.

And so I turned to Petfinder and searched for a homeless beagle to adopt. My hands shook slightly as I began the process. Up popped Petfinder's dog-finding menu and away I went, searching for my walking companion and eliminating thousands of dogs each time I clicked:

> Breed: beagle
> Age: adult
> Gender: n/a
> Location: ON
> I have: dogs, cats
> Search: *click!*

Page after page of small icons appeared on my screen, a cornucopia of little hounds, eager, panting, and smiling, she so pretty, he so handsome, and all needing a home: how could I possibly choose? And then I saw him, his head cocked inquiringly, mouth agape, huge eyes fixed on his photographer: What? he seemed to be saying. Why?

Never let it be said that you can't fall in love with an image, because I fell in love with Bonzi's. This intense dog with energy pulsating straight into my ken, a little guy whose adorableness was showcased without artifice, his orange collar hardly noticeable in the tiny Petfinder icon: *veni, vidi, me vicit:* I came, I saw, and he conquered me. I stared and stared. I'd found my new dog.

"Bonzi Billy Beagle Boy was pulled on a cruelty case," his biographer had written. "Bonzi loves other dogs and kittens, does not mind cats, and loves people. He loves to play, go for walks, and just is so sweet. Bonzi's right front leg turns outward. But that does not stop him from running and playing. Bonzi will have to be crated when not being watched. He loves to use his hunting skill to find things he should not have and then destroy them. However, with the look of 'I'm so cute,' how can you not forgive him? Bonzi has been in the prison program. Please tell everybody you know about Bonzi Billy Beagle Boy. He deserves a good home."

Perfect. Bonzi was spirited, an enthusiast, and he loved to go for walks! Except that as I began to pore over his detailed biography, something puzzled me: Bonzi Beagle was in Ohio, not Ontario. My heart sank. I must have keyed in OH instead of ON. On the QWERTY keyboard, H is right above N. My finger must have slipped.

Damn and double damn! I tried again—ON—no mistake this time. Clicked, and once again got OH, Ohio. Sweaty with anxiety, I closed Petfinder, calmed myself, went back into it, tried again: ON. And there on the screen, OH.

Petfinder was still overwhelmed by the relentless surges of desperate Katrina animals loaded onto its website. Petfinder wasn't to blame, and I didn't blame it. But I felt sucker-punched. I wanted to adopt Bonzi, but now I couldn't.

Or perhaps I could. I debated for an entire week, and on December 1, decided to submit an application for him, Ohio or not. I completed the form and pressed Send. Then I composed an explanatory email. "To Whom It May Concern. I have fallen in love with Bonzi Billy Beagle and would like to adopt him. I am Canadian, from Toronto, but hope this will not pose a problem as I can provide vet and dog-related references, and arrange for pickup in Ohio. I hope to hear from you soon so that we can proceed with Bonzi's adoption."

Belatedly, I remembered my Ohioan ancestry and fired off another email. "My maternal grandfather," I wrote, "was American, and one of my ancestors was from Ohio. Her name was Lucy Cooley, and I have her original copy of *Uncle Tom's Cabin,* inscribed with her name and Rose Cottage, Ohio. So although I am not from Ohio, I can boast of a genetic Ohio Connection!"

Hours later, Betty Peyton, the Humane Society director, responded that she'd already adopted out five dogs to Canada that year, so Canada was not a problem. "Bonzi is a major sweetheart," she added. "The office will call you in a couple days."

I did not have to wait that long. The next day, at 11:45 A.M., shelter manager Cathy Leistikow left me a message. My application to adopt Bonzi had been approved. I was ecstatic. But years later, I discovered that Cathy was not ecstatic at all, and that my Ohio ancestress did nothing to lessen her angst.

Betty had been puzzled. What was the problem? The vet reference was solid and included "Great woman!" Everything checked out. So what if she's up in Canada? What could go wrong?

"When Betty told me Bonzi had an application and that the lady lived in Canada, my heart skipped a beat," Cathy recalled years later. "He'd been adopted out to local people, and so his trips back when they returned him weren't a problem. But here it was, messy winter, holidays, and *Canada*? What if he didn't 'fit in' right? What if the adopter decided that she really didn't like him? If he got away from her, would she truly look for him? Would she really understand his personality? Would she be honest and call us if it wasn't working out and help us to get him back? Boy, was I a worrywart! I pestered Betty till she promised me that she'd keep in touch with you and be available for any questions you might need answered."

Meanwhile, I was struggling to arrange transportation to bring Bonzi "home" for Christmas. I knew that the Katrina rescuers either availed themselves of existing transport networks like the Canine Underground Railroad or improvised convoys of vehicles to drive homeless animals to receiving shelters throughout North America. But I had no idea where to start, and after six frustrating days, I told Betty Peyton that I'd decided to redeem my frequent-flyer points, fly down to Columbus International Airport, pick up Bonzi, and then fly right back to Toronto where we would live happily ever after.

My plan had one flaw. Columbus International was more than thirty miles away from the shelter. Conquering this final obstacle wasn't easy, because my arrival coincided with the shelter's Christmas bake sale, adoptions, and preparations for Santa Claus pictures. Betty's solution was to enlist welding engineer and beagle rescuer "Beagle Bill" Ballis to collect and drive Bonzi to the Columbus City Center where Beagles R Us was holding an adoption fair.

"Whereabouts in the mall?" I asked.

"You'll know," Betty replied. "Just listen."

The morning of December 16 broke biting cold, with a blizzard of swirling snow that snarled roads, triggered traffic alerts, and forced Pearson International Airport to cancel flights. Friends and neighbours, wearily shovelling snow, told me I was insane to try to get to Ohio, or even to the airport. I agreed, but nothing short of a flight cancellation could stop me. Thanks to the vagaries of snow, winds, and mysterious weather patterns, our modest turboprop was cleared for takeoff. Less than two hours later, I landed at Columbus's sparkling airport and flagged a taxi.

My driver was a voluble Pakistani wearing an outsized woollen tuque his sister-in-law had knitted for him in the green and white colours of their native land. He liked it, he said, because it kept him warm, but the frigid air wasn't his problem, finances were, and even more, the incompetence of certain other people, people you'd think you could expect better of.

He was still talking as he let me off at the shopping mall and handed me my only luggage, an empty dog crate. "Just ring me and I'll drive you back to the airport," he said, handing me his card.

"I'll have a dog with me," I warned him. "And he won't be in the crate."

It took him two seconds to decide. "Not to worry, ma'am. You ring me."

I hurried into the Columbus City Center lugging my crate. Once inside its cheery brightness, I stood still and listened—and began to laugh. Piercing the air and drowning out the din and clatter of hundreds of busy shoppers was a cacophony of wailing and howling and barking as a baker's dozen of beagles strutted their stuff at the adoption fair. As I rushed toward the sound, my heart started to pound, because one of those beagles was mine.

"Beagle Bill" was a calm presence as he presided over the frenzy of a dozen uncrated beagles, assisted by several eager high school student volunteers. I introduced myself and Bill pointed to a whirling dervish of a little dog, much smaller than I had visualized, a madcap mostly-beagle who was racing up and down the small enclosure chasing after another dog, up down back forth in out, and who didn't even glance at me when I called him. I leaned down to try to catch him, but he eluded my grasping hand. I was a human stranger; why waste time on me when he had another dog to chase?

A big beagle sidled up against my legs, and, as I leaned over to pet her, slobbered kisses all over my face. I also picked up and cradled the prettiest, softest puppy. And then, after a brief discussion with the student volunteers—"You're from Toronto? Do you know the cast members of *Degrassi High*? You don't? Not even *one*?"—I hung my head and retreated to a Subway kiosk where, over a gobbled sandwich, I filled out Bonzi's paperwork.

Back at Beagles R Us, Bill caught and leashed Bonzi while I borrowed a cell phone and called my taxi driver. Ten minutes later, in the back of the cab, Bonzi sat on my lap submitting to my caresses. Up front, the driver resumed his litany of complaints—ineptitude! bungling!—interspersed with extravagant expressions of gratitude for his good life as a Columbus cabbie.

At the airport, Bonzi and I strolled around until our flight was called. Everything interested and nothing fazed him, and he greedily accepted a giant oatmeal cookie and sipped water from a portable cup. But when I had to crate and hand him over to an airline representative, I felt terror. She checked the crate and then heaved it onto a luggage cart, all the while assuring me that he'd be fine, just fine. Then she pushed my little dog out into the freezing, blustery winter's afternoon, and I was not allowed to follow.

I hadn't transported a dog by air since I brought poor Tommy back from Haiti. Tommy had survived the trip. Would Bonzi, in what I prayed really was the heated interior of the cargo hold?

The airline must have dealt with countless other panicky customers. Minutes after the plane took off, the flight attendant leaned over my seat and handed me a little orange card: "Our Very Special Cargo. Hi! My name is Bonzi. I'm onboard also!" I read the message over and over but did not cease praying. Good, he was onboard—but was he alive and warm or had he frozen to death metres beneath me?

He had not. At Pearson International he scrambled out of his crate and shook himself as if the journey in the belly of the aircraft had restored his energy, and now—let's go go *go*! Tail wagging, he led me outside, where I apologized as I recrated him for the bus ride to the subway, and then transferred him into the subway to be whisked across the city, freed to ride the streetcar on my lap and finally, to trot happily in front of me as I tried my best to keep up with him while carrying the crate.

Bonzi rushed me through the park as if he knew we were going home. Inside the warm house I collapsed onto the sofa and watched Alice, Pumpkin, and Old Olive react as their new dog-brother sniffed around the house, lifted his leg, peed lustily on the decorated Christmas tree and then pooped on the carpet, the first and last accidents he's ever had, barring rare bouts of illness. Afterward, he followed his twitching nose into the kitchen and polished off all the dog food.

Welcome home, Bonzi!

# SEVENTEEN

# Getting to Know the Beagle of Madison County

The girls kept cautious track as the newcomer roamed throughout the house, inhaling exploratory nostrils-full of information about us. "He's just one busy, busy explorer," I emailed late that night to Betty and Cathy.

Betty answered straight away. "YAY!! I hope you really do get along. He is a sweetheart, but also a beagle. If you ask him if he is a good boy, he will do a little howl and look at you. I have to tell you that the whole staff cried today. And I should also warn you that the dog warden also deputy sheriff Gary Kronk will be calling you to check on him. See, Bonzi was his cruelty case. He fell hard for the boy. So do expect him to call one day. Take care of the boy and yourself and thanks for opening your heart to a homeless hound."

By Day Two, I knew that Pumpkin and Olive liked Bonzi, and Alice was falling in love. Instead of the ailing Pumpkin to cuddle with, she now had a young male dog who accepted her yielding little body pressed against his as if she belonged there.

That night, I lifted Bonzi onto my bed and Alice, watching from my pillow, slithered over and nestled against his side. We all slept soundly until early morning, when I picked Alice up and lowered her onto the floor. Bonzi contemplated leaping down after her, but my bed is high and he decided against it. He looked at me with his big brown eyes, telling me he needed help. I eased him down and he flexed his limbs, shook his head until his ears flapped, and then bounced out of the room and downstairs, followed by Pumpkin and Old Olive.

I threw my winter dog-walking coat over my nightgown, thrust my feet into my boots, and led my convoy of dogs outside, Alice in a red coat decorated with embroidered sprigs of green holly, Pumpkin in royal blue, long-haired Olive *au naturel,* and Bonzi in a yellow coat that had been Rachel's. He looked puzzled but stood still while I fastened it around him. As soon as I stood up, he jiggled slightly, as if to test or shake off this unaccustomed encumbrance. When it stayed right where it was, he gave up and pulled ahead of his new sisters as I walked my pack over to the dog park, with Alice, as always, in the crook of my elbow.

Soon the girls wanted to go home. Bonzi did not. Ignoring all his prison training, he resisted my command and, mutinously, plopped himself into a snowbank and refused to move. I remembered Betty's email—"If you ask him if he is a good boy, he will do a little howl and look at you"—and so, as he sat on his freezing haunches trying to wait me out, I asked him: "Bonzi, are you a good boy?" He looked right at me but neither howled nor moved. At that particular moment, he let me know, he was not a good boy.

I dragged everybody home, removed the girls' coats and harnesses, and then tugged at Bonzi's leash and headed back outside. He was ecstatic as we approached the park, where at least ten dogs were playing. "Are you a good boy, Bonzi?" I demanded. Bonzi wagged his tail, rewarded me with the semblance of a truncated howl, and, as I let go of his leash, flung himself into the thick of the dogs, where he played and played until he was so cold that he allowed me to lure him away. Back inside the house, he skittered around until he discovered the heater and sagged down right beside it.

I emailed a description of this eventful walk. Both Betty and Cathy responded right away. "Sounds like Bonzi will be working out," Betty wrote. "The dog park will be his favorite place to go. I can tell you that. He loves to run and play, and he does love his walks. [Yes! My walking companion!] That boy does not know a stranger and he is so damn cute you can't help but want to pet him. I would love to get a picture of him in that coat. As for the prison program, Bonzi's handler Jake got a Shih Tzu and told me she is the easiest thing after him. I will make sure Jake knows Bonzi is doing well."

One small dog with so many people at the end of his leash! From the moment Betty accepted my adoption application, Bonzi's human pack had drawn me into it. Betty and Cathy and I had exchanged so many emails and phone calls that I felt I knew them.

I was also grateful to the inmate dog trainer who knew my dog better than I did, as his caring and intelligent report made obvious. "Everything Jake says is true," I emailed Betty. "Bonzi is hyper, submissive, will chew things (chair leg, sofa cushions) but will stop when you tell him, loves to play with his rawhide bone, likes to fetch balls but doesn't retrieve them, and is very, very, very sweet. He's really fun to walk, so interested in everything, tail wagging like mad the whole time, stops passersby to be petted, wants to play with all passing dogs, is obviously enjoying every minute."

I decided to send a card to Jake, letting him know how much I appreciated his work and how happy Bonzi was. Time and again I composed a polite note in my head. But the weeks turned into months, and I never got around to writing it out and sending it.

Nor did Deputy Sheriff–Dog Warden Gary Kronk ever call me. I was disappointed. I badly wanted to hear his account of how and where he found Bonzi, but I could not convince myself to pick up the phone.

Despite the wintry weather, Bonzi and I began taking long walks. As a walking companion, he was everything I could have asked for, except for occasional angry lunges at dogs he instantly—and, I was to learn, unchangeably— disliked. Usually they were big dogs. They were never puppies.

One of Bonzi's sterling qualities was that he loved puppies and always greeted them with play-bows and patience. Nothing a puppy did ever irritated him. When other people grabbed their dogs apprehensively as puppies approached, I never had to. But if a very muscular and intensely focused dog stalked into the dog park, Bonzi would unleash his highest-pitched chihuahua-ish bark and launch himself at the offending animal, snapping and warning that he was a canine force to be reckoned with. He identified doggy enemies as quickly as friends, and never forgot which was which.

At home he blended with the other dogs as if he'd always known them and, cuddly and loving, welcomed Alice's gentle warmth as she clung to him. "Alice is his personal heating pad," a visitor joked.

Once, early on, I picked up the phone and called Betty. "I don't want to panic," I said, "but Bonzi has been chasing the cats, and they've never been chased before."

Betty was unconcerned. "He just wants to play with them. He'll never hurt them."

Hortense, my tiny, delicate, ailing thirteen-year-old tortoiseshell, put a stop to Bonzi's teasing. After fleeing from him up the stairs, she suddenly stopped halfway, turned around to face him, rose onto her haunches, and hissed and spat so ferociously that I could hear it clearly downstairs. Bonzi, a few risers beneath her, froze. Their drama lasted a few seconds longer.

Then, as Hortense glared at him, Bonzi sheepishly backed down the stairs. He never chased her again.

Snoopy was another story. Large, powerful, healthy, and only six years old, Snoopy was everything a dog who loved chasing could want, a black and white streak who engaged endlessly in the game he didn't know he was playing. But one day Snoopy rebelled. He slowed down, zigzagged back into the kitchen, sipped long and thirstily from the animals' water bowl, and never ran away again. He didn't have to. That was the last time Bonzi chased him.

Two months after Bonzi's arrival, my sick old Pumpkin surrendered to renal failure and slipped away as serenely as she'd lived. She'd been the kindest and gentlest of dogs, whose one misdeed had been to wander out of the house when a contractor left the door open. In freedom, she'd done what she loved best—ambled through the park, stopping to sniff at every tree trunk—until a concerned neighbour alerted me that a one-eyed beagle with a red harness was on the loose. I'd sprinted down to the park and found her right away, making her unhurried way back home to her family, to me.

To honour Pumpkin, I decided to foster a dog, a worried-looking beagle–basset senior I found on Petfinder. S.O.S. Quebec-Ontario Dog Rescue had arranged to pick up a vanful of puppies and young dogs from a struggling rural shelter. As an act of kindness they also took Maggie, recently pulled from death row at an even smaller pound. Because of her age, they estimated that I could expect to foster her for two to three months before she was adopted.

But Maggie was a failed foster. She arrived emaciated and in urgent need of complicated, frighteningly expensive surgery for a smashed hipbone socket. She must have been struck by a car, the surgeon said, and was in excruciating pain. She was also terrified of people, including me, and refused to walk.

Days later, Maggie had her operation. That night she whimpered so much that I finally took her into bed with me. Within a week she'd fallen in love with all of us, admiring young Bonzi, snuggling with Old Olive, and romping with Alice in an awkward slow-motion ballet.

As she healed she grew happier and fatter—before her surgery, the poop position had been so painful she hardly ate. But Maggie was impervious to housetraining, and I gave up trying after Dr. Black examined her and discovered that she had no sensation in her nether regions and therefore no advance warning from either bowels or bladder. I did the only thing I could. I acquired fifteen pairs of denim diapers, lined them with baby-diaper rags, and laundered loads of ten every second day. S.O.S.'s coordinator praised me to the skies for my devotion. Then she lowered the boom. Because she was clearly unadoptable, Maggie was mine for life.

When I promised to keep in touch with Bonzi's Ohio mentors, I meant it. A month or two after Bonzi's arrival, when Betty phoned to say that her husband was driving up to Toronto on a brief business trip, I invited him to dinner.

George was portly, long-haired, and flannel-shirted, a no-nonsense, soft-spoken, intelligent man who shared his wife's passion for dogs, including the pit bulls and Labrador retrievers they called their children. That's why he subjected himself to a gruelling work schedule and long hours: so that Betty, who'd worked three jobs to support him as a young would-be rock star, could devote herself to animal rescue.

After dinner, I sent George off with a boxful of items for the Humane Society's auction sale. Bonzi, tail wagging and whining hopefully as he staked out the dining table, reassured him that life was good, and that George didn't need to scoop him up and drive him back to Ohio.

In late 2006, I read an emailed announcement promoting the Humane Society's annual fundraising banquet. I glanced idly through it until one notice caught my attention: the first recipient of the brand-new Bonzi Award would be Gary Kronk. My heart raced. The Bonzi Award? Whatever was that? And how could I not have known?

Ever since 2000, when she had accepted the unpaid but demanding position of Humane Society director, Betty and her colleagues had talked about establishing an award for helping animals. Instead of lamenting the neglect, abandonment, and cruel treatment of so many of the dogs and cats taken into the shelter, they would honour the good people who dedicated themselves to saving animals and improving their lives.

Until Gary Kronk's joint appointment as deputy sheriff and dog warden, the county's dog wardens had lacked the power to do anything more than rescue at-risk dogs and take them to the shelter. In the most egregious cases, they could report their findings to the police, who alone had the power to prosecute but rarely did so.

In 2005, all that changed. Gary's enhanced authority gave the dogs of Madison County the defender and advocate they'd never had. And in May 2005, when he rescued Bonzi, Twinkle, and Velvet and successfully prosecuted their owner, Betty, Cathy, and the other shelter caretakers rejoiced that justice had finally been done.

But Betty was determined to acknowledge the courage at both ends of the leash, and in the whole wretched affair, who'd been more courageous than little Bonzi? It was true that he'd presented a series of daunting challenges that had pushed her to take the calculated risk of sneaking him back inside the Ohio Prison for Men for a second Second Chance at improving his life skills and smoothing over his rough edges. But there was just something about him, his quirkiness, his crazy, crooked little legs, his happy-go-lucky personality despite abuse and the crappy hand he'd been dealt, that made Betty, along with everyone else who met him, fall in love.

And so the Bonzi Award was born, and Gary Kronk was its first recipient. When all was said and done, how could it have been otherwise?

The Bonzi Award became institutionalized in the HSMC's ethos, and is promoted as "an annual award given to individuals, businesses, and groups who have made a difference in the life of an animal or the lives of the animals we serve. Named after Bonzi, our first successful neglect prosecution case who has a happily ever after life with his forever family in Toronto, Ontario, Canada where he now enjoys dual citizenship. His story and the people who played a part in it illustrate why we do what we do."

Betty had no need to notify me. My role as the person to whom she'd handed over Bonzi's leash was already enshrined in his legend.

# EIGHTEEN

# The Nanny Dog

The years passed, and Bonzi walked with me as I wrote. *Sugar: A Bittersweet History* was published to critical acclaim followed by several international editions. But on the same day that an advance copy arrived at my door, Old Olive's congestive heart failed, and she left us. A dog's death at seventeen is more triumph than tragedy, and Old Olive's rescue and subsequent happy life was why I adopt needy older dogs. But no matter how often I reminded myself of this, I ached for the loss of my perfect Olive.

Ten months later, I was mourning little Alice. Her first surgery for breast cancer, the occupational hazard of puppy mill breeders, had been successful, but when she was thirteen the cancer reappeared, and blood tests revealed that she was also in the terminal stages of renal failure.

I'd promised her that she'd spend more time in her happy life with me and Bonzi than her seven years in the mill. It was a promise almost fulfilled: when she crossed the Rainbow Bridge, Alice was just months short of fourteen. I loved her so much, and Dr. Black almost wept with me as we let her go.

Bonzi and I continued our walking marathons. As I mused and mentally planned out my next book, he indulged in his relentless pursuit of snackable morsels of bread and the rare bone, and in developing relationships with both humans and dogs. Humans called him the "Hood Clown" and "The Bonz," and petted and spoiled him. After I mentioned that Jake, his prison trainer, had concluded his exit journal with the comment that "Bonzi tries hard to be the best dog he can be," dog-park wits would comment, as Bonzi howled or chased a garbage truck or struck out at an enemy dog, "Bonzi's just being the best Bonzi he can be."

At a fundraiser for Big on Beagles, an Assistance Agency for Beagles Experiencing Troubled Times, Bonzi pigged out on doggy carrot cake, snatched treats from the edges of tables, and instigated so much trouble that he spent half his time aloft as event volunteers carried him around in Time Outs. Sixty off-leash beagle buddies were overwhelming, and in the excitement, Bonzi forgot all his carefully inculcated training.

What he never forgot was a friend, and his were friends-for-life. He loved all the neighbourhood puppies, even when they disappointed him by growing up and towering above him. But with a curious breedism, he hated other equally nice dogs, all pit bulls, huskies, and dogs with curled-up tails. Whenever one of these encounters ended badly for him, he would limp sadly home, where I would wrap him in a comforting throw and cuddle and croon to him while he gobbled down morsels of soy cheese and bread.

n 2009, my personal Year of the Downward Dogs, Bonzi came into his own as a Nanny Dog. Both Maggie and I were in a downward spiral. She'd become an immobile invalid who lived, ate, and slept on her Kuranda bed in the living room. To cart her outside, I'd pull her on a dolly covered with thick fleece, heave her onto her wagon, and then trundle her along the streets of Toronto. Without that rickety wagon, Maggie's circumscribed life would have shrivelled into house arrest. Instead, she rode around until her peaceful passage over a year later.

When it came, Maggie's death was a release for both of us. I'd loved her with such sad protectiveness, easing her pain and making her difficult life more pleasurable. By the time she lay dying, refusing to eat or drink, her skin flabby and her eyes bloodshot, she leaned into me trustingly and surrendered herself, knowing that she was my great love.

She did *not* know that I had my own medical problems. My spine had badly deteriorated, a legacy of my long-ago car accident. Walking and even sitting had become torments. After months of resisting, I was using a cane and travelling by Wheel-Trans, the transit service for the disabled. Cycling was the only normal activity I could manage; I'd bike briskly across the city to my medical appointments and then hobble through the slick, hard hospital corridors leaning on my cane.

Suddenly my luck turned. A neurosurgeon decided that I was a good candidate for surgery. No guarantees, but I might be able to walk properly again, at least for a while. I rejoiced, and perhaps Maggie understood how hopeful I suddenly was. But it was too late for her, and she had to leave us two months before my surgery restored me. Unlike me, Maggie could not be fixed.

In the practical way that dogs perceive the world, Bonzi seemed to know that Maggie's problems were beyond repair, but he did not give up on me. He play-bowed and asked me to take him for another of the walks that were getting shorter and shorter. But no matter how curtailed his outings had become, he showed me his great enjoyment of whatever I did manage. And when he nudged me, asking to be cuddled, he chose just those moments when I was saddest or most anxious. "I'm so lucky to have you, Bonz," I'd croon. And, in remembrance of Maggie, and without giving myself enough time to reconsider, I applied to adopt a special needs dog, a tiny one I could easily carry. Not long after, Petey, my fragile, fear-biting toy poodle, came to live with us.

Loyal Rescue had rescued Petey after nine years in an Amish puppy mill. The assessment provided by Ingrid Czerwenka, his foster mother—"Petey is very, very shy and scared. He is not housetrained, has not been on a leash. We have not gotten this far"—did not put me off. Alice had had an equally disturbing résumé, and I was up to the challenge.

I met Petey in the parking lot of a shopping mall midway between my house and Ingrid's. As he lay rigid and silent on my lap, I dangled his trousseau in the air: a bright blue collar and matching leash. Ingrid frowned. Petey was a flight risk, she said, and could not leave my fenced backyard. "If you ever let go of the leash, he'll take off and you'll never see him again," she warned.

Then she handed me his adoption folder. His veterinary records included an X-ray of his heart and a note that Petey had advanced heart disease and had to avoid all shock and strenuous exercise. I would discover soon thereafter that he also had the genetic disease micropthalmia, which had left him with one blind pinpoint-sized eye and one sighted small one.

The adoption folder also included an article titled "Adopting the Puppy Mill Survivor." As I riffled through its stark headings—"Terror of Human Hands, Aversion to Eye Contact, I'm Afraid of My Food, Marking/Housetraining, Flight Risk, Fear of Water, Fear Biting"—it dawned on me that Petey's challenges might be considerably more complex than I had anticipated.

And yet: hadn't I successfully cared for Alice, another puppy mill survivor? And wouldn't gregarious, fun-loving Bonzi ease Petey's transition to beloved family pet? Ingrid certainly thought so. "It's always best to place mill dogs in a home with existing dogs," she said. "It's what they know and where they're comfortable, so it's a huge plus that you have a couple of friends for him already. Petey will take his cues from them and hopefully, over time, develop confidence in himself."

The first day was easy. Petey lay on the faded blue sleeping cushion Ingrid had given me, and didn't move. But the next day, as I picked him up, he bit me. First, he growled. Then he lunged at my hand, and I was too shocked to let him go until he'd bitten me with vampire-like ferocity, spattering blood onto the floor. When I put him down, he scampered away then turned and fixed his tiny near-blind eyes at me, grumbling steadily, his mouth open slightly as if he might chomp at any moment.

Not a good start, and it didn't get any better. If I moved even an inch toward him, my furious little poodle would leap away and press himself against the wall, glaring at me and shaking in misery. It didn't take me long to learn what it was he couldn't tolerate: any movement that suggested I intended to pick him up. He was a strictly defensive biter, and that was his trigger to attack.

From the second he woke up, Petey was on high alert, ready to flee at the first sign of danger. He could not go outside for walks. The stress of the bustling streets, open spaces, traffic, and—most frighteningly—people would burst his wonky heart. He could not go farther than the backyard garden, where he encountered only my dogs and cats and the occasional squirrel.

But how to get there? Petey was terrified to pass by my feet as I stood at the kitchen door. As he tried to summon up the courage to go outside, barking and growling, dancing from side to side, he'd make a series of false starts toward the door. Sometimes he conquered his fear and rushed past my shoes. When he couldn't, I'd retreat, flattening myself against the stove until he'd made it safely out the door.

Yet he seemed to like me. He would bound up the stairs to my study and peep at me, wagging his stub of a tail until I made even the slightest movement—turning my head a fraction, coughing, putting on my glasses, turning a page in my book—which would send him skittering back downstairs.

Eating was another problem. Unlike Alice, but like many other puppy mill survivors, Petey was so deeply scarred by nine years of fearful eating that no matter how hungry he was, he couldn't eat if anyone, dog or human, looked at him. Petey needed utter solitude. Otherwise, he'd either jump away or simply sit staring in the direction of suspected intruders … and not swallow a single bite. Petey defied the conventional wisdom that "when he's hungry enough, he'll eat." Petey couldn't and wouldn't, except when he was unobserved. Eating "publicly" nearly paralyzed him with anxiety.

How, I wondered, could I ever make a breakthrough with this bite-sized creature? I contacted his rescue, pleading for help. Janet Robertson, a woman with decades of experience fostering rescued puppy mill breeders, responded. "Leave a leash on him at all times so that you can control him without getting bitten," she advised. It was brilliant advice. From that day on, Petey wore a thin green-and-pink leash that became his second tail. It was also our lifeline for peaceable coexistence. I could calmly step on it and control him without terrifying him.

But most of all, Petey cemented himself to Bonzi. Whatever Bonzi did, Petey tried his best to do too. Wherever Bonzi went, Petey followed. And there was one place Bonzi taught Petey to relax with me, and that was on my bed. Though Petey couldn't tolerate my lifting him, he devised a way to bypass any close contact and still get onto the bed. He jumped into a dog bed and stared at me until I lifted it onto my bed. Then he jumped out, faced me, and metamorphosed into a different dog.

This Petey-on-the-Bed play-bowed to me, inviting me to join him. I pounced and bounced, and he laughed and bounced back. He stole my bed socks and shook them wildly with his teeth. He chased the ball I threw for him then dropped it so that I could toss it again. It was a flabby red ball that he'd torn but he much preferred it to his Kongs with peanut butter, his pop-up dragon, the stuffed animals he unstuffed and discarded. When he was tired, he curled up against Bonzi, sighed deeply, and abandoned himself to sleep.

Petey worked very hard to make his life good for himself.

Most of his self-confidence came from Bonzi's physical presence and his endless patience, though it can't be agreeable to always serve as another dog's cushion or hiding place or therapist. Poppy, a large senior beagle mix I adopted nearly a year after Petey, proved this when she bared her teeth at him the first time he tried to snuggle with her, and the years have not mellowed her. Your issues, Poppy growled, have nothing to do with me, so bug off, useless little dog.

Bonzi, on the other hand, was endlessly gentle and forbearing, a Nanny Dog to this neurotic and needy puppy-sized old dog, just as he'd been to Twinkle and Velvet in that cold, dark shed back in Ohio. Bonzi, who refused to accept life as an underdog, made underdog Petey feel secure, confident, and loved even in the scariness of the world he inhabited in his head and his memories.

# NINETEEN

# Saints, Sinners, and Second Chances at Life and Love

In 2010, two months after *A History of Marriage* was published, I had my spinal surgery and, after a rapid, joyous recovery with Bonzi snoring away at my feet, set to work on *Haiti: A Shattered Nation*. Then I plunged into this book and began to meet some of the many people who'd been at the other end of Bonzi's leash before I ever laid eyes on him.

One of the most extraordinary, whom I came to know through her memoirs and now through personal correspondence, is Sister Pauline Quinn, the patron saint and founder of hundreds of prison dog-training programs across the United States, Canada, and many other countries. Like all the others, the Ohio Prison for Men's Second Chance program owes its existence to Sister Pauline.

In childhood, Sister Pauline endured abuse, institutionalization, and anguish. In her teens, she was raped and impregnated by a policeman, and then forced to put the infant up for adoption. She was uneducated, sometimes homeless, and always desperate. But in the 1960s, a German Shepherd Dog named Joni came into her life. "Joni," she writes in her book *Paws for Love*, "would not let people hurt me anymore." Through Joni, the despairing young woman felt God's love and started to heal.

Years later she took vows as a Dominican nun. "The word *Dominican* comes from the Latin words 'domini' for God and 'cani' for dogs," she told *Compass* magazine. "Dominicans are dogs for God." As a Dominican "working like a dog for God," Sister Pauline conceived the idea of bringing canines into a women's prison to be trained as service dogs. "God gave us dogs to be our friends, and we must be a friend in return," she argues in her book. These programs would save unwanted dogs from destruction by training them to help the disabled, the mentally challenged, and the elderly make their lives more complete and meaningful.

The first program opened in 1981, after Sister Pauline managed to convince the warden of the Washington State Correction Center for Women to authorize a trial program that became the prototype for all other prison dog-training programs. (*Within These Walls,* a 2001 film starring Laura Dern and Ellen Burstyn, dramatizes Sister Pauline's struggles during that trial year.)

Sister Pauline's philosophy of rehabilitation and the treatment of prisoners was simple, sensible, and eminently compassionate. In *Paws for Love* she decries vengeance, reminding us that "Saul persecuted the Christians ... then changed his life and became Paul, and then later Saint Paul.... Many [prisoners] ... have hurt, scared and damaged so many lives. All the while, their own lives rot away without meaning and much of the time without hope. They are warehoused and often forgotten. Who knows what they went through in their own lives to have brought them to be incarcerated?"

But one day most of these convicts will be released, and "changing the way we treat prisoners will help bring safer societies." These prison animal programs, Sister Pauline taught, "help to bring back respect, dignity and especially love, which is the main ingredient in motivating change."

The Ohio Prison for Men's Second Chance program was rooted in Sister Pauline's compassionate principles. When Betty became involved in it, Second Chance was training puppies to be good family dogs—housetrained, obedient, and well socialized. When the training was completed, the shelter put the pups up for adoption.

At the urging of the warden, who supported her work and wanted the prison to get credit for more community service hours, Betty oversaw the expansion of the program from eight to thirty or forty dogs. This helped the Humane Society as much as the prison by freeing up kennel space in the shelter so that more dogs could be rescued. And because of their reputation for reliability, most of the prison dogs spent less time languishing in the shelter.

On the human side of the equation, more dogs required more trainers. When Second Chance was first established, a professional trainer came into the prison to teach the rookie trainers. By the time Betty took over, the program relied almost exclusively on journeymen inmate trainers like Shane Livingston to work with the newcomers.

There was much to be said for this arrangement. It's true that a dog is a dog is a dog, but it's equally true that a prison has unique challenges and rules not found outside the fences. Everything you do has to be considered from often competing perspectives: first, that of normal life, and second, that of the security-obsessed prison. It isn't even a balancing act. It's more like a crazy juggling game, trying to keep fifty alien items aloft in the air. Shane Livingston's two-hundred-page *Canine Program Training Manual* was designed to do that by addressing conditions in the Ohio Prison for Men.

Choke chains and leashes were examples. Many trainers used to recommend choke chains as training tools. But in prison, the damage that a ripped and angry man can inflict on an uncooperative dog is appalling, and so, in a world where CDs are banned because they can be broken into weapon-like shards, choke chains are strictly forbidden. The veterinary First Aid kit was a similar story. There could be no narcotics; scissors were blunt-nosed; forget about syringes.

Betty also cared deeply about the trainers, most of whom lived only for their dogs, as she never tired of telling people. You could see it in the compassion, empathy, and love they radiated. Their dogs would relax contentedly beside them.

But Betty dealt in the daily realities, not the Big Picture, and yet—when she stole time to stand back and contemplate, wasn't all this part of the Big Picture? Wasn't it redemptive? Didn't it dig deep inside the trainers' souls and reveal what was good? Didn't it inculcate discipline? Didn't it release tension and bring clarifying, purifying tears?

And wasn't it good for the dogs? Almost always.

And good for the men? Always.

Put those two kinds of goodness together, and what you surely had was the Big Picture. Even if it was so much work, with more always waiting around the nearest cage and cell.

← 12 - Betty Peyton, shelter director, rescued the entire litter of her pit bull mix, Alarm, from death row at another shelter.

↓ 13 - Sister Pauline Quinn, founder of prison dog training programs in the U.S., Canada, and South America, with dogs Nicky and Reni.

14 - Julie Beaver of Winnipeg knitted splendid leggings and a necktie for Bonzi after Leggings for Life connected us.

15 - The sight of homeless dogs in packs or pairs is common throughout Serbia and galvanized me to commit to Mission Airlift.

16 - Jelena Kostić and long, model-thin Linda as a young dog. Linda is now twelve, and still Jelena's "most favourite of creatures."

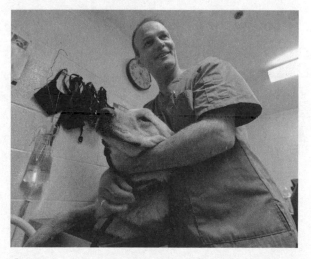

17 - James McLean of Toronto Animal Services with Ernest, rescued from the James Bay area. James was a crucial link in the human chain that made Mission Airlift possible.

18 / 19 - Little Sivkica in Jelena's shelter snuggling in a food bowl and in Toronto, after Cam MacInnes groomed her. I renamed her Hannah Joy.

20 / 21 - Wendy, Jean and Laurance Bird's beloved companion, was the first dog Jelena sent to the U.K. Below, in the shelter, Wendy claws at Jean's arm to catch her attention.

22 - Cathrine Lowther, with Magic and Jimmy in Ottawa, believes that "there can be nothing, *nothing*, more important than this life, right here, right now."

23 - Jelena is reunited with thirty-five of her former shelter dogs and their grateful adopters in Austria, 2011.

24 - Dora Sesler, CEO of the international cinematographic company Sesler and a great friend to the rescue community, with Logan in Niagara-on-the-Lake, Ontario.

25 - Katija is a folk hero among Serbian rescuers. For years she single-handedly rescued and fed hundreds of dogs on her modest plot of land.

26 - Jack, the first Serbian dog that Mission Airlift brought to Canada, whale watching with Emily at Cap-de-Bon-Désir, Quebec. His family calls him "the salty wonder-dog."

27 - Smile, renamed Pochi, responds to Catherine Draper and Nathan Goold's "Want to go for a walk?" Below, she and Nathan enjoy a long ramble.

28 - Lorraine Houston, director of Speaking of Dogs, with her two family dogs, Cora and Cracky.

29 - Second Chance dog trainer and program aide until his release from prison six years ago, Shane Livingston grooms his dog Roy.

# TWENTY

## Full Circle: My Return to Ohio

Almost eight years after I brought him home, I prepared for a return to Bonzi's birthplace to meet all the people at the other end of his leash. I told Betty that I'd be attending the Bonzi Award ceremony, and that I wanted to interview her, Gary Kronk, and Cathy Leistikow as well as that year's award winners, and to tour the new shelter. Visiting the prison and meeting inmate handlers would add depth and richness to my book, though I realized that it would probably be impossible to arrange.

Betty's response, by telephone, was concise and stunning. Gary Kronk will meet you at the airport, she said, and you'll be staying with Marge Hopkins, who fosters cats for us. Come down on Thursday, because on Friday you'll be visiting the prison. Afterward we'll go to the shelter and Cathy will give you a tour. The banquet is on Saturday night, and you'll be the guest speaker, but you don't need to dress up fancy.

Talk about getting things done! Talk about people working and pulling together! I was thrilled. "Imagine," I wrote, "what a loving and fun-loving little dog with crooked legs, a stout heart, and an enthusiastic approach to life can inspire!" I began to pack.

The flight was smooth and short, and soon I was traipsing through the gleaming corridors of Columbus International Airport looking for Gary Kronk, the silver-haired man I knew so well from photographs. And there he was, holding aloft a pink sign inscribed in block letters: ELIZABETH. I was startled at his casual civilian clothes instead of his familiar deputy sheriff's uniform, but as he stowed my luggage into the trunk of his car, he reminded me that he'd recently retired and that I'd meet the new deputy sheriff–dog warden at the Bonzi Award dinner.

And speaking of Bonzi: "I'd hoped you might bring him, but Betty told me he's too old," Gary said.

"Too old and his tracheal problems are too serious for flying. I wouldn't risk it even to come down and see you. But if you and Liz ever come to Toronto, you've got a place to stay—and it comes complete with a little beagle who can outsnore anyone!" Gary laughed and nodded. "But Gary, please tell me all about how you rescued Bonzi. What was the place like? What about his horrible owner? And first of all, tell me about the very first time you saw Bonzi!"

As he drove me through the lush green Ohio countryside, the former dog warden carried me back with him eight years to that frosty May morning when he first laid eyes on the dog with the peculiar legs, chained to a wooden box on a rural back road. For the half hour it took us to reach London and Rothwell's Neighborhood Restaurant, I listened spellbound as Gary confronted the pit bull, summoned backup, vowed to rescue Bonzi and prosecute his owner, and later discovered the shed with the two miserable chow-retriever puppies he would also liberate.

"I just wanted them to know that someone cared for them and loved them," he said as we pulled into Rothwell's parking lot. "And I wanted their owner to be convicted because of the awful things he did to them."

After lunch, Marjorie Hopkins drove me down the road to her house. The first thing I noticed in the living room was an acrylic statue bearing an image of Bonzi, the image I'd fallen in love with on Petfinder. Marge smiled. "Oh yes, some years back I won the Bonzi," she said. At my urging, she reeled off what she'd done to deserve such a distinction. "I foster Humane Society cats, I knit cat and dog blankets for them, and I make quilts they auction off to raise money."

I stared at the Bonzi in its place of honour in this modest Ohio home. "Marge, did you ever meet Bonzi?"

"Oh, I don't think so, but over the years I've heard so much about him. I'm out at the shelter fairly often, and Cathy still talks about him all the time. An underdog if ever there was one, but somehow he never saw himself that way!"

"Marge," I exclaimed, "someone else just told me almost exactly the same thing! Her name is Julie Beaver, and she reminds me so much of you."

It's my daily ritual to click first on the Animal Rescue Site to "help fund food and care" for rescued animals, and then on FreeKibble to earn kibble and litter for shelter animals. One morning the Animal Rescue Site featured a video of Willow, a cat with such severely disabled back legs—they faced backwards—that she could only drag herself around.

Halfway through the video, Willow's useless legs were encased in pink leggings crocheted in a soft, airy wool that was firm enough to support her and enable her to walk. It was a draggy, shuffling sort of walk, but how happy

Willow looked sashaying around the living room. "Look at me now!" the caption read, prompting streaming tears of happiness across the virtual world. "I wear my Leggings for Life every day. I am never without them. Now I do almost everything the other kitties do."

Willow's miraculous transformation inspired her human, Wendy Matthews, to found Leggings for Life, a non-profit international network of needlewomen who commit to providing a lifetime's supply of leggings to a disabled animal.

Willow, scurrying about in her pink leggings, made me think of Bonzi. By 2013 he was ten years old, portly and noticeably gimpy as his deformed legs now made even short walks so painful that I pushed him around in a Dogger stroller instead and gave him a daily painkiller. But just imagine the comfort of soft, padded leggings to warm and protect his always aching legs! Not knowing what to expect, I applied to Leggings for Life and included Bonzi's photo.

Across the country in Winnipeg, Julie Beaver had also clicked on the Animal Rescue Site and discovered Leggings for Life. Julie's personal mission was to provide comfort for needy shelter dogs and cats, and she'd already knitted more than 350 blankets for them through the Snuggles Project, an arm of the Oregon-based Hugs for Homeless Animals. These blankets not only calm and soothe frightened animals but also brighten the shelter's industrial atmosphere, encouraging visitors and volunteers to remain longer.

Now Leggings for Life offered Julie the chance to establish a lifelong connection with a damaged dog, and after her application was matched with mine, she sent Bonzi a wardrobe of leggings in fantastical themes: Scandinavian, Candy Stripe, Street Crossing Guard, Lumberjack. She added a shimmery Princess Pink scarf for Poppy and a mohair halter for Petey, who bit me when I tried to put it on him.

Julie had been ecstatic when I sent her photographs and added that I was going to Ohio to attend the Bonzi Award ceremony. "What a guy Bonzi is," she wrote. "Cuter than I even imagined! I feel such a bond with him because of his leggings. Bonzi has touched so many lives by saying 'I survived, and look how good I am.' An underdog if ever there was one, but he just doesn't see himself that way!"

Prison day arrived sunny and cold. I'd given the matter of what to wear some thought. And when I modelled my outfit—a black skirt with a black pashmina draped over a brand-new teal Mark's Work Wearhouse sweater decorated with little black dogs—Marge nodded her head approvingly: "Yes, I think that'll do quite nicely."

Betty arrived in jeans, the only thing I'd ever see her in, munching little packets of cheese and crackers. "All I could find in the house," she said. "No time to get to the store."

"I've been reading all about you online," I began as we drove off. "For instance, you're one of [Columbus radio station] Sunny 95's 2011 Twenty Outstanding Women You Should Know."

Betty inclined her head.

I consulted my notes. "And for nine years you haven't had to authorize a single euthanasia at the shelter." Betty nodded. "And you participate in the Tour for Life that sends two tour buses from state to state finding homes for death-row dogs and cats." Betty nodded again. "And you and George have adopted four dogs from your shelter, two pitties, and two chocolate Labs?" Betty grinned. "And you've initiated a weekend foster program so that the dogs get a break from the shelter and get socialized and maybe even adopted by their fosters." Betty nodded and smiled. "And George is the man behind the woman, the guy who makes it possible for you to do all this and run the prison program too."

"George is my biggest supporter," Betty said. "Without him, I'd be out working and lucky to volunteer a couple of hours a week. See, George is my rock star." She coughed. "And here we are—see over there? That's where we're going, that's the prison."

This wouldn't be my first visit inside prison walls. After Haiti's devastating earthquake of 2010, I twice visited the prison in Jacmel, chatting with prisoners, handing them toiletries and Bibles through the bars of their communal cells, collecting the notes thrust out to me. At least thirty men were crammed in each cell, where three-level bunk beds occupied most of the floor space and a bucket served as an emergency toilet. The few women prisoners shared a cell with two windows and more light. The sick bay outside at the edge of the courtyard was inhabited by hollowed out, grey-skinned, visibly ill inmates afflicted with AIDS, tuberculosis, or cholera.

But neither that experience nor a special tour of Toronto's historic and long-empty Old Don Jail had prepared me for the tense atmosphere of the Ohio Prison for Men. Its large, low buildings are set within an extensive campus of manicured grass, the whole enclosed by a high chain-link fence and security cameras. We pulled up into the parking lot next to the Humane Society's boldly painted van just in time to see a young shelter worker walk inside hanging on to two leashed dogs.

"They're going to the other zone," Betty said, leading me into the reception area, where we underwent an airport-style security check that included removing our shoes and stowing our handbags in a locker. After I surrendered my passport, a prison pass was pinned to my coat. Then an impassive correctional officer escorted us through the grounds to the higher-level-security cell block A, where the inmate dog trainers lived. We passed several prisoners, all in state blue, the tension palpable. The only smiles I saw were among three men playing basketball, feinting with the ball and teasing each other.

Inside the cell block, sullen men clustered and chatted in low tones. Then Sergeant Basil Whyte appeared, trailed by three dog trainers. Betty introduced us, and, to my astonishment, they insisted that I inspect their cells. "We tidied up just for your visit," one inmate said.

"Why thank you very much, that's so nice of you, and I'd love to," I said, forcing myself to step inside and look around each of their cells. I've already described them, but omitted one detail: that the men have to use a toilet in full view of their cellies and of any passersby, including correctional officers.

Afterward, Sergeant Whyte invited me to use his office to interview the trainers, insisting that I sit at his desk while he stood in a corner looking on. The inmates sat on chairs facing me. I'd been permitted to bring pen and paper but no recording device, laptop, or camera, and so I pulled out some small coiled notebooks from my coat pocket and began to ask questions.

These trainers were not only experienced and articulate; Betty had also identified one of them as Bonzi's trainer. After a minute of great excitement, though, we realized that he hadn't even been in the program during Bonzi's era. The same thing happened a second time, as another inmate struggled and failed to remember having ever trained a beagle named Bonzi. I shrugged off my disappointment. It had been more than eight years! What were the chances that Bonzi's trainer was even still incarcerated?

I asked my questions, listened, jotted in my notebooks, encouraged conversation. The men were eager to share their vision of dog training. "I'm a rapport trainer," one man said. "I'm firm, fair, and consistent."

"We need to have a lot of patience with both dogs and people," said another. "And you learn a lot by observing. For example, an abused dog shows you the direct effect of his abuse. It's like human bullying. Dogs pick on other dogs, too."

When I mentioned that I'd heard about the trainers pitching in to create arts and crafts projects that the Humane Society auctioned off, they responded enthusiastically, listing their offerings: paintings, jewellery and jewellery boxes, toy motorcycles made from Popsicle sticks. "We wanted to raise money to pay for surgeries for two shelter dogs: kidney stones and an eye operation."

"And did you?"

"More than enough! We had some left over for other vet bills."

I was delighted, and asked for more stories. They reflected, and then one man leaned forward and eagerly told me how much the trainers know about veterinary medicine. "We diagnose all sorts of health issues—kennel cough, coccidiosis, whip/hook/tape/round worm, ear infections, conjunctivitis, parvo, coronavirus—and we often dispense their meds. We have a huge storage box of medicines here."

"We're almost like vet techs," another inmate chimed in.

I smiled and told them that while researching Second Chance, I'd come across a rescue community website that described how Betty had pulled a small Benji-type stray dog, along with the nine fluff balls she'd just delivered, from a shelter's death row. During the lengthy wait until the pups arrived at the prison, the Second Chance trainers had paced "like impatient expectant dads" waiting for their new charges.

The men, leaning back in their chairs, nodded and grinned. Yes, they'd loved those puppies, even though it had been a lot of work getting up every couple of hours for feedings.

I'd noticed that every time I broached what was clearly an unexpected topic, the trainers would glance at Sergeant Whyte as they answered. This happened when I asked about the No Snitch rule. Each trainer looked at the others. Finally one said, as much to the sergeant as to me, "You have to defend the dogs. But it's hard. Fisticuffs could get you kicked out of the program—that is, if a correctional officer didn't see the incident." With an almost imperceptible inclination of his head, Sergeant Whyte indicated that this was an acceptable answer.

I made one embarrassing faux pas. The material I'd read about prison dog programs had emphasized that trainers were carefully vetted before being accepted into the program, and that certain crimes made a prisoner ineligible, with rape, child or elder abuse, and murder heading the list.

Discussing qualifications for admittance into the program, I said brightly, "Of course you're careful about the trainers' backgrounds. You don't accept anyone who's committed rape or murder, for instance?"

After a long, puzzling silence, Sergeant Whyte answered sternly, "No! I don't look at a man's crime. His past isn't what matters. I base my judgments only on his character, how he conducts himself inside, how he gets along with other inmates. Prison is about redemption as well as punishment. I'm interested in redemption."

"Ah!" I said, nodding sagely. "That makes such good sense."

"My crime doesn't define me as an individual," one trainer burst out. "The program lets me give back so that I'm an asset to the community, not a liability. Training dogs is beneficial to me. I take away things I'd never learned, and it builds my character. I'm a better person for it."

Later I researched the conviction records of each of these inmates: murder, rape, aggravated assault, involuntary manslaughter. No wonder Sergeant Whyte had chided me. Each program is different, and at the Ohio Prison for Men, redemption does not discriminate.


Soon after my unintended blunder, Betty knocked and opened the door, propelling an older inmate in front of her. He was short, compact, bearded, and bespectacled. He looked confused and uncomfortable. "I've found him," Betty said triumphantly. "Trainer Browning. *He* was Bonzi's trainer."

For a second everyone in the office stared at trainer Browning. Then I jumped up. "Are you *sure* it was him? Are you *sure*?"

"I knew the minute he walked across the range," Betty declared. "The Beagle Guy. And when I asked him if he'd trained Bonzi, he spread out his right hand all crooked, just like Bonzi's leg. And I *knew*. But when I told Browning that Bonzi's mom was there wanting to talk to him, he said, 'Noooooo! She's in *Canada*!' So I said, 'No she's not, she's right there in Sergeant Whyte's office.'"

Browning's solemn expression softened. "Bonzi was my dog," he said simply.

I started to leap out of my chair to embrace him, but then I caught Sergeant Whyte's look of admonition. "I'm so excited to meet you," I said instead. "So happy. What's your name, by the way?"

"Jake," he said.

"Jake, what can you tell me about Bonzi? What was he like when he lived with you?"

Jake smiled. "We loved him. He was a bundle of joy, easy to train, and just a happy dog." I must have looked expectant, and he understood that I wanted more. "Bonzi liked to chase another dog for hours, playing tag, with him always doing the chasing." He searched his memory. "He was a little dog with a bigger-dog attitude," he said.

Sergeant Whyte signalled that time was up. His shift was over, and he wanted to go home. I walked just behind him with Betty, keeping my hands pressed against my pockets stuffed with my precious notebooks. I'd met Bonzi's trainer! I was euphoric, a human helium balloon, impervious to danger as we walked briskly past long lines of inmates returning to their cell blocks at the end of their work assignments.

etty and I headed back to West Jefferson, to the shelter, where Cathy Leistikow took over as my minder while Betty disappeared into the office and plunged into paperwork. I'd corresponded with Cathy off and on for years, but here she was in the flesh, a trim, energetic woman who flashed smiles as she spoke and never stopped working throughout our entire shelter tour, shuffling through a pile of paper, checking supplies, tossing a load into the washing machine that runs non-stop to keep the busy shelter's soiled bedding and towels clean, leaning over a cage to speak to a special dog or cat.

Back in the office, Cathy demonstrated how, in the old office, she would barricade Bonzi inside the reception area, and how he would escape. "You know what I'm so happy about?" Cathy confessed. "That you've always kept in touch! It's so hard sometimes, when we just don't know how a dog or a cat has made out after they leave us."

I hugged her as I bade her goodbye in the shiny new cat room with its replica living room furniture and sunny graphics. Lucky Bonzi, to have had such a compassionate and dedicated woman at the other end of his leash.

The next evening at the banquet, I was seated between Marge, resplendent in red corduroy pants with a matching red turtleneck top decorated with black dogs, and Gary Kronk. At one point Gary handed me his cell phone, which displayed a photograph of an intricately executed model motorcycle. "That's the one the inmates made," he said. "Imagine. Just Popsicle sticks."

After dinner, dozens of photos of Bonzi flashed up on a big screen while I gave my speech. Then a Bonzi Award was presented to four Humane Society volunteers, Anne O'Connell-Null and Kevin Null, Belinda Ewing, and

Morgan Skeldon, a ten-year-old whose grandmother drives her to the Humane Society several times a week to feed and brush the cats, clean their cages, and walk smaller dogs. Morgan dreams of becoming a veterinarian, but Betty has also promised her that she can have a job at the Humane Society any time.

The following morning I flew back home, where Bonzi greeted me at the door with spurts of happy howling and a little shuffling dance. Beside him, rubbing against his side, Petey wagged his tail and play-bowed. The cats watched me from the stairs. Poppy, almost stone deaf, hadn't heard me coming and was upstairs sleeping in my study.

"Little Bonz!" I crooned. "You've inspired so many people to do so much good stuff! And I met Cathy and Betty and Jake, can you believe that I met Jake?" Bonzi threw back his head and howled, loudly this time. Petey, his shadow, danced around delightedly. Life was good. We were all back home together. It was time for me to sit down and write Bonzi's story.

# PART 5

# DOGS WITHOUT BORDERS

# TWENTY-ONE

# Barking Free in Belgrade

By the hot, humid summer of 2006, when the Canadian embassy in Serbia invited me to be a special guest of the Belgrade Book Fair where I'd be launching the Serbian edition of *A History of Mistresses,* Bonzi had comfortably settled into his role as walking partner. But he was much more than that—he'd become my Continuity Dog, the only one of my dogs whose imminent deterioration or death I had no reason to fear. Bonzi was young, healthy, and energetic, and the physical deficits that might ultimately affect his quality of life wouldn't likely shorten it.

I had constant reminders: Pumpkin had died in February, and six months later, my graceful little cat Hortense had slipped away as I cradled her on my lap. When I accepted the Serbian invitation I was still grieving, and grateful that Bonzi wouldn't test my emotional fortitude until we were both much older.

As Bonzi and I walked—as he greeted people, play-bowed to friends, and snarled warningly at enemies—I mentally reviewed my latest sections of *Sugar: A Bittersweet History,* the book I was currently writing. And up until my October departure date, when I was actually at the airport heading for Belgrade, *Sugar* was mostly what I had on my mind.

But less than two hours after I landed at Nikola Tesla Airport, I was stalking a pack of docile homeless dogs at the bottom of a steep hillside park just beneath the Balkan Hotel, where I was staying. The dogs lounged and played until an old woman with a black headscarf shuffled into sight and sagged down onto a crumbly stone wall. As the dogs raced over to her, she reached into a paper bag and pinched off pieces of a stout sausage she tossed to one dog after another. They wolfed it down, lingered briefly, and then ambled away to new adventures. They also set me off on the path to Mission Airlift, a mini-airlift of Serbian dogs bound for new lives with Canadian families.

At dinner that night, Vladislav Bajac, my publisher, elaborated on what I'd seen. These homeless dogs roamed everywhere in Serbia, he said, and reproduced in such numbers that the problem had grown steadily worse. And as I must have noticed, many were purebred or had recognizable breed characteristics, indications that they'd been recently abandoned.

"You can even date it to 1999," he said, "when the seventy-eight-day NATO bombardment killed over two thousand Serbs. Hundreds of thousands were left homeless and forced to take refuge wherever they could." Their dogs, abandoned on the streets, were NATO's collateral damage. From then on my handbag was redolent of leftovers from every meal; every morning thereafter, I would feed and follow the dogs. I also spoke to them in Serbian, consulting a list of commands handwritten for me by a helpful Serb (who also provided a list of vegan dishes I could order in restaurants).

*"Ne!"*—No!

*"Dobro!"*—Good!

*"Dođi!"*—Come!

"*Sedi!*"—Sit! (Something that no dog in Serbia ever did for me.)

The city of Niš, Serbia's third largest, was as dog-ridden as Belgrade. After I deposited my luggage at the historic Banovina, now part of the University of Niš, Dr. Vesna Lopičić, literature professor and future vice-rector, escorted me on a walking tour of the handsome old city. Before we'd gone more than a few yards, a pair of homeless dogs strolled by. I sank to my knees to photograph them, but by the time I'd fished into my handbag for my camera they had disappeared down the street. Vesna stopped trying to show me landmark buildings and launched into her own story about finding a litter of motherless puppies and taking them to the dog shelter run by Jelena Kostić.

By dinnertime, Vesna had arranged for me to meet Jelena the next day, right after my lecture at the university. Jelena, she told me, was a recent graduate of English literature and history at the U.K.'s Open University's Newbold College. She'd returned home to Niš, but instead of finding a job she was able to devote herself full-time to animal rescue because her father—an official translator, renowned sculptor, and, in this Eastern Orthodox nation, a devout Seventh-Day Adventist—supported her financially. How will I know her? I asked. She's young and very pretty, with long brown hair, Vesna said, and she'll be carrying a puppy.

Later, as we said goodnight, Vesna assured me that Niš was so safe that I could tramp through the park behind the Turkish Fortress, alone, without the least worry. "You say you would like to see what the dogs do on their own. Why not spend an hour observing them?" And so I wandered through the Turkish Fortress park in the darkness—few of the street lamps were functioning—watching the dogs. Mostly they slept, sprawled together on grassy knolls, uninterested in me or the occasional lovers who sauntered by hand in hand. I tried to take a tally but couldn't see well enough to count the furry mounds sunk into the shadows. Nor was listening helpful. Except for a yelp here and a warning growl there, the park dogs slumbered in silence.

After my lecture the next morning I stayed to chat with the students, who had all learned their extraordinarily fluent English in Niš, where they could choose either British or American accents. The conversation soon turned to the homeless dog situation. It was clear that the students were well aware of it; it was just that they lacked solutions.

Unlike Jelena, who'd taken action, quixotic though it was—except to the hundreds of dogs she saved from certain death in the local *kafilerija,* one of the municipal pounds infamous for their primitive, brutal ways of disposing of unwanted dogs. (Another word is *sinteraj* or *shinteraj,* a name stemming from *shinters,* the dogcatchers.) At the time of my visit, some *kafilerijas* slaughtered weekly. Others waited until they were full.

Vesna dropped me off at my rendezvous point, and soon Jelena appeared, wearing a pale blue T-shirt and jeans and carrying a fluffy white puppy she intended to adopt out. Is there an adoption fair? I asked, hurrying alongside her through the bustling streets into the central courtyards where people idled at café tables, drinking coffee and smoking cigarettes. Jelena chose a table with an unobstructed view—so that we can see everyone who passes by, she explained in her gently accented English. She declined my offer of coffee and sat gazing around the crowds of pedestrians, thrusting the puppy up in the air each time she identified a possible candidate. Several people looked but all moved on, shaking their heads. "Isn't this a difficult way to adopt out puppies?" I ventured. "How do you know the adopter is a good person?"

"I ask questions, I look, I take care," she said. "I get their address and I check on the dog after." She shrugged and brushed back her long tawny hair. "It's not the best way, but it's my only way right now."

She exhorted another passerby to adopt her adorable puppy, and this time her target slowed down and reached out for the puppy, feeling his head, stroking him. "What do you want for him?" he asked Jelena.

She waved her hand: nothing. The pup was up for adoption, not for sale. All that was required was a pledge to care for him until the end of his days, and of course, to accept that she'd visit sometime in the future. Oh, and the potential adopter must agree to neuter him.

The man was taken aback. Neuter him? Why? Male dogs can't have puppies! Patiently, Jelena explained that unneutered dogs can procreate, that they're susceptible to certain diseases, that some are aggressive. Neutering, she said firmly, was non-negotiable.

Soon the man was seated at our table, frowning with concentration as he filled out an adoption form. Among its clauses: the adopter must commit to providing nutritious food and comfortable housing, to vaccinating the dog, to allowing Jelena to make two home visits a year, to notifying her of any change of address, and, if at any time he no longer wanted it, to returning the dog to her. Jelena checked over the form. Without another word, she handed over the wriggling puppy.

The man's face lit up as he held his new dog. "Thank you!" he said. And then, surprised, a repeated "Thank you!" when Jelena handed him a package containing a few embroidered napkins and household items, a thank-you gift in turn for adopting the puppy.

As the man and his armful of soft fluffiness moved off out of sight, Jelena composed herself; the fleeting sadness across her finely sculpted features disappeared. Well, she said briskly, I have to go out to the shelter now. Vesna said you wish to accompany me? And so—she stood up—we should leave right away.

paid for a cab that delivered us, clunking and bouncing, to the shelter's rented field and the muted baying of well over a hundred dogs. We tramped down the rutted mud road to the ruins of an agricultural depot where ten feral cats had settled in as squatters—along with Alekandr, an alcoholic who for twenty-five years had lived there in unspeakable squalor. Now, in return for that privilege plus fifty euros a month, Alekandr helped with the dogs.

Outside in the pleasant treed field, dogs chained to doghouses or confined to wire enclosures played, barked, or dozed in the sunshine. A few cowered away from us or from other dogs. I picked my way along the hard-packed earth, trying to sidestep poop and the occasional lunging dog, and followed Jelena into the damp mouldiness of the depot. A middle-aged volunteer she introduced as Sonja was lighting kindling to fire up a vast iron vat. There Jelena and her associates proceeded to cook hunks of donated meat, bones, and assorted vegetables with gallons of water, the mix eventually rendered into a slurry stew to which we added pieces of hard white bread that we broke apart from a pile of loaves. As it simmered, Sonja stirred it and Jelena and I went outside to water the dogs.

"It might be too hard for you," Jelena cautioned as she picked up a huge plastic container, pumped it full of water, and set out along the path. If a petite, delicate-looking woman like Jelena could do it, I thought, how could I possibly fall down on the job?

Within minutes, my arms (I needed both to hold the pail) were quivering with the effort and already aching. My hands were rubbing raw. Because I kept slipping, precious water slopped onto my running shoes and ran down my jeans. When I poured it into the dogs' bowls, my hands shook and I missed my target. By the time I'd emptied my pail, Jelena had decided that stirring the pot would be much more useful and would free Sonja to carry water. "We're used to it," Jelena said kindly. "It takes a while."

I looked at her—swaddled in a mud-spattered nylon man's jacket and knee-high rubber boots, her masses of hair dishevelled and swiped back into a messy ponytail with pink plastic clips—and marvelled. For all her ethereal appearance, this young woman had been cast in marble. And because of her, more than a hundred dogs had escaped the *kafilerija* and were enjoying something approximating a decent life.

That night at dinner with Vesna, I could scarcely speak about anything but Jelena and the shelter. "I'm so glad I was able to connect you," Vesna said, lighting up a cigarette and exhaling into the night air. "And before you leave Serbia, there's another animal lover you should meet, the wife of the Canadian ambassador. I've heard that she also rescues dogs and cats, though of course not nearly so many as Jelena."

"Another crazy lady?"

Vesna tapped ashes into the ashtray. "Some people say so. You'll like her. And she'll like you."

# TWENTY-TWO

# Crazy Ladies Who Rescue

Back in the capital, I spent my days at the Belgrade Book Fair, an immense international literary event held near the Sava River with its floating dockside restaurants. Booklovers stopped to flip through the just-launched Serbian version of *Mistresses* while a scrum of literary journalists convened at the Canada stand to interview me about it. When they concluded their interviews with "personal interest" questions— Was this my first time in Serbia? What was my impression of it? What had I heard before I came?—I mentioned my last-minute preparations for the trip: *The Bridge on the Drina,* Ivo Andrić's classic novel about the real-life complexities of the Balkans; a Lonely Planet guidebook; and twenty-two small containers of soy milk, two for each day.

When pressed for more, I expressed my admiration for the Serbian passion for literature, and told the story of how doctoral student Ivana Durić Paunović, a co-translator of Julian Barnes's *Arthur and George,* had introduced herself to me: "How do you do? I'm George."

I praised Serbia's agriculture, which, for want of money for fertilizer, produces luscious organic vegetables and fruits. And I spoke about the homeless dogs, which led to a spirited discussion about the culprit—the NATO bombing—but not potential solutions. When the interviews ended, I assuaged my hunger—fried potatoes slathered in Serbian-style ketchup had been the only available vegan food that day—by imagining the feast awaiting me at that evening's reception.

The event was held at the Canadian ambassador's official residence, an imposing building perched on a hillside next door to its American counterpart. The tables were loaded with food and the throng of guests in the reception room all carried heaping plates. As perhaps the only non-carnivorous guest, I wasn't so lucky. But alcohol was flowing: why not dull my hunger with gin and tonic? By the second glass I'd decided that this was a good, even brilliant plan. Then a hand plucked at my arm, and I turned to see that it belonged to Ambassador Robert McDougall.

"My wife would like to see you," he said.

"But didn't you say she was too sick to come downstairs?"

The ambassador dismissed my remark. "Come with me," he said. And, as I hesitated, "Why don't you bring your drink?"

And so, gin and tonic in hand and not entirely steady on my feet, I accompanied him up the wide polished stairs to his private quarters. He opened the door, ushering me inside, and then turned back to his official duties downstairs. The apartment was massive and elegant, except for the large sacks of cat litter piled high against the walls, presumably for the two handsome cats who observed me coolly from the sofa.

A woman appeared, small and fine-featured with a shaved head and a cigarette clamped in her unlipsticked mouth. She wore all black: a baggy T-shirt and sweatpants, both furred with cat hair. "I'm Cathrine Lowther," she said, sticking out her hand. "Cathrine with no *e*."

Without relinquishing my gin and tonic, I held out my left hand and shook hers. "How do you do. I'm Elizabeth *with* an *e*."

"Come in," Cathrine said, leading me into a den lined with stacked cages, each containing a tiny kitten. "They've all got this fucking virus," she said, "so I couldn't do the official hostess thing because if they don't get their meds on time, we'd probably lose them." She sat down with a kitten in her lap, and, squinting her eyes against cigarette smoke, pinched the skin on the tiny creature's neck. Then, with a practised movement, she slid in a hypodermic needle and released the plunger. She gently replaced the kitten into a cage, and, as I watched, repeated the process until the last kitten was medicated. Finally she sank back into the office chair, exhaling cigarette smoke and relief.

By then I'd learned that only two of the felines were hers, the tabby Posey and the Persian Gus-Gus, whom I'd seen in the living room. The sick, motherless kittens were Cathrine's fosters, and would stay with her until they were healthy and weaned from the bottle she fed them every few hours. And as soon as they were adopted out, new orphans would replace them.

I glanced around her could-be palatial apartment, and, my tongue loosened by the gin, wondered aloud how Ambassador McDougall put up with it all. "He loves me," Cathrine said, "and he's the love of my life." And, as the next few years were to prove to me time and again, that was why the woman who became my partner-in-rescue could focus so mightily on her rescue activities. Her husband was her confidant and her strongest supporter.

When I mentioned Jelena's shelter and the homeless dogs I'd seen all around Belgrade and Niš, Cathrine nodded. She too rescued dogs, she said, but kept them out in the courtyard because the embassy residence couldn't accommodate them inside. "I'll take you down to visit them," she said suddenly, peering up at me. "Come on. I want you to meet Whisky Jack."

Minutes later we were in the dimly lit courtyard, where dogs in large wire and wooden cages blasted the still night with their frenzied barking, lunging forward as we approached. Whisky Jack was a medium-sized, cream-coloured terrier with an endearing expression that won over humans but not, apparently, other dogs, who bullied him.

Cathrine explained that an expatriate woman had noticed him scrabbling for food on a slag heap in front of a pharmaceutical company. He was alone, an emaciated puppy afflicted with a skin condition that left him with infected sores and almost furless. It took the woman several visits to capture him and bring him to a veterinarian, whom she begged to find him a home because, as is common in Belgrade, her apartment's strict rules forbade dogs. "And by then," Cathrine continued, "the vet knew just who to call: me. And so Whisky Jack joined my growing pack of Serbian street dogs, and finally his skin cleared and his coat grew in, and lo! A handsome fellow."

Then she added, "Why don't you take him back with you to Toronto?" Much later, when we'd become good friends and dog-rescuing allies, she described my unexpected appearance at her door as the answer to a prayer: a dog lover who could find good, solid Canadian homes for her dogs. Surely, Cathrine pleaded, Whisky Jack would appeal to a family back home? She'd failed to find him a good home in Serbia and was increasingly worried about what would happen to the nearly two dozen dogs still living in the courtyard when Rob was transferred to his next assignment.

I have always regretted that I didn't leap into action and whisk Whisky Jack back to Toronto with me. But I was taken by surprise, and with only a few event-packed days left before I flew home, I promised Cathrine only that I'd think about it. And then, still clutching my now-empty tumbler, I said goodbye to her and returned to the clamorous reception while she climbed back upstairs to her needy feline orphans.

On the shuttle bus back to the hotel with my literary compatriots, the conversation, in English and French, was of books, Serbian authors and literary stars, the unexpected impressiveness of the Book Fair, and the geniality and generosity of Ambassador McDougall, our host.

"Yes, and he was so composed during his welcoming speech, when he was nearly drowned out by the dogs howling outside. Did you see how calmly he walked over to the window and slammed it shut?"

"Stray dogs everywhere, eh? But it's nice to know that they plague even the patricians up on the hillside!"

"Too bad his wife was sick. She'd have been interesting to chat with."

I slumped back into my seat and said nothing. Interesting? Well, yes, but also so intense and purposeful that I'd escaped her with just enough strength to haul myself back to my hotel room.

My trip rushed on: a stay in Novi Sad, where I lectured at the university and took photos of the city's synagogue and other historic sites to show Dora Sesler, the volunteer dog transporter who years earlier had brought me Old Olive, and who'd been born in Novi Sad. Back in Belgrade I attended a reception at City Hall and, at the Book Fair, signed books and conducted interviews in the manner of the Grand Old Book Tour that now exists only in fond memory in North America. And every morning and evening, visits to the dog pack that had staked out the parks and streets south of the Balkan Hotel.

As I sat on the plane during the long flight back to North America, I was exhausted, exhilarated, but also vaguely guilt-ridden about leaving Whisky Jack behind. Had Cathrine actually expected me to bring him? Would she really entrust him to someone she'd never laid eyes on before? All across the ocean I argued with and finally forgave myself, only to begin worrying about all the unlucky dogs I was winging away from. Finally, I slept.

Toronto plunged me back into the welcoming world I'd left eleven days earlier. My dogs leapt at me and danced around the room. The cats emerged and strutted past me into the kitchen, meowing for treats. Apart from the hundreds of emails clogging my computer, everything in my life was the same—except me. Without my realizing it, Jelena, Cathrine, and the nameless Serbian dogs had changed me.

I kept in touch with Vesna, with whom I was developing a warm friendship as our professional relationship, rooted in the Canadian literature she knows more about than I ever will, expanded comfortably into the personal. I sent her scholarly articles and books on autobiography, the subject of her next book. Vesna delivered my gifts to

Jelena—a sweater, a shirt, and a cell phone case "so that she can enjoy her awful work caring for all the dogs a bit more."

Jelena appreciated my gifts, but was inconsolable at the prospect of a scheduled slaughter of stray dogs in Niš and other Serbian cities. At her request, I sent letters of protest to the authorities, pleading that "these animals deserve a better fate than execution." Only later did I discover that the recipients didn't read English. More practically, I wired Jelena money to buy food and medicine for the dogs she kept safe in her shelter.

But shelters were clearly a stop-gap solution—when I'd visited that October, Jelena's had had 160 dogs, the majority females, of whom only twenty-eight were spayed—but by Christmas that number was up to nearly two hundred and steadily rising as people left boxes of puppies and tied older dogs to the gate. What the situation cried out for instead was a radical shift in policy toward homeless animals.

Vesna warned me that the real enemy was the strong macho mentality that denigrated animal advocates as crazy women who should be breeding children instead of fussing over dogs. "This isn't cynicism," Vesna said, "it's reality." But as frustrating and often heartbreaking as it was, the slow, steady advance of caring animal advocates was making inroads into Serbian cultural mores and, occasionally, into its official policy on homeless dogs.

I corresponded with Cathrine, who wowed me with her intelligence and mordant wit and never reproached me for having left Serbia without any of her dogs. Instead, she described how, after first arriving in Serbia with Gus-Gus and Posey in her carry-on luggage, she was almost magnetically sucked into animal rescue. "It wasn't a love of dogs, it was the sight of pregnant cats dragging their bellies across busy streets, of mangy dogs digging in garbage, of dead kittens in a trash bin, of blind old dogs abandoned to the mercies of wholly inadequate shelters. What struck me was the realization that I could do something, however small, to help the Serbs who were trying to meet that need."

She began by petting dogs in a shelter that locals had nicknamed the "Concentration Camp for Dogs," where, for four hours, she and other volunteers would stroke hundreds of dogs, repeating endlessly, *Dobar pas.* Good dog. "And a miracle occurred. Four hundred dogs crowded around four strangers, with almost no fighting. Every one of them wanted his or her turn getting an ear rub, a muzzle scratch. Every one of them wanted to hear those words, 'Good dog. Good, good dog.'

"Yet these dogs were killers. They lived in a constant turmoil of dominance fights, often with severe consequences, because of the number of new dogs coming into the shelter every week. Some were insane with rage; others were mad with terror. You'd never have known it on that Sunday. Every dog, of every size and temperament, came for those few seconds of affection and attention." On that day, every dog was a Good Dog, and they transformed Cathrine into a dog rescuer.

Each story Cathrine told me, and each new disaster reported by Jelena, strengthened my resolve to help. So when Vesna invited me to return to Serbia—to launch the Serbian edition of *A History of Celibacy* at the Belgrade Book Fair, to present a paper at a Canadian Studies conference with heavy Eastern European attendance, and to lecture once again at the universities in Belgrade and Niš—I accepted. One year after checking out of the Balkan Hotel, I checked back in. But this time my luggage included a large, airline-approved dog carrier.

I presented my paper and lectured on "Marriage: Where We've Been and Where We're Headed," the subject of my next book. The following morning, after taking the bus to Niš, I met Jelena for a bumpy ride out to the shelter in a taxi—whose driver had adopted two of the shelter dogs and regaled Jelena, who translated for me, with stories about their antics. Before she opened the gates, Jelena handed me my outfit: a thick pair of rubber boots and a man's mackintosh, both mud-spattered, and a kerchief, faded but clean. She also introduced me to Anabela, a gracious senior dog who marched to the beat of her own rhythms and, although a shelter resident, wandered freely around the large property.

I patted Anabela and followed Jelena down the rutted road to the shelter. The twelve months since my first visit had seen drastic changes. The number of dogs had doubled to over three hundred. Most were on chains. Others were in wire enclosures with access to a shared cage. Only Anabela and a few puppies roamed free, playing happily but also at risk of attack if they happened too close to an aggressive— or crazed—chained dog.

A horn honked at the gates: the delivery van with its load of twenty flats packed with loaves of bread already stacked on the ground. While Jelena spoke to the driver, I heaved up a flat and began the first of more than a dozen staggering trips along uneven beaten earth, slipping and sliding in patches still slick with dew, my arms aching under the unaccustomed burden. Twice I was bitten by dogs I'd passed too close to. One dog smiled before she lunged, the other bared his teeth; both grazed the back of my right thigh, nipping through my jeans. I didn't mention the bites until hours later, when we finally returned to Niš. What did it matter? My single terrible day was a microcosm of Jelena's whole life.

After the cooked food had cooled, we ladled it into pails and served it. I observed as I worked and took notes in my head. Though double in number, most dogs were much better housed than they'd been the previous year. Jelena had spent donations from European supporters on well-constructed cages, most built onto little posts that kept them dry during floods. When the rains were relentlessly long and hard, the dogs could escape the muck and mud by climbing onto the rooftops.

But even this was fraught, because an unlucky few had hanged themselves when they slipped off and their chains got caught around their necks. And so when the Europeans asked her to describe the most suitable way to secure and house the dogs, Jelena chose strong mesh fencing that would keep them safe, with no chains needed. The enclosures were well built, and although the dogs they sheltered were never taken for walks, they could still socialize and play and run around on their own.

As we went the rounds with food and water, Jelena greeted each dog by name and told me each one's story. In this primitive shelter she had created a world of Limited Liberation, and all but the most traumatized or fragile dogs thrived.

That day, watching Jelena work and grieve—she found an old, sick dog dying in his enclosure and carried him into the depot, where he lay in comatose comfort wrapped in Alekandr's old coat until he stopped breathing—my heart swelled up with admiration and respect. Jelena was a dedicated, resourceful, indefatigable, and productive shelter founder–director–manager–worker–fundraiser. She had committed herself to an impossible mission, and she was succeeding.

But there were ideological stumbling blocks that drove her to lock horns with many of her strongest supporters, including me. At our first meeting Jelena had aggressively sought out likely strangers to adopt a puppy, but she had no confidence in foreign adoptions. Foreigners, she believed, euthanized at the drop of a hat; she preferred to keep her charges safe in her shelter rather than murdered abroad. "In all Western countries dogs are tested, and if they show the slightest aggression, whether food aggression or against other dogs, they are killed. That is why you don't have aggressive dogs there," she declared.

That belief explained why she had no robust adoption program geared to Western Europe, where she was gaining more supporters: she was convinced that if one of her little ones nipped or growled in Amsterdam, Bruges, or Vienna, they'd be immediately dispatched.

Much later that evening Jelena and I sat in a café, scrubbed clean and garbed in fresh clothing, Jelena wearing the sweater I'd brought her but not the modish shirt that was, she said unapologetically, too risqué for her. She also declined coffee in favour of fruit juice, and dismissed the pastry platter without a second glance. (I dismissed it too, but only after a thorough examination that failed to reveal even one vegan goodie.) A strict vegan, Jelena trusted only her mother's home cooking. Once again, I marvelled at how a woman so delicate and guileless had both backbone and principles of steel, and could be converted but never bullied into compromising them.

Jelena's single-minded determination to help every last creature in her ken consumed her time and energy and invaded her family's home, which she'd crammed with nine dogs and an assortment of cats, rabbits, and birds. But it had also brought her Linda, her "most favourite of all creatures." In the months before the shelter opened, a friend's brother had spotted puppies hiding under a building and contacted Jelena. Although she'd rushed over, the puppies were gone; neighbourhood children told her that the dogcatchers had already been there and caught a two-month-old puppy born without a tail. That evening Jelena arranged for someone to sneak over to the dogcatchers' vans—where the dogs stayed overnight, piled in one on top of the other, without food or water or even air, until the dogcatchers drove them to their likely deaths in the morning. When the young man reported that he'd been unable to locate the tailless pup, Jelena ordered him to return to the vans and look more carefully. This time he found her.

Jelena named the tailless pup after the supermodel Linda Evangelista: she had the same kind of beauty—a long, slim body that reminded Jelena of a swan—as well as the grace of a ballerina and, with her cream-coloured, black-spotted head, the elegance of a fashion model. Linda's breed is uncertain, but when I suggested retriever lineage, Jelena replied with a resounding "Nooo!" What then? I asked. "She is Linda! That is what she is. And if I can choose which dog to put in your book, I choose Linda!"

Years later, Linda still fills Jelena's huge heart with her familiar loving presence. And after our long conversations about her dogs, Jelena said only this: "Thank you so much for telling Linda's story, and giving it—and her—eternal life."

# TWENTY-THREE

# Whisky Jack,
# Canine Ambassador

After a circuitous bus trip back to Belgrade and a rushed supper in my hotel room, the Canadian ambassador's residence was an oasis of stability. Cathrine, the epitome of order and efficiency, had checklists for the launch of Mission Airlift, through which she would place as many of her rescued Serbian dogs as she could in Canadian homes. My duty was to arrive at Nikola Tesla Airport no later than 5:00 A.M., be as accommodating as possible with airport officials, and then, once in Toronto, claim Whisky Jack and transport him to Animal Services, where my friend James McLean, the shelter's veterinary technician, would be waiting.

There was an urgency to the transport. Cathrine and Rob had arrived in Belgrade two years before, and Rob would soon be reassigned elsewhere. Before that happened, Cathrine had to find homes for all her remaining dogs. She'd already placed hundreds with rescues in Western Europe, among them a French organization dedicated to special needs dogs. These groups were now swamped and could take only a few more. Canadian homes seemed her only remaining option.

But why was she so adamant about sending Whisky Jack first? Why not, for instance, Dunja, the very pretty dog in the cage next to his, who would surely be easily adoptable? "I have to get him out of here because he's so emotionally needy, and the locals consider him 'too ugly.' Whisky needs to bond with someone who'll focus on him and give him all the love and attention he needs but that even I can't give him because he's one of so many." That made sense, and so through the bars of her cage I told Dunja that when she finally made it to Canada, Whisky Jack would show her the ropes.

The next day at the Book Fair, I answered questions and posed for photographers at the launch of the Serbian edition of *A History of Celibacy*. After that I didn't waste time sleeping; at 5:00 A.M. I was at the airport. Cathrine, holding tight to Whisky Jack's leash and visibly anxious, reviewed what was about to happen. First, she thrust a sealed envelope at me, packed with the dinars I'd need to put Jack on the plane. Then, lowering her voice, she emphasized the importance of keeping him quiet. Not long ago, an irate airport official had refused to let a dog onto the plane because it wouldn't stop barking; its distraught human was forced to remove it from the airport. To avert that nightmare, Cathrine had given Whisky Jack a generous dose of tranquilizer.

Although all her previous orphans had travelled by road in vans and these were the first to fly, Cathrine had planned Mission Airlift very well. The paperwork was in order, we were on time, the tranquilizer was working. When Whisky Jack, dozy in his crate, was wheeled away well before the boarding call, we listened intently but heard no alarming howling. The call came to board. Cathrine and I embraced and reassured each other that all would be well. As soon as I strapped on my seatbelt, I fell asleep.

Whisky Jack was in good hands. Frankfurt Airport, where we'd get our connecting flight to Toronto, has superlative facilities for dogs in transit. They're taken to an animal station with strict security and professional caretakers, who clean the cages and replace soiled bedding, water and walk the dogs, and keep them in climate-controlled pens until their next flight. Whisky Jack would be fine. It wasn't until I reached Toronto that my real Mission Airlift work would begin.

At Pearson International, I opened Whisky Jack's cage—still dry ten hours after he left Frankfurt!—and raced him outside, where he had an impressively long pee. The effects of the tranquilizer having worn off, he was bubbly and friendly and pulled hard on his leash, eager to keep walking. Then, during the cab ride into the city, he perched himself on my lap and happily looked out the window until we reached the shelter.

Now came the hard part: We're not going home, Whisky Jack, I'm abandoning you. But leaving him in the state-of-the-art shelter with James McLean, a towering, beloved figure in the animal rescue community, didn't feel like abandonment, at least to me. First came the delighted compliments—He's so *cute*! I *love* him—which prompted me to boast that Whisky Jack also knew his commands. When I pronounced them in halting Serbian—Sit! Down! Come!—he diligently complied, preening at our enthusiastic praise.

As I was about to leave, Whisky Jack looked at me in confusion. But when James said "Come!" in a Serbian that sounded just like mine, Whisky Jack wagged his tail and followed him upstairs to the kennel, where James planned to keep him until he acclimatized. Before he was put up for adoption, I provided a phonetic list of his Serbian commands and composed an engaging write-up to attract people to consider him.

One week later, Whisky Jack went home: James had adopted him out to a woman named Sian Miekle and her family. And Sian, a Trinity graduate and University of Toronto's digital services librarian, was very willing to keep in touch with me. I was as thrilled for Cathrine as I was for Jack. "All your hard work, unstinting love, and (Rob's) money have given this fine dog a great home," I wrote her. "James was very careful to choose special people. He told them something of WJ's story, and that'll make them even more tolerant of any mistakes he makes. He said about them: 'They are sooo nice.'"

The news hit Cathrine hard. "I'm sitting here with tears just rolling down my face, splashing on the keyboard! I know, I know, I should be happy, and maybe I am, but I can't help but think, That's MY dog! When I get over this bout of grief for myself, I'll be very happy for him, really I will. And I know I can't keep them all. I just really, really hope his people will treat him with love and understanding, and if *anything* goes wrong, I will always be here for him. Sniff, sniff (sleeve getting gooey ...), he's such a loving, good dog...."

And then, as joy trumped self-pity, a hopeful P.S.: "If Whiskey Jack can find a home that fast, then I'm more ready to hope for others."

I smiled to myself. *Après Jack, le déluge.* Mission Airlift was well underway.

From that October on, we conducted the selection process for dogs-to-go as if we were a search committee. As the candidates multiplied, we agonized, debated, and occasionally lobbied for our favourite. And we never forgot the pioneering work of Whisky Jack, who'd proven that a good Serbian street dog could find true happiness with a North American family. Who could have guessed that Jack (Whisky-less now), ensconced on the Miekles' living room sofa, could ever have become such an ambassador? And who could have guessed that Jelena, mesmerized by photos of an uneuthanized Jack, would now be lobbying as hard as Cathrine for the chance to send some of her orphans?

I turned my attention to the daunting task of finding an individual or a rescue willing to accept the next dogs on Mission Airlift's transport roster. But that was just the first step. We then had to find the money for their vetting and transport and provide airline-acceptable crates to ship them in. Cathrine had to prepare their "pet passports," arrange their trips within Serbia, and send me engaging photographs along with honest but inviting descriptions of each dog. I had to find them a place at a shelter or foster home, meet them at the airport and transport them there, and then act as liaison until a permanent adopter took the dog home for good. Without the sustained support of an ever-widening network of animal advocates, Mission Airlift would have deflated and crashed.

Who could have imagined that a British rabbit lover's earnest request for information about Jelena's shelter would prompt her little group—along with like-minded German, Austrian, and French women, all bound together as Wolf Spirit—to join forces with Mission Airlift? In an official request for information, Jean Bird wrote:

"Dear Ambassador, I have been helping to fund a dog shelter in Niš, Serbia, owned by Jelena Kostić that I believe your wife has recently visited, and I would be very grateful to learn of her impressions of the sanctuary. Our small group in England really want to help Jelena, but none of us has visited as yet and I would appreciate another opinion. Thank you so much."

Rob forwarded the request to Cathrine, who explained to Jean that I, not she, had visited the shelter; as Cathrine told me later, she also urged Jean, "in the strongest terms," to continue supporting Jelena.

I did the same, but laid out the shelter's rudimentary conditions and stressed my conviction that the goals should be to spay and neuter and to give priority to the dogs' quality of life. "Given a choice," I wrote, "many might prefer to live rough in packs in city parks, depending on the kindness of strangers to feed them, enduring hunger and sometimes cruelty, but having nonetheless something approximating a life. But with the dogcatcher busily rounding them up and euthanizing, living rough all too often ends in miserable death. Jelena's shelter at least keeps them alive, and the possibility of adoption provides hope and should be a crucial goal."

These lofty ideals were much easier for us outsiders than for Jelena, who faced relentlessly nightmarish days keeping the operation going—collecting at-risk dogs, browbeating locals for donations of anything they could give, and worrying about paying the bills, all while at the mercy of the heavens as they unleashed snow, rain, hail, freezing cold, or broiling heat down upon her open shelter. Still, thanks to Ambassador Jack, our goals were merging. "I have become obsessed with adoptions!" Jelena wrote. The Wolf Spirit women were sending money, and unlike Mission Airlift's more limited mandate, they were making arrangements to start bringing her dogs to Western Europe on an ongoing basis.

After two weeks with the Miekles, Jack was thriving. He'd begun to play with other dogs, and now felt safe enough to roll over for tummy rubs. "He's quite transformed life in general for us," Sian told me. "We all agree that life is better with a dog, and most particularly with Jack." And she invited me to visit. As I sipped tea in their living room, Jack lounged on the sofa—happy, confident, and as far as I could tell not the least bit interested in me, a forgotten piece of his forgettable past. Later, as Sian and I walked and Jack bounded up and down the ravines near their home, he kept turning back to check that she was just where he'd left her.

Gracie, one of Cathrine's rescues and the second Mission Airlift dog to seek her fortune in Canada, had an adoptive family waiting for her, my friend Heather Conway's aunt and uncle, Joyce and Dominic Senese. Nicknamed Spacey Gracie—she'd been obsessed with her first toy, a ball she chewed, chased, growled at, play-bowed to, buried, and then dug up—she disembarked in Newark, New Jersey, with her tail between her legs, redolent of vomit. But she recovered quickly during the long drive to her new home outside Niagara Falls: Joyce had given her a brand-new ball. Inside the house, ball clenched between her teeth, Gracie greeted the five cats. Boomer the dog fell in love with her on the spot. Her tail began to wag. Gracie was safely home.

Next in line was Bak, a seven-month-old pedigreed black Lab and the grandson of a multiple international champion; his owners in Niš had been about to chuck him out because he had hip dysplasia and his breeder had offered them a replacement puppy. Despite Bak's worrisome disabilities, Joan Znidarec of Labrador Retriever Rescue Ontario had agreed to take him. Then there was Pippin, a fragile, vulnerable fluff ball with glaucoma who had arrived from Jelena's shelter needing to be shaved from ear to tail to remove the mini-bricks of mud and poop stuck in her fur. She was a sunny, sweet-natured little dog, and by a great stroke of luck, Carol Thorpe accepted her into her volunteer-run Happy Tails rescue, which specializes in small breeds. As the Happy Tails website notes, "The dog immediately becomes part of a foster family where it is loved and nurtured back to a stable physical and/or mental state, and only then will it be adopted to a fully screened, loving family or individual." Back in Niš, mucking out the shelter and laboriously feeding and watering its residents, Jelena rejoiced at Pippin's good fortune.

Cathrine's friend Vedran Vucić, Serbia's premier Linux/ Open Source geek, shepherded Bak and Pippin on the flight to Toronto; before he continued on to Montreal, he helped me push my two exhausted, smelly charges outside to our meeting with dog rescuer Bonnie Hall, whom Dora Sesler had recruited to drive me.

Bonnie, waving, was pulling up in her car as Bak awkwardly spilled out of his crate onto the pavement. I waved back at Bonnie but she was staring at Bak, transfixed. I was startled and alarmed. What was wrong? Was she having second thoughts about fostering such a large dog? But no, Bonnie was having an epiphany, a long moment of déjà vu. Her eyes glazed and face frozen, she was seeing in Bak the reincarnation of her beloved Spud, who had passed away a year earlier.

"Spud has come back to me," Bonnie told me later. "Bak is his embodiment, and I just love him." One look, and Bak's foster mother became his permanent adopter. It didn't matter that Bak was grotesquely overweight, could scarcely walk twenty feet, panted and drooled, gobbled his food, and guzzled every drop of the dogs' drinking water. All Bonnie saw was his flawless temperament. Bak was frighteningly smart, understood everything, and was in love with Lennie the cat, whom he carried around in his mouth when the two weren't cuddling and licking each other. He was Spud in spirit, and Bonnie was ecstatic.

Pippin, too, would find a home. During her brief stay at my house she was playful and affectionate, and mesmerized Bonzi. By the time Happy Tails volunteer Janet Lewis was ready to foster her, my guitarist–dog groomer friend Cam MacInnes had transformed Pippin into a fluffy princess with a matching collar and leash. Cam, who with his wife, Lana, rescues Airedale terriers, had offered free grooming to the Serbian dogs, and before Mission Airlift ended, he had beautified several of them.

The grooming process was often recorded by Fred Ni, a computer animator and volunteer dog walker who was documenting Mission Airlift. Fred was a surprise adjunct to our rescue project. He'd met Whisky Jack at Toronto Animal Services, where he learned about us. He was already photographing adoptable TAS dogs for its website and would showcase them on his blog, One Bark at a Time. "Fred's blog helps us one thousand percent," James McLean told me. "The phone rings off the hook about every dog he features." Mission Airlift would be Fred's first documentary, and I invited him to film any and all stages of our work.

Cam's grooming and Fred's photography paid off: within days, Pippin had clocked in over nine hundred hits on the Happy Tails website. Janet Lewis began the laborious process of vetting adoption applications; she also house-trained Pippin and assessed her character, reporting that loving and adorable though she was, the former street dog was bossy with other dogs and stole their toys. Potential adopters were advised that Pippin should be their only dog. Her glaucoma-afflicted eyes would deteriorate, and one would likely have to be removed.

Despite her visual deficits, Pippin was soon adopted; Carol at Happy Tails went on to receive updates from her delighted humans. When I reported this to Jelena, who'd already rejoiced at photos of Pippin lounging on my sofa with Bonzi, she added a new task to her frenetic work schedule: identify other fluffy little dogs who might also become Happy Tails.

# TWENTY-FOUR

# Diplomatic Dog Delivery

In late May, when Ambassador Rob McDougall was about to fly out of Belgrade for official meetings in Ottawa, Cathrine had packed everything he would need. That included crates containing two of her rescued dogs, Dunja and Kojo.

Dunja had spent her entire young life in a shelter run by Katija, a tiny widowed peasant woman so poor she could barely feed herself. Her *azil*—a field about the size of two large North American lots and secured by a high stone fence with a rusty metal gate—housed about three hundred dogs along with geese, chickens, turkeys, and a few cats. It was so close to the *kafilerija* that people about to dump their dogs there often deposited them in front of Katija's gate instead.

Days after Cathrine had first arrived in Belgrade, Libby Oliver, wife of the Australian ambassador and unofficial volunteer coordinator for diplomatic wives, suggested that she walk dogs at Katija's shelter. The mostly collarless dogs were bedraggled and dirty, but safer than they'd been as street dogs. Katija had also browbeaten the local butcher and baker into donating their leftovers. But then Katija's neighbours, who hated her and her hundreds of dogs, took her to court in a bid to shut down the shelter. They were foiled. The internationally renowned film director Goran Paskaljević (*The Dog Who Loved Trains,* 1977) and his French wife, Christine Gentet-Paskaljević, were socially powerful dog lovers who bought Katija's property for a token price. The court case dissolved, the shelter continued to operate, and Katija, by then (in Cathrine's words) "as wizened as a little monkey and as tough as an old boot," was able to retire with nine of her favourite dogs to a proper little house where, for the first time in her life, she enjoyed electricity and indoor plumbing.

Before the advent of the Paskaljevićs, Dunja had been tossed over the fence into Katija's shelter. After Cathrine brought her to live in their courtyard, the pretty terrier impressed her with her canine beauty and intelligence. Dunja would do well in Canada, she decided.

"Dogs sedated, and fast asleep when they left. Husband not sedated, also asleep on his feet," Cathrine emailed me on departure day. Hours later, at Pearson, Rob handed me Dunja and Kojo and continued on to Ottawa.

This time the rescuer who'd offered to pick me up at the airport was Christine Ford, future founder of Oh My Dog! I'd already leashed Dunja and Kojo—my massive airport bag included collars and leashes, kibble, and water as well as cleaning supplies—and as we stood waiting on the sidewalk, they wagged their tails happily and lapped up the water I'd poured out for them. Christine drove up minutes later. When she saw Dunja, her jaw dropped. "She's not going to the pound," she said as she hopped out of the car. "I'll foster her." So without the least effort on my part, Dunja trotted off with Christine—who, with Dora and others in the rescue community, mounted an intensive campaign to find a perfect home for this perfect young dog.

Kojo, meanwhile, was headed for the municipal pound. An odd-looking dog with a toothy leer for a smile, he quickly charmed a young woman, who renamed him Marley and made him her constant companion.

But lovely Dunja, sponsored by Lorraine Houston's Speaking of Dogs rescue and happy with Christine in what she didn't realize was her foster home, took longer to find her humans. "I cannot tell you how in love with her I am!" Christine raved. Dora Sesler also felt a special connection. "She's quite attached to me too," she wrote. "I explained to her that we were born in the same country, so I think she knows that. The other day as Christine walked her, she went up to my house when they were on my street. What's amazing is that she'd never been here! We'll find her the right home—the one she's meant to be at."

That home was in Ottawa, with Lori Duncan and Ryan Hunter, who made two separate trips to Toronto to see her. Christine, Dora, and Lorraine were enchanted. Lori and Ryan were active, responsible people who'd done all their homework about caring for a dog. In Ottawa, a fellow rescuer's home visit confirmed these impressions. After an emotional leave-taking from her Toronto friends, Dunja went off to her new home.

Rescuers salvage as many dogs as they can, but their victories are always clouded by the knowledge that for each life saved, scores more are lost. So if they're to continue their work, they have to find ways to conquer or at least manage their despair. Their most powerful weapon is usually a gift:

news, preferably accompanied by photos, of a rescued dog's happy new life. Rescuers also encourage themselves by saving a favourite dog—of which Coco, Dominik, and Pinky were living, barking examples.

Coco was a friendly, floppy little mutt whom Jelena had urged the Wolf Spirit women to sponsor; her joyful adoption through Happy Tails gave Jelena a much-needed lift. Dominik was a healthy, muscular, very slender young dog with an erect carriage whom Cathrine had sent me in the hopeful expectation that the husky-wolfish look that repelled Serbs would appeal to Canadians. She was right, and off he went to live with a veterinarian technician and her partner in Toronto's dog-loving Beach community.

Last was Pinky, a handsome street dog whose good looks and pink nose made Cathrine feel "all smooshy" and catapulted Pinky into the queue for Mission Airlift. But Pinky's adoption did much more than give Cathrine a boost even better than her beloved double-chocolate ice cream. It also introduced me to Michele Erker, then an executive member of Toronto Cat Rescue who fostered cats and transported dogs and had agreed to drive me and Pinky from the airport to Toronto Animal Services.

At the last minute, just as we approached the door to the shelter, Michele banged her head on the steering wheel. "I can't leave her here," she groaned. "I just can't do it. I'll foster her myself." Then another, louder groan: "Damn! But what about the cats? I have fifteen at home right now, my own and a bunch of fosters. How is she with cats?" I shrugged, my initial elation evaporating. "No clue," I told Michele. "We'll have to ask James to test her." And so we hauled Pinky out of the car and into the shelter. Fifteen minutes later we were giddy with relief. "Pinky!" I exclaimed, ignoring her perplexed expression, "you got an A plus! And now you're going to Michele's house until we find you a forever home."

Pinky integrated into Michele's menagerie as if she'd always lived there. "Last night the little lady slept soundly on my bed among cats and my other dog Milo, snoring," Michele told me. "She takes the cats in her mouth and carries them around, plays with them, loves them and is loved by them. She'll make a family very happy with her silliness."

Once again Lorraine Houston helped me out, this time with a courtesy post for Pinky on her Speaking of Dogs website. It didn't work out quite as expected, though. At the all-important home visit to her potential adopters, my doubts began as soon as Michele and I walked into the well-kept suburban house with the large deck and huge garden—and the white wall-to-wall carpeting. It was Pinky who delivered the final deal-breaker: she squatted suddenly and had diarrhea on the wooden deck. The family's two boys looked at her and at each other—Was that terror I saw on their faces?—and then nervously produced the cleaning supplies I'd requested. We could all tell that this wasn't the family for Pinky. But as we headed back to Toronto, Michele and I burst out laughing. No need to say more: we'd just done our first and last home visit. Pinky already had a home. She was Michele's dog, and we were wasting our time pretending not to know that.

"Cathrine," I emailed that night, "Pinky won't let Michele get rid of her. It's the fifteen cats. Pinky's in love with at least ten of them." I'd be in permanent touch with her, I added, and Michele would be delighted to have Cathrine visit. Over in Belgrade, Cathrine responded to this news as if to a shot of adrenalin. For at least another day, she told me later, she'd hummed and sung aloud as she scrubbed and medicated and walked and cared for her charges in the courtyard.

Belatedly, Cathrine learned that a friendly acquaintance was heading to Toronto and was willing to transport a dog. The roster of candidates was long, but because the bigger cages were in Toronto about to be shipped back to Belgrade, only small dogs could be considered. Which is why shy, delicate Trinket was chosen.

Little Trinket had a sad story. She'd been tied to a doghouse with a short, slender wire, and in her struggles to free herself the wire had bitten deeply into her neck. The wound became infected and the flesh around it died. Eventually, Trinket got free and was found by someone who brought her to Cathrine. It took months for the wound to heal. Her throat had to be shaved every week and cleaned and disinfected every day. After it healed completely, you could still see a deep groove where the wire had left its mark in her neck. Trinket's other scar was her extreme shyness, although she did slowly learn to trust; after that she loved to be picked up and cuddled, lying contentedly in someone's lap. She was a quiet dog, and good with all other living creatures: children as well as adults, puppies as well as dogs. She was one of the few dogs who never got into fights and would only growl if other dogs crowded her.

Since Trinket's arrival was a last-minute affair, I couldn't arrange transport from the airport. A taxi would be prohibitively expensive and airport buses refused to take dogs, so I'd have to use public transit: an express bus, a subway, a streetcar, and finally some serious walking.

I did not arrive unprepared. As soon as her Serbian transporter handed Trinket to me, I rushed her outside onto a grassy patch, carefully opened the cage door, and leashed her. Then I pulled her out into the sunshine where she stood frozen, refusing to budge. I tied her leash to my waist and began the nauseating chore of scraping, spraying, scrubbing, and drying the cage, tossing the soiled bedding into the garbage and lastly, masking the stench with an artificial fragrance that I hoped wouldn't get me kicked off the TTC. Meanwhile, Trinket lay flat on the pavement and wouldn't move.

The next challenge was sneaking her onto the bus. By then it was rush hour, when no dogs are allowed. I confided my predicament to the young man ahead of me in line, and he agreed to help me by carrying the empty cage while I hid Trinket in my bag of cleaning supplies and shuffled along in the crush of commuters, entering the bus sideways to conceal my ungainly baggage.

Once aboard, my smiling accomplice handed me the cage. I slid it toward the back of the bus and stuffed Trinket back inside. Then I collapsed into a seat and sighed deeply. Success!

But Trinket had been crated for eighteen hours, increasingly stressed as her sedation wore off, and she began to pass gas in a steady stream. Nearby, people sniffed the air tentatively, unable to locate the culprit, while I looked innocently away, as if I were enjoying the scenery. One irate man complained to the driver, but by then we were almost ready to disembark. I pushed the cage briskly toward the back door and out onto the street.

Next came the subway, easier to navigate because it was air-conditioned and more spacious, with no TTC agents in sight. Trinket and I rode unchallenged across the city; then I repeated my bus stratagem and stealthily lugged her onto the streetcar. The farting that had been diluted by the subway's air conditioning resumed at full force, and before long the woman next to me opened the window and stuck her head out while all around me passengers were eyeing each other suspiciously and covering their noses.

At last I slunk off the streetcar, set the cage down, and tugged Trinket out onto the pavement. Still she refused to walk, so I carried her pressed against my chest while I dragged the crate with my other hand, staggering the thousands of miles (or so it felt) to the shelter.

James, too, wrinkled his nose. Then he popped Trinket into a big washtub and began to bathe her. Afterward, I sat on the floor towelling her off, trying to get into the mind of a dog who'd never before been in a house. When she was dry, James led her into a cage that looked very much like a prison cell; as I squatted next to her, she gobbled her food and drank. When I finally left her, Trinket was wagging her tail.

I remembered Tommy, so frightened in his quarantine kennel, and contrasted his pain with Trinket's pleasure. Unlike Tommy, Trinket was happily surprised by incarceration in the shelter cage. She had her own comfortable bed and bowls full of kibble and water, as much as she could eat and drink. She could sleep where she wanted, without having to compete with other, bigger dogs. To Trinket, this was a luxurious experience.

That evening I spoke to Fred, who promised to walk her and report on her progress. "I'm exhausted," I groaned, "and I still have to power-wash the goddamned crate. But who cares? Trinket's saved!"

Trinket's stay at the pound was short. When Erica McArthur saw her profile online, she told her husband, "That's my dog." And so Trinket, renamed Zora, went off to her new home with the McArthurs. Years later, Erica enlightened me about Zora's refusal to walk: the trauma of the wire embedded in her throat had caused a permanent horror of collars. But as Erica had discovered, Zora was happy walking with a harness. Before our conversation ended, I couldn't help asking Erica if Zora still delivered pungent smells. Erica only laughed. I took that to be my answer.

That summer, Cathrine made a brief trip to Canada with more dogs from her courtyard. I recently watched Fred's video to refresh my memory of the day she arrived. It began as Cathrine, in an elegant striped silk shirt and with a cigarette between her lips, went from cage to cage introducing her charges. When she got to the smallest cage, her voice changed and she spoke with aching tenderness about the little dog with the rigid front leg. At two months old, she'd been struck by a car and brought to Cathrine, whose vet named her Smile—because even in the worst pain, the little brindle mongrel pup would lift her head and offer him a great big smile punctuated by a tail wag.

The vet had operated for six hours, pinning the back leg, casting the front leg, aligning the pelvis. Afterward Smile spent two months in a small cage in the residence's courtyard garage, immobilized. Her only human contact was when she was lifted out to be cleaned, when she was fed, and when someone put their hand in the cage to rub her ears and get their fingers nibbled. During it all, she smiled at the presence of any human. She also developed a one-paw swipe through the bars of her cage to steal food and toys from the cage next to hers.

The surgery was successful, except that her smashed right front leg ossified into rigidity, and Smile walked with a pronounced limp. She remained happy and affectionate, though she barked like a machine gun at dogs who encroached on her space. She was winsome and affectionate, the perfect family dog that no family showed any interest in adopting.

In Toronto, Smile's luck changed. "Adopted!" James notified me, less than two weeks after she arrived. I even got to meet her new owners after Vesna brought Smile's X-rays with her when she came to Toronto for the summer. Through James, I contacted Nathan Goold, Smile's adopter, and took the X-rays to his workplace. When I saw Nathan coming to meet me, pulling himself forward in a wheelchair, my heart softened. Then Nathan explained what had attracted him and his wife, Catherine, to their lame little dog: her broken legs, her beauty, her calm, sweet temperament. And her ease with Nathan, as if she'd been around wheelchairs all her life. "Pochi"—her new, Japanese-inspired name—"is one of the most loving dogs we've ever met, truly a remarkable and special dog," Nathan said. "She has more playful energy than she knows what to do with. I think she's about the only one who doesn't know she has a limp." In a letter to James, Catherine added, "She had us wrapped around her paw in no time. Words can't express how grateful we are to the many people who were responsible for caring for her and giving her a chance at life when her prognosis did not look good."

The second dog to arrive in company with Smile/Pochi was the bouncingly pretty young Irene, another of Cathrine's rescued street dogs, whose sunny personality and ability to get along with humans and dogs alike made her stand out from most of the pack. But Irene, quiet and unaggressive, had a problem: other dogs picked on her, especially the larger ones.

Like her travelling companion, Irene was quickly adopted. Young Emily Cocarell had spent an entire year searching for the right dog until she found Irene at Toronto Animal Services. But a posh young couple had already applied for Irene; when Emily arrived, they were out walking her, making sure she was right for them—they wanted a black dog because they had a black couch. Emily waited nervously. Then a miracle happened: the couple decided she wasn't right for them after all. That day Irene walked out the door with the human who years later can't imagine having ever lived without her.

Emily changed Irene's name to Pickles, and treated her like a princess. Pickles ate homemade dog food with her kibble. At night, before she fell asleep, she would pile her favourite toys at the foot of the bed she shared with Emily. And, to alleviate Pickles's severe separation anxiety, Emily arranged for a steady rotation of friends and relatives to visit when she was at work. (The cost of failure was high. Left alone, Pickles shredded couches.)

Just five weeks after she merged her life with Emily's, that anxiety nearly cost Pickles her life. Emily was in the shower, getting ready for her birthday party. Her brother and her cousin were in the living room with Pickles when Pickles suddenly escaped out the door. Until Emily emerged from the shower and discovered she was gone, nobody gave chase. Emily wasted no time. With a towel wrapped around her and flip flops on her feet, she raced down the street screaming Pickles's name.

Emily's brother belatedly joined in the search, jumping onto his bicycle and pumping hard. He caught sight of Pickles and tried to corner her, but Pickles fled from him and ran out into the street—where a car hit her. Then, dragging herself away, she disappeared into someone's backyard.

Within minutes, a hastily dressed Emily arrived in a taxi and began a methodical, increasingly panicked search for her dog. Finally, after nightfall and several false sightings, she returned home and waited until morning to resume the hunt. Just after dawn came the truth that was stranger than fiction. Emily received a call from Animal Services informing her that Pickles was at Cinderella, a Korean restaurant, and to please come down and fetch her as the owner's family wanted to go to church.

When Emily arrived the entire Korean family was waiting impatiently, dressed in their Sunday best and carrying tasselled white leather Bibles. The irritated father, who just wanted the whole episode to end, told her that Pickles had appeared in the restaurant the night before, triggering a visit from the police and a potentially costly warning that dogs aren't allowed in food-related establishments.

He'd wanted to push her out onto the street, but his teenage son had other ideas. And so, at considerable financial sacrifice, Papa announced an early closing. Then the son brought two duvets downstairs, one for Pickles, the other for himself, and the pair spent the night side by side until morning, when Animal Services opened and he reported finding Pickles.

But Emily represented a discordant subplot. How, Teenager wondered, did Pickles get injured, and why did she run away? The conclusion that fit all the facts as he knew them was easy: Emily had abused Pickles, and Pickles had fled to Cinderella for safety. So when Emily arrived at the restaurant, Teenager (but not his father) was reluctant to surrender Pickles to her tormentor. But at the sight of her beloved human, Pickles whimpered with joy and hauled herself across the room toward her—a tearful, rapturous reunion that made the son question his assumptions.

After that, what could have been the saddest story in the world suddenly had a beautiful ending. Pickles never ran away again.

# TWENTY-FIVE

## Hannah Joy, Heartbreaker

When Vesna Lopičić arrived in Toronto for a summer of library research, she brought more than Pochi's X-rays. She also brought a small, matted dog from Jelena's shelter, the former street dog Sivkica. "I would like to get this dog to Canada like Pippin and Coco," Jelena had written. "She is so smart and has a very good nature. What do you think, Elizabeth? Is she adoptable?"

It was a rhetorical question. If ever a dog was adoptable, Sivkica was that dog.

"Please, pretty please," I pleaded with Cathrine. Although she was frantically trying to place the remainder of her own large pack before Foreign Affairs plucked Rob out of Serbia and sent him elsewhere, with her usual good grace she agreed to take care of Sivkica's paperwork and transatlantic flight. Jean Bird of Wolf Spirit rushed to raise the funds. Vesna volunteered to be Sivkica's official transporter. In Toronto, Carol Thorpe agreed to accept her into Happy Tails. And with no foster home immediately available, I signed up to foster her myself.

Jelena had first seen Sivkica in the city centre, where she lived on the street in front of the Mega Store and survived by eating food scraps tossed to her. As Jelena scooped up the puppy she'd come to rescue, she also spoke softly to the grey street dog. Then she turned and left, the puppy in her arms. The grey dog followed Jelena all the way home, where her other dogs chased the little intruder away.

"The saddest thing is that, as she is such a loving dog, she would follow anyone who said something nice to her, like I did, but usually no one ever noticed her. Luckily the dogcatchers weren't around just then," Jelena recalled. The next morning the little grey dog was outside waiting for her. Jelena gave in, named her Sivkica ("greyish" in Serbian), and installed her in the shelter. There she spent two years chained to her doghouse, sometimes snuggling into her food bowl, and wagging her fluffy tail whenever Jelena or one of her harried colleagues petted her.

At the airport, Vesna told me of the nightmarish episode at the brink of their departure from Belgrade, where a baggage mixup almost prevented Sivkica from boarding the flight. At the last minute, the error was discovered and the small dog crate was carried into the belly of the airplane. Shuddering at the thought of the near-miss, I hugged Sivkica close.

When I carried her into my house and introduced her to the dogs, Snoopy the cat lurked nearby, cautiously observing her from the safety of the dining room table. We cuddled for a while, and then Cam MacInnes appeared: he had agreed to treat the smelly, bedraggled long-distance traveller to a "spa day." Fred Ni recorded the transformation, including the moment that Sivkica, exhausted by the long flight, fell asleep in the bathtub.

Afterward, in the park, Fred took more photos. Sivkica saw her first squirrel and playfully pawed at its tail. That night she slept on my bed with Alice and Bonzi; when I woke up, she wagged her tail. She was a skinny, dainty, adorable bundle, and within a day I'd renamed her Hannah Joy in celebration of her soft sweetness, her beauty, and her loving joyfulness.

I made a terrible foster mother. I'd fallen in love with Hannah Joy and could barely stand to give her up. I took her to a book signing at the World's Biggest Bookstore, where, for two hours, she sat on the table next to a pile of my books. I wrote an impassioned biography for Happy Tails: "Nobody must ever get mad at her ever, never a sharp word much less a blow, never a door left carelessly open, never a sadness inflicted. Her new family must understand the awful life she's gotten through, the hunger, living tied in a field night and day, fed when there was food, watered when there was time and someone to do it, surrounded by scary dogs who sometimes killed each other, hot in summer, freezing in winter.

"Some of her behaviour comes from being tied on a short chain. She can jump up on a table from years of jumping on top of her doghouse to escape snow and rainy mucky mud; she finds her poop spot by turning in tight little circles. But she is such a perfect dog, quiet as gold, loves her walks, peaceful at home, sleeps on my pillow, wags her tail all the time. She's sensitive, staring into your eyes to make sure she understands what you want, and she jumps at startling sounds: she didn't hear cars, horns, trains, etc. in the rural Serbian field. But she's not a nervous dog, just a sensitive one. A princess, without any airs, just wanting to please and to love."

Hannah Joy was adopted by a couple in their fifties, who were everything we could have dreamed of: one spouse stayed at home, and because they had no children, Hannah Joy would be their child. "We left as they were putting her

in their car to take her to buy her a whole new 'trousseau,'"
Carol reported happily. "We think being doted on will suit
Hannah to a T."

"Oh, isn't it lovely?" Jean Bird exclaimed when I
emailed her the great news. "That image of that little dog
sitting in her food dish in Niš comes into my mind, and it
makes me laugh and cry to think of her now!" I laughed
and cried too, and if ever Hannah Joy's people can no longer
keep her, I'll fly to wherever she is and reclaim her.

Mission Airlift was on emergency standby: Rob's appointment as Canada's high commissioner to Bangladesh had
been confirmed. With the incoming ambassador having
agreed that one arthritic old dog could spend the rest of his
life in the residence courtyard, Cathrine's menagerie was
now down to two unadoptable dogs and three more for
me to find homes for. And so, taking matters into her own
hands, Cathrine flew to Toronto to deliver them.

Little Erin, a tri-pawed tyke who looked like a
mini Rottweiler, was pre-approved for James and Debra
Edwards—*if* he got along with Precious, the family cat. He
did, and his adoption was joyously confirmed. Speaking of
Dogs placed Angela, a young terrier from one of Jelena's
foster homes in Niš, with a welcoming family.

Only seven-year old Meda ("bear" in Serbian), a
quivering giant schnauzer–sized mass of emotion with
cloudy eyes and uncertain health, was problematic. Cathrine
bravely pledged to take him with her to Bangladesh if all
else failed. But Meda was in luck: not only did he find a
home, but his adopter, Jackie Thorne, refused to give up
on him. It took a while before Meda finally understood in

the depths of his being that he would never be abandoned again. Then he became Jackie's soulmate, and her family's great joy, until his death four years later.

"I'll never get over losing him," Jackie told me. "Our home is full of pictures of him and my head is full of memories. I adored Meda, and was so blessed to have that time with him. I just wish I'd had longer to adore him."

# TWENTY-SIX

## *Dobro, Dobro!*
## Mission Airlift Goes Down

Before Cathrine left Belgrade, she still had two crazed dogs to remove from the courtyard. Magic and Jimmy were so flawed that nobody anywhere would take them. Magic, born on the street, had witnessed the brutal killing of her mother and siblings. From then on she'd been relentlessly aggressive, the permanent alpha in the courtyard's ever-shifting pack. Magic also hated people—except Cathrine—and attacked anyone who came near. If a cat strayed too close, it did not survive. Cathrine was desperate. "I'm a cat person! What will I do with an aggressive dog who thinks cats are breakfast?"

Jimmy, rescued from the *kafilerija* in puppyhood, suffered such frantic global fear that he hid away, refusing to emerge even to eat. His skin erupted with infections, including mange, and he lost his tail to necrosis. Jimmy was as cowed as Magic was aggressive, cringing when strangers approached and screaming if they attempted to pet him. In a home or a shelter, he would expire from fear or disease. Cathrine was stuck with Jimmy as well.

But Cathrine wasn't Jimmy's hero; Magic was. And Magic played the role to the hilt, defending Jimmy even from Cathrine if that seemed necessary. So Cathrine had a dog, and her dog had a dog. She had two choices, neither one appealing: euthanasia or carting them off to Bangladesh with her. "They hated my beloved cats, distrusted my True Love"—Magic attacked Rob whenever he tried to kiss Cathrine—"needed constant attention and care, were dangerous to strangers, and I didn't like either of them," she confided. "But I had a moral obligation to them because I'd taught them to trust and rely on me." And so off they went with her to Bangladesh. What else could my poor friend do?

Magic continued to terrorize people, and even bit a security guard. Jimmy, sickened by the food and water and riddled with intestinal infections, needed so much care that the vet threatened to move into the official residence. But slowly, almost imperceptibly, things changed. Cathrine arranged for visits to an untouched property where the dogs could run free. She let them sit on the sofa beside her and would cuddle them at bedtime. One memorable night, Jimmy slowly and tentatively put his head on her lap, whereupon Magic bit his nose and put her own head there instead. Her dogs had come to love her, and Cathrine realized that she'd come to love her dogs.

During Mission Airlift, Cathrine would stay at my house whenever she returned to Canada. It made simple sense: the money she'd have otherwise spent on hotels and restaurants would go directly into rescuing more dogs. And Cathrine was an easy guest. She pitched in to help with the animals and the garden and required only an odd but simple diet that had to include Häagen-Dazs Double Chocolate ice cream and Coke Zero.

These infrequent visits cemented our friendship. Cathrine also credits them with an epiphany: observing my diapered, terrified, limping, struggling, helpless old Maggie treated as one more member of the family impressed on her that disabled dogs are just as deserving of rescue as the able-bodied. ("Don't tell Rob that," I pleaded. "Don't lay that burden at my door. He'll hire a hit man to do me in.") But she was right: with Maggie as a measure, it'd be hard to deem any dog unadoptable, even Magic and Jimmy.

I met the difficult dyad after Rob's assignment in Bangladesh ended. Cathrine had arranged two flights, a day apart, from Dhaka to Toronto: the first was for her, Rob, and four cats, the maximum number of animals allowed; the second was for Magic, Jimmy, and another cat.

Cathrine sent me a list of tasks. "Elizabeth, Beau has no bowel control. I'm likely to be running low on diapers by the time we get in. Is it possible to have some waiting, xx-small or x-small? Also, one roll of cheap paper towels or sturdy toilet paper to make a special poop pouch that keeps him from smearing poop all over himself." For transport, I cajoled Michele, Pinky's human, to drive the menagerie in a gigantic rented van to Ottawa, where Rob and Cathrine would be living next.

The first load descended on me on my birthday. After cramming four cages into my small guest room, Cathrine set to work cleaning, medicating, grooming, and soothing four traumatized cats, three with special needs and one so grumpy that only she could get near him. I peered into the room through a slit, careful not to let anyone escape. Meanwhile, my dogs and cats were on high alert, pacing and scratching and whining outside the door, intent on challenging this noisy band of intruders.

The next day, Cathrine and Rob taxied out to the airport to pick up Magic, Jimmy, and Gus-Gus the cat. When they returned, pandemonium ensued. To walk their two dogs was a feat of bravery and dedication, given that under no circumstances could either escape or go near other living beings. And Gus-Gus, in no mood to celebrate his return to his homeland, expressed his displeasure in loud squalls of misery and reproach.

Later that day—a day that every one of the eleven animals stuffed into different rooms in my narrow row house was already hating—we sat waiting for Michele, who was at the rental office pleading for a vehicle that would accommodate two passengers, one driver, seven caged animals, and eleven massive suitcases. She finally arrived in a truck. Then, as curious neighbours watched, we began to carry all the cages downstairs and outside to the street. But no matter how cleverly we packed, disregarding vision requirements by stuffing the interior right to the ceiling, it wouldn't all fit.

Finally, shuffling and reshuffling cages as their disoriented, unhappy inhabitants meowed, hissed, screamed, barked, and howled, we surrendered to the facts. Cathrine, a small woman, Michele, an even smaller one, and Michele's medium-sized friend whom she needed for company on the drive home would squash together in the front seat. With the seven animals and four suitcases in the back, they'd drive to Ottawa where Rob and the remaining suitcases would join them the next day.

Early the next morning, when Rob's taxi arrived, the driver loaded the remaining seven enormous suitcases into the trunk. Then Rob headed off to Union Station and a relaxed train ride to the capital.

It was over. *Dobro, dobro!* The last of the dogs in Mission Airlift were safely home.

# TWENTY-SEVEN

## Dogs Without Borders

While it was underway, Mission Airlift made just enough sense to keep me slogging away at it, transporting street dogs from Eastern Europe to Toronto where I moved heaven and earth to find them good homes. Sometimes I wondered, Was I out of my mind? Other people, more tactful, asked me why, with so many homeless dogs in Ontario, I was spending so much time and money on faraway Serbian dogs. Only after Mission Airlift and its relentless pressures and worries ended did I have the time and distance I needed to sort out the reality of what it was all about.

Cathrine and Jelena, both intense, hard-driving women with no time to waste on fripperies, had drawn me into Serbia's homeless dog crisis, but it was the dogs themselves who clinched my decision to commit to Mission Airlift. Once I'd gazed into a dog's eyes, or fed and watered her, or heard even snippets of her life story, she transcended all political borders and became only a dog who needed my help.

Cathrine and Jelena felt that obligation and much more, which is why both were saddled with overwhelming numbers of homeless, unwanted dogs. Not Serbian dogs. Dogs. *Their* dogs.

Remember Whisky Jack? "That's MY dog!" Cathrine had wept when I told her about Jack's wonderful new life in Toronto. I also received dozens of emails from Jelena, courteous but insistent: What was happening to Pippin? to Sivkica? to Erin and Angela? If I hadn't been able to forward her a constant flow of photographs, I think Jelena might have collapsed with anxiety and grief.

In Toronto, when I reached out to established rescuers I'd met in my previous modest rescue work, they unhesitatingly pitched in to help my Serbia-born orphans. Why? Toronto Animal Services' James McLean, who's received awards for his work in homing dogs, believes that dogs have no borders. "I've never thought it was wrong to rescue a dog from somewhere else if it needs a home," he told me. Although TAS has an open policy for admissions, it does take into account such things as the current shelter occupants and possible health issues, for example any viruses a dog might carry. If accepted, non-Toronto dogs are evaluated and their stories and place of origin recorded. It's often those stories that attract people to consider them. And it helps, James noted, that many dog-loving Torontonians eschew breeders and pet stores and ask specifically for rescued dogs. Taking in the occasional puppy or healthy young dog, rare among Toronto strays and owner surrenders, helps keep adopters away from pet stores with their ailing puppy mill "merchandise."

Lorraine Houston credits teamwork and shared resources for making the rescue movement work. And when Dunja, Pinky, and Angela landed in Toronto, Speaking of Dogs fostered and sponsored them until they found their forever homes.

Carol Thorpe, too, saw only homeless little dogs whom her rescue could transform into Happy Tails. An indefatigable dog rescuer, Carol, now president and director of Happy Tails and a college daycare manager, cares for her own three dogs, all Yorkies, and provides loving palliative care for the terminally ill dogs James sends her from TAS. When she was vetting potential candidates to adopt Hannah Joy, Carol was also tending to two of James's unadoptables, who would finally die in her arms. "They all take a bit of my soul with them," Carol told me, "but someone has to be there for them at the end."

Nearly eight years later, Jelena's shelter has become a happier story that wouldn't have been happy at all if I'd told it earlier. My visits there took place during what we now call "the dark days," although by my second visit in 2007, the first slight improvements were evident. Years later, light and shadows have banished the darkness.

The dogs are no longer chained to flimsy crates or lean-tos; now they live unchained in fenced enclosures, the majority with wooden flooring so that they're no longer mired in mud or frozen in icy snow. They have insulated doghouses, the older ones with sloping roofs designed for easy drainage but not for dogs leaping up to escape the mud and snow, which happened so often that the roofs are now built flat like improvised patios to accommodate their canine residents.

Instead of stale bread supplemented by cooked meals concocted from random donations and kibble, the dogs are fed regularly with healthier canned and dry food. The monthly 4500 euros that costs is raised through donations, auctions, and online sales by what I call the Serbian Dog Connection, a coalition of European dog rescuers that replaced the now defunct Wolf Spirit. Foster homes prepare dogs for adoption in Serbia and Western Europe. Paid employees feed the dogs and clean the kennels, removing some of the burden from Jelena's slender shoulders.

These women—Jean Bird, Lindy Payne of SOS for Serbian Dogs, and Jovana Ivastanin of Serbia's Forgotten Paws, all in the U.K.; Nancy Dequeker, founder and president of the Stray Dog Association of Belgium (Oprichter en Voorzitter at Voorzitter Vereniging Straydogs Belgie); and Iris Hafele of the Austrian Animal Welfare Sun (Tierschutz sonne)—have united to help the dogs in Jelena's and other Serbian shelters. They all visit Jelena's shelter, Serbian-speaking Jovana frequently, and share their experiences. They haven't all met each other, but they regularly communicate by email and the occasional conference call made in English, their lingua franca.

The most heartening news of all is that since 2007, when Whisky Jack made his pioneering trip to Canada, each dog's chances of adoption have soared. Adoptions to Austria, Belgium, Holland, and (since the relaxation of its stringent quarantine regulations) the U.K. have risen dramatically. "Even 'oldies' are getting out of the shelter," Jean Bird says.

Jelena has sacrificed her entire life to the dogs. She'd been drawn into the quagmire of operating the shelter at a young age, and bore the brunt of responsibility when her associates stepped away from it. "It's not the dogs' fault," she has said more than once. "Someone has to take responsibility for them, and I'm the one chosen to do that." And so her life plays out: working at the shelter in mud-splattered gear, the remainder of her waking hours spent on the phone or computer, connecting with Jean, Nancy, Iris, and her other associates, keeping track of and supervising operations, and forever tackling the shelter's crucial fundraising.

The daily realities of hundreds of dogs cannot be rationalized away. They remain as both albatross and purpose. Jelena's is a conflicted existence, and one shared by many dog rescuers.

Cathrine used to be one of them. "Rage and despair were my ground state," she told me recently. "But rage and despair are like the two beams in a particle accelerator: when they come together, they create an enormous amount of energy. The way to do the impossible is to harness that energy and aim it. I may not have discovered the Higgs boson, but I might have made the world an ever so slightly better place, at least for the creatures in my care."

"You can't make everything right all the time. But look at how things are improving. That's what it's all about!" Jean Bird exclaims.

Cathrine would agree. During Rob's assignment in Bangladesh, she spent her vacations in Belgrade, hosted by her former animal-rescue comrades-in-arms, doing what she'd always done: rescuing dogs and cats. She was pleased to learn that the Belgrade *kafilerija* had been shut down and replaced by three old-style pounds where dogs were put up for adoption, at least for a while, and had access to outdoor dog runs from their cages.

Belgrade also established a "Trap, Vaccinate, Sterilize, Return" policy that includes special collars so that dogcatchers, knowing the collared dogs' status, will ignore them. The most gratifying outcome of these various new policies is that the number of street dogs has dropped dramatically.

Mission Airlift ended years ago, but the memories linger. We had tackled the unfathomably giant problem of homeless dogs by targeting just a tiny chunk—and we changed their lives. "From garbage heap to paradise in one short lifetime," Cathrine once marvelled. "G-d grant the same journey to all the lost, abandoned, and unwanted."

# EPILOGUE

# Redemption Does Not Discriminate

It took a prison officer to nail a fundamental truth: redemption does not discriminate, and that's as true for dogs in unfortunate circumstances as it is for the convicted felons Sergeant Basil Whyte selects for Second Chance. Whisky Jack, Bonzi, Hannah Joy, Pinky, Pochi, and Pickles ... the list goes on and on ... all deserved to be rescued, as does any dog who's not part of a loving family. This is equally true of sad, sick, lonely, imprisoned, or just plain dog-deprived people. Our human and their canine ancestors interacted and evolved into two interdependent species that are made for each other. Which is why, trading with the gifts God gave me, I became a dog rescuer blessed with a life gloriously enriched by dogs.

It took me years to identify that calling, and to add interpretative witnessing to my rescuing efforts.

My comings and goings had caught the attention of a neighbour, the poet Ken Babstock, whom I'd once implored to adopt Dunja. Two decades after Tommy's death, as I passed by his house with two of my dogs, Ken waved me over and then held out a slim volume of his latest poetry,

*Methodist Hatchet*. "Uh, you're in it," he said, pointing to a single yellow Post-it.

"*I'm* in it? You put *me* in one of your poems?"

Ken smiled enigmatically. "I hope you like it."

I rushed home, unharnessed the dogs, and popped on my reading glasses. "Thank you for lending your identity," Ken had scrawled on the title page. I flipped to the Post-it, and in the second part of "Russian Doctor," dedicated to David Foster Wallace, read this passage:

The worst of the glare slid behind the sales lot tinsel and she wasn't
a stranger at all. No stranger; my
neighbour, Liz. Elizabeth Abbott. You may know her
work: *Celibacy*

*Mistresses*, something on *Haiti*, and recently, *Sugar*.
Her home a hospice for dying dachshunds
way station for incoming rescues from Serbia (we nearly
took in Dunja last month.) So, animal

rights activist, retired academic, vegan, but here's where
the Danish gets sticky.

Without even knowing Tommy had ever existed, Ken had encapsulated my old dog's legacy—and how I've lived my life—into a few lines of poetry. In 2012, when *Methodist Hatchet* won the Griffin Poetry Prize, the world's richest ($65,000) award for poetry, I joked that "If it hadn't been for Tommy, I wouldn't have become what I am, you wouldn't have written 'Russian Doctor,' and then some other lucky dog might have won the Griffin!" Meanwhile, my home remains a way station for needy dogs whose lives I want to memorialize by telling their stories.

My reunions with the Serbian dogs are the happiest to recount. When Emily Cocarell walked into my house with Pickles (Irene), Mission Airlift took on new meaning. Sweetest of all, every July Emily honours her beloved dog's adoption by donating goods and money to a shelter or rescue organization.

When Nathan Goold opened his condo door to me, Pochi (Smile) licked my face in greeting. Then, despite her stiff leg, she leapt gracefully from sofa to bed and back as Nathan and Catherine shared their stories about her. One went straight to my heart: "We know several people who've adopted dogs because of Pochi. They wanted a dog just like her."

My friend Michele Erker's Pinky is still the pink-nosed beauty Cathrine went "all smooshy" over. Tri-pawed Erin Teddy is inseparable from his cat Precious and is Debra and James Edwards's pride and joy, just as Gracie is Joyce and Dom Senese's. Touchingly, Dom sees in Gracie the spirit of his grandmother, Ana.

Jack the Ambassador Dog who powered Mission Airlift into operation is a portly, bumbling, gentle soul whom Sian Miekle describes as "splendid and middle-aged—he's a very good boy indeed and hilariously set in his ways: he lets us know when it's bedtime, walk time, and dinnertime. Jack also loves camping, but he frets if he loses sight of any of his people, and on one trip stayed up all night because they were sleeping in two tents and he couldn't see them all at the same time."

In Ottawa, Cathrine's Jimmy and Magic, kept securely on a separate floor from her many cats, including her fosters, are maturing into almost-civilized dogs she no longer needs to walk at 1:00 A.M. to avoid other living creatures.

At the other end of the leash, the humans who rescued these dogs continue their work and are faring equally well. Jelena Kostić, Jean Bird, and their associates in the Serbian Dog Connection have refined and expanded their rescue operations. Betty Peyton, Cathy Leistikow, and their fellows at the Humane Society of Madison County, Ohio, are as immersed as ever in their rescue work. The Canadians who came to my assistance all remain active and committed. And because the rescue movement is borderless, they're in constant communication with U.S. rescuers.

As well as overseeing more than twenty foster homes and rehoming dogs, over a thousand since 2001, Speaking of Dogs' Lorraine Houston focuses on "educating and enlightening people about better understanding canine behaviour and positive training teachings and techniques. Most dog behavioural issues stem from miscommunication between dog and owner, with many owners turning to punishment and coercion, which generally leads to a confused, defensive dog and a compromised relationship."

That's exactly what prison dog-training programs aim to correct, as two Ohio Prison for Men's ex-trainers continue to remind me. Shane Livingston, author of the *Second Chance Canine Program Training Manual*, was freed several years ago, is married to his childhood sweetheart, and has earned a bachelor's degree in business administration with a 3.96 GPA. Eddy Stackhouse, who knew Bonzi when his close friend Jake Browning was training him, is out on parole. And making good on his vow to adopt his current Second Chance dog, he now lives with his superbly trained rat terrier, Rexy, and with Cherry, his new wife's chihuahua. Both Shane and Eddy cooperated unreservedly with this book because they believed, as I do, that almost uniquely among prison experiences, dog-training programs work extraordinarily well for both inmates and dogs. In that sad and violent world, they are beacons of light and hope.

But in return for their confidences and recollections, both men insisted that I portray Second Chance truthfully, with all its triumphs but also its flaws, so that people would believe me and hopefully work to make necessary improvements. Shortcomings notwithstanding, everything I learned and experienced about Second Chance reinforced my conviction that it's a superlative program that benefits both man and beast. The men agree.

"I can still never get over how much we were able to accomplish with so little," Shane marvels. "It was what served as the catalyst to transformation for some handlers, myself included. It's a vital community service, and institutions should embrace it."

Prison dog-training programs are all about redemption. They improve a prison's public image by offering significant benefits to animal rescue groups and to the citizens who adopt prison-trained shelter dogs. Loving and caring for the same dog a prisoner has loved and cared for broadens people's minds and opens their hearts to forgiveness.

One day Shane asked me to include the following passages in my book.

"Inside prison, hatred and vitriol are the air that you breathe, initiative and self-esteem are frowned on, and I felt like a subhuman, a cockroach. Prison labels and treats prisoners as pariahs, and as we know, pariahs—dogs and people—always try to cover their tracks and are slow to trust.

"It made me question myself—maybe everyone is right? maybe I am a cockroach?—and that kind of self-doubt can be crippling. But when you get a dog and become a trainer, you are forced to reclaim your initiative and sense of self-worth and with it, enough empathy to do the dog and its training justice. You learn to let go of anger, to try to be better. Working with dogs has been the vehicle I always needed to get in touch with myself, to put the anger and the old wounds to bed once and for all."

So much is happening! So many people have reached out to so many dogs—and to each other—in a borderless rescue movement peopled by self-financed, volunteer-manned organizations that compete and criticize but mostly cooperate with each other because their driving force is the power of love and redemption, and trading with the gifts God gave them.

My greatest gifts have been my dogs. I have loved—and been loved by—all of them, but Tommy, whose soulful photograph has watched over me from the wall of every study I've ever worked in since even before I brought him home, was the dog who set me on the path to rescue and to memorialize the dogs at the other end of my leash.

# AUTHOR'S NOTE

In Parts 3 and 4 I describe a prison dog-training program and the inmates involved. I was granted permission to visit that prison on condition that I not use its true name, and so I've given it the pseudonym The Ohio Prison for Men and called its program Second Chance at Life and Love. I've also changed the name of the correctional officer who allowed me to interview inmates in his presence.

For reasons of security, I've not only invented the inmates' names but also scrambled their identities, including pairing men as cellmates who were not cellmates and as colleagues who were not colleagues, and altering details of stories to reflect the reality of the prison dog trainers' world without leaving tracks that could identify individuals. When I'd finished writing, two former inmate trainers read the manuscript for errors or slips that could identify people.

# PHOTO CREDITS

21 Jean Bird

22 S.M.M. Kabir

23 Jelena Kostić

24 Dora Sesler

25 Patricia A. Andjelkovic

26 Sian Miekle

27 Nathan Goold

28 Lorraine Houston

29 Shane Livingston

# ACKNOWLEDGMENTS

In Haiti, Claudette and Josette (RIP) Fabien cared lovingly for my dogs, and I am forever grateful. Yvonne and Joel Trimble jumped right in to help me rescue Tommy, and kept making the impossible possible.

Sharon Evans, ageless and indefatigable, welcomed me and my little dog Rachel into Mount Sinai Hospital and was my advocate and support. In retirement, she became my friend and helped me as I researched this book. Joanne Fine-Schwebel and Lesli Herman of Mount Sinai's Volunteer Service Department kept the Pet Therapy program going and helped as we refined and expanded it.

I lived and worked at Trinity College for thirteen years, and so much of my life there involved dogs. Many of Henri Pilon's kindnesses are described in this book, but his rescue of dear old Pepper, found standing beside his dead owner's body, must also be mentioned. Isabelle Tanner, who adopted Pepper, was the epitome of compassion and commitment, and her story remains to be told. So does the story of Reverend David and Mary Neelands, who took in the leaky old dog Peef and gave him the happiest of endings. Professor Jill Levinson's two poodles, Tovah and Matan, who ate student Shannon Robinson's essay, "Female Evil in Macbeth," are legendary at Trinity, and their story will be retold elsewhere. My gratitude to all the students who participated in Pet Therapy, with special thanks to those who helped me document those years with their recollections and files: Zinta Zommers, Karen Fung, Gillian

Bowers, Sarah Munro, Chana Hoffmitz, Jess Langer, Claire Hicks,Vanessa Scott,Jeremy Burman, Kes Smith, and Emma Peacocke. And to Paulette Bourgeois for lending us Dixie, and Father Mark Andrews of St.Thomas's Anglican Church for Molly, and for their reminiscences.

In my ancestress Lucy Cooley's home state of Ohio, Betty Peyton, director of the Humane Society of Madison County, deserves bold-face type acknowledgment for facilitating my adoption of Bonzi Billy Beagle, and eight years later, orchestrating a dream trip to Ohio and introducing me to all the people she knew would be invaluable resources for this book. As time went on, many of us have also become friends. Cathy Leistikow, manager of the Humane Society of Madison County, Ohio, loved Bonzi and kept him safe, and protects him still. Cathy, you are a gem! Gary Kronk, deputy sheriff–dog warden (retired), rescued Bonzi and worked heroically to obtain a cruelty conviction against his owner, and then to ensure that Bonzi was happily adopted. Gary was also an enthusiastic resource for this book, and I've portrayed him as the hero that he was, despite his more modest self-portrait. Marjorie Hopkins was the most gracious hostess, and made my Christmas shine with her gift of a treasured Marge Hopkins quilt.

In the state prison I've called the Ohio Prison for Men, "Sergeant Basil Whyte" gave me unparalleled access to the dog trainers' cell block and allowed me to interview trainers in his office. His reflections on the purpose and value of the program also inspired the title of my epilogue: Redemption Does Not Discriminate. Sergeant Whyte, you are a good man. The three trainers I interviewed in Sergeant Whyte's office were, as I have described, articulate and helpful, and I wish them all the very best in their futures Inside and (hopefully soon) Outside the fences. Jacob Browning was the first human to live with and love Bonzi, and long before I met him, I intended but failed to thank him for caring for my boy. Thanks, Jake, for all your reminiscences, for caring for so many other needy dogs, and for your cheerful friendship.

Outside the Fences, Eddy Stackhouse and Shane Livingston, former dog trainers in the prison program, have been my teachers and resources and have tirelessly responded to my questions and concerns. They also read and critiqued my manuscript, and made it so very much better. Thanks also to Sister Pauline Quinn, a heroic figure who is as generous as she is inspirational.

In Serbia, Vesna Lopičić introduced me to Jelena and is always ready to help save more dogs. Jelena Kostić's perseverance in abysmal circumstances continues to inspire scores of us. We lost track long ago of the astronomical number of dogs who owe their lives to her. Vladislav Bajac inadvertently changed my life by publishing my books in Serbian.

During Mission Airlift and long after it landed, Cathrine Lowther's devotion to rescuing dogs and cats, and to her friends, has been fierce and unwavering. Robert McDougall is the kind and calm behind-the-scenes presence who makes Cathrine's rescue ventures possible, and who encourages her to continue. Jean Bird is my never-met soulmate, and a driving force behind Jelena's shelter. James McLean is a towering figure in the rescue community, and his kindness in taking in my Serbian orphans has made so many dogs and their new people happy. Fred Ni documented Mission Airlift and helped me focus on how and why it operated. Cam MacInnes calmed and beautified frightened dogs who had never been bathed or pampered before.

In the frenetically busy animal rescue community, Lorraine Houston of Speaking of Dogs is at the head of the pack. Carol Thorpe of Happy Tails has time for every dog and their rescuers, just none for herself. Joan Znidarec accepted Bak into Labrador Retriever Rescue Ontario, saving his life. Bonnie Hall of Your Dog Rescue meant to foster Bak but fell in love with him instead, and since then she and Bak have been living happily ever after. Christine Ford of Oh My Dog! fostered Dunja with love and transformed her into a princess. Jenn Windt of Barlee's Angels brought me my wonderful Rosie, and years later sponsored Meda. Ann and Pete Wilson, of Ann and Pete's Rescue and Foster Home for Dogs, brought Russell and Pumpkin into my life, and I'm so thankful to them.

Dora Sesler's good deeds are sprinkled throughout my book because she's such a trooper when it comes to rescuing dogs.

From the time Michele Erker banged her head on the steering wheel as she wrestled with leaving Pinky at the pound and fostered and then adopted her instead, I've enjoyed being her friend.

I am so grateful to my readers, Heather Conway, Greg Gray, Dawna Dingwall, Dave Rider, Mary Beth Bourke, and Laura Repas. Your comments were so helpful and made the often lonely writing process that much easier. And for over a decade, Heather Conway has been a close friend, confidant, and fellow dog-lover.

My brother Steve has been my biggest supporter and cares for my menagerie when I have to travel. I am so grateful to have the world's best brother. Thanks to my sister, Louise Abbott, for her excellent work resuscitating raggedy old photos and making the images sparkle.

Ever since Julie Beaver and I both clicked on the Animal Rescue Site one morning and discovered Leggings for Life, Bonzi's sore leg has been comforted by Julie's leggings and passersby have been entranced by them. Thanks too, Julie, for the hundreds of blankets you've knitted to comfort shelter dogs and cats.

Heide Lange, my agent for almost thirty years, stopped me in my tracks when I couldn't find my way and steered me in exactly the right direction. My editor, Helen Smith, made the writing process less lonely, and cheered me on with her spot-on editorial critiques, even when she killed my darlings. Andrea Magyar made my dream for this book come true, and has been with me every step of the way. Copy editor Karen Alliston sniffed out my howlers and faux paws like a bloodhound, and made this book better.

Ingrid Czerwenka and Janet Robertson of Loyal Rescue saved my Petey and helped me through the worst of the little guy's nightmares. Dr. Robert Black has doctored all my animals, and I couldn't have wished for a kinder vet for them.

Sian Miekle, Debra and James Edwards, Nathan Goold and Catherine Draper, Emily Cocarell, Bonnie Hall, and Joyce and Dom Senese have kept in touch and allowed me to visit the Mission Airlift dogs they adopted. These are the things that keep rescuers going.